All Man!

PDC

MAN'S
MAGAZINE

SEPTEMBER 35c

HEMINGWAY'S
PRIVATE WAR WITH
ADOLF HITLER

BOOZE HELL
MY SIX NIGHTMARE DAYS IN
BELLEVUE'S ALCOHOLIC WARD

HOW TO PROLONG
YOUR SEX LIFE

ERNEST HEMINGWAY

THE MAN WHO DEFIED
CHICAGO'S MOBSTERS
THE DAY CUBA EXECUTED
25 AMERICAN CITIZENS!

All Man!

HEMINGWAY, 1950S MEN'S MAGAZINES, AND THE MASCULINE PERSONA

DAVID M. EARLE

The Kent State University Press
Kent, Ohio

© 2009 by The Kent State University Press, Kent, Ohio 44242
Library of Congress Catalog Card Number 2009007201
ISBN 978-1-60635-004-1
Manufactured in China

All Man! was designed and composed by Darryl ml Crosby

LIBRARY OF CONGRESS CATALOGING-IN-PUBLICATION DATA
Earle, David M.
    All man! : Hemingway, 1950s men's magazines, and the masculine
persona / David M. Earle.
        p. cm.
    Includes bibliographical references and index.
    ISBN 978-1-60635-004-1 (alk. paper)∞
  1. Hemingway, Ernest, 1899–1961—Criticism and interpretation.
  2. Hemingway, Ernest, 1899–1961—Psychology.
  3. Masculinity in literature.
  4. Men's magazines.
  5. Pulp literature—Periodicals.
  I. Title.
    PS3515.E37Z58579 2009
    813'.52—dc22

                                            2009007201

British Library Cataloging-in-Publication data are available.

13 12 11 10 09   5 4 3 2 1

Contents

Preface and
Acknowledgments

The idea for this book was gestating for a long time—since childhood, even before I read any Hemingway, because his was a household name in my family. I grew up with Ernest Hemingway. Not literally, of course. I was born seven years after he died, but I was born in Sun Valley, Idaho, only a few miles from his Warm Springs home. My parents lived there through the Hemingway years. Dr. George Saviers, who delivered me, was Hemingway's best friend. My mother was one of Hemingway's nurses during his last year, and my father—one of the three surgeons in Sun Valley at the time—operated on Mary Hemingway's arm after her hunting accident. I grew up knowing a Hemingway who was much more human than the public myth. I was aware of that other, larger-than-life Hemingway, but he was tempered by firsthand accounts of a real man, gentle, failing, and frail.

I never knew the Sun Valley Hemingway knew. My family moved to Cleveland when I was two years old. But Hemingway's Sun Valley, and my parents' Sun Valley, crystallized in my young mind through stories and photos of its hey-day. My father told of George Saviers's skill with a shotgun, of avalanches threatening our Warm Springs house, of the trout fishing and pheasant hunting. He told me about seeing Gary Cooper, about the time he gave Jimmy Stewart oxygen because of the altitude, about Marilyn Monroe filming *Bus Stop* there. My mother told me stories about listening to jazz in the Duchin Room and riding in the Sun Valley Lodge elevator with Louis

Armstrong. But mostly my parents told stories about Hemingway's last years. Or perhaps that's what I asked about most. My Sun Valley was captured in photographs from the 1950s and early 1960s, my mother in capri pants and my father in black Ray-Bans, images of a time and place that seemed sophisticated and adventurous, glamorous and rugged. Sun Valley, a cultural oasis in the midst of the wild Sawtooth Range, seemed to embody the two sides of 1950s masculine culture: the glamorous side of martinis and jazz and the rugged side of fishing and hunting. These aspects were what the men's magazines of the era sold: travel, fishing, cocktails, and, of course, Hemingway.

When I returned to Sun Valley in the 1980s and 1990s, a new college graduate, what I found was an overdeveloped, touristy, corporate characterization of its former self. It was so far from my imagined Sun Valley. And though there were still traces of Hemingway—his memorial, photos hanging in the lodge—his persona had been co-opted by the Sun Valley Corporation, making so apparent the disparity between the "mythologized" Hemingway—adventurer, hunter, sportsman, boaster—and that private, soft-spoken man I had grown up with. Years later, when I went to graduate school, I also encountered the problem of the disparity—or set of disparities, to be more exact—of Hemingway's public myth and private life, which is also the disparity between high-brow literature and popular culture, a problem within the very heart of modernist literature.

This book is not a biography of an author but an examination of a public persona, of a specific type of popular magazine, and of a distinct era in American history. Therefore, innate to the goal of this book is an exploration of the time when twentieth-century literature crystallized into a popular form that, by its own definition, wasn't supposed to be "popular." The mythologizing of Hemingway during the 1950s was so extreme and sensational that it flies in the face of what modernist literature is traditionally said to be.

Many, many people helped with this book, foremost my editor, Joanna Hildebrand Craig, who understood my vision and the need for this book from the moment I plopped a stack of moldy men's magazines on her desk. This book could never have been accomplished if not for her tireless editing and thoughtful insight.

To a certain extent, this book is an extension of my dissertation, a further illustration of its argument. I'd therefore like to thank my dissertation committee at the University of Miami, Pat McCarthy, Zack Bowen, and Anthony Barthelemy.

Many collectors and archivists helped with the research as well, whether hound-dogging permissions, making available parts of their pulp collections, or digging up tattered copies of magazines. I thank Mike Zubal of www. zubalbooks.com; the library staff of the Ray and Pat Browne Popular Culture Collection at Bowling Green, who aided in my early days of searching; Doug Ellis; Walker Martin; Laurie Austin in the audio and visual collection at the JFK Library; Susan Wrynn in the Hemingway Collection at the JFK Library; Maria Charalambous and Suzanne Goldstein at Photo Researchers; John Gunnisen at Adventure House; and Dian Hanson. Matt Bishop also gave me some additional information about his father, who wrote for *Confidential.*

I am particularly indebted to Bob Weinberg of Popular Publications for generously granting permission to reprint excerpts from *Argosy;* to the Kennedy Library for making their manuscript and photo collections available; and to Carol Pinkus from Marvel Comics for granting permission to reprint material from the Martin Goodman line of magazines. I also thank Susan Beegel, Kirk Curnutt, James Meredith, and the Hemingway Society for their support in awarding me the Smith-Reynolds grant to support my research.

I'm indebted to Hemingway scholar Carl Eby for his careful, nuanced reading and many valuable suggestions. I also thank Robert Trogdon, Bridget Haas, and Alison Kelly for their help with earlier drafts—Robert for his inexhaustible Hemingway knowledge, Bridget for her support and encouragement and for letting me bounce my ideas about trauma theory off her, and Alison for keeping it from getting too academic. I give a general and heartfelt thank-you to all my friends in Cleveland who kept me sane with coffee, food, and booze while I was writing this book, especially everyone at Gypsy Bean, Talkies, Bar Cento, 55 Degrees, Lola, and Lolita.

Finally, I must give credit to my parents, who knew the man during his final, failing years and humanized him with compassion and honesty. At an early age they introduced me to a man at odds with his public reputation, a man every bit as fascinating as any of his fiction. I dedicate this book to my parents and thank them for supporting me and my literary (and collecting) passion, for instilling in me an unprejudiced academic hunger that resulted in this project.

A Note on the Illustrations

T his book is about a product of our cultural history—pulp magazines—so denigrated that not only have academics neglected them but so have the companies that published them. In my research for this book, finding the actual magazines was a large and difficult task—but an easy one when compared with the effort involved in trying to hunt down reprint permissions for the various articles and illustrations.

The majority of these 1950s men's magazines are not housed in traditional archives; they are not collected in libraries or digitized like "respectable" literary journals or even the mainstream news and lifestyle magazines of the era. It is much easier to access little magazines, such as *transition* or *The Little Review,* since these periodicals get the attention of literary critics. So, not surprisingly, my primary "archive" has been eBay, where a huge number of these pulps are available.

Pulp magazines and popular reprints were read by everybody in the 1910s and 1920s, including Hemingway and a myriad of other modernist authors. Yet such popular magazines are the great ignored literary product of the twentieth century, one that had a gravitational pull on all other American literature. Unfortunately, most literary archives and collections contain only what the academy considers worth studying, and we study what is available in the archives. So missing as a source for literary critical work is this most influential brand of literature. One aim of this book, therefore, is to expand our idea of what should be collected and studied. These magazines reflect cultural, political, and literary tensions and interesting, amusing, and insightful perspectives in danger of being lost due to dismissal and neglect.

Given the disposable nature of these magazines, tracking down ownership and copyright is not a simple or easy task. Many of the individual publications were owned by pulp conglomerates or subsidiaries of magazine or paperback publishing companies now long out of business or subsumed again and again into larger companies. As the companies were sold off, often only the paperback or comic book line was continued, and the magazine titles folded. Some of the magazines were never copyrighted in the first place. All of this contributed to a long and winding paper trail and many dead ends. After sending countless emails and letters and making numerous phone calls to track down possible rights ownership, I found that more often than not companies had no idea whether they owned the magazines.

Just as troublesome was the relatively lackadaisical attitude many of these magazines had themselves with attaining permission to reprint and giving credit to photographers, artists, and contributors. Many times the photo credits just listed initials; more often they didn't list any credits at all. The staff of the John F. Kennedy Library's Hemingway Photo Collection has been invaluable in finding photographers and rights holders. To cover all the bases, I have tried to gain permission from both the magazines and photographers, though more often than not this was impossible, despite a week at the Library of Congress's copyright office and a flood of unanswered emails.

Copyright issues are complicated in the clearest of situations, but especially so when dealing with fifty-year-old magazines that were often operating below scrutiny and without permission cares. The more respectable magazines, such as *Argosy* and *True,* serve as examples. Because of its long pulp magazine and pulp hero background, *Argosy* and Popular Publications' copyrights were bought en masse by a pulp historian who was only too happy to grant reprint permission. But *True,* a Fawcett Publication, has a nebulous ownership. Originally a pulp house, Fawcett expanded to paperbacks and comic books in the 1940s. It sold off the comic book line in the 1950s and was bought in 1977 by CBS, Inc., but by that time *True* was sold in quick succession to Petersen Publishing and then Magazine Associates in 1975, who became Primedia, Inc. But somewhere along the way, *True* folded. The magazine's 1950s copyrights were never renewed. This illustrates not only the conglomeration of media since the 1970s but also how even the best-known and most widely respected men's magazine, *True,* was allowed to fade away unnoticed.

In short, I made every possible effort to secure permissions and acknowledge rights for all the illustrations and text included in this book. That information can be found in the captions for the photos and on the copyright page for the articles.

Introduction

In the July 1957 issue of *The Nation*, Milton Moskowitz offered an overview of a new trend in magazine publishing, a "Newsstand Strip-Tease" that was "burying newsstands under a sea of pictures and literature whose common denominator is sex." Moskowitz's tone is one of unwilling respect for the phenomenon, stating that "in the publishing industry, these magazines are being watched (even as they are scorned)." His respect stems from the magazines' proliferation, their success, their sheer magnitude of production:

> Here are some of the magazines which have been introduced in this country recently: *Revealed, Duke, Night World, High, Ho, After Hours, 21, Fling, Monsieur, Hollywood Confidential, TV Scandals, Behind the Scenes, Suppressed, Personal Psychology, Mr., Celebrities, Answer, Plowboy, Trump, Scamp, Rave, Sensational Exposes, Duel, Impact, Challenge for Men, True Men's Stories, Uncensored Confessions, Hunting Adventures, Casanova, Inside, Frauds, Inside Story, Cabaret, The Lowdown, Escapade, Exposed, Gay Blade, Good Humor, On the QT, Bachelor, Expose Detective, Adam, Rogue, Nugget, Tip-Off, Caper, Dude, Gent, Jem, Uncensored, Top Secret, Rage, Man's Illustrated, Men's Digest, Satan, Tiger, Relax, Ogle, Sh-H-H-H, Pleasure, Rugged, Hush-Hush, Battle Attack, Real Action, She, Hue, Bare, Pose, Pin-Up, Spick, Swagger, Span, Male Point, Tomcat, Dazzle, TNT, Humbug.*

And this imposing list is by no means all-inclusive. Has there ever been another three-year period in which seventy-five consumer magazines were born?[1]

If anything, Moskowitz is underestimating the number of such publications. Between about 1952 and 1961, hundreds of new men's magazines were published. Some titles only lasted a few issues; others lasted for decades and had circulations in the millions. Moskowitz breaks them into three broad categories: the "Playkids," offshoots of *Playboy,* what I call the "bachelor" magazines; the "Peeping Toms," or the celebrity gossip tabloids; and the "He-Man Adventures," offshoots of the old pulps, "25-cent packages of blood-and-thunder." He even starts to conjecture about the reasons behind this explosion of new titles but stops short, writing, "Magazines, they say, mirror the times. If so, what portion of our times is illuminated or reflected by the Playkids, Peeping-Toms and He-Man Adventures? They will, no doubt, provide future historians with interesting food for thought."[2]

This idea of the newsstand striptease captures the visuality of these magazines, a visuality I have tried to emulate here in the use of illustrations—sensational, extreme, kitschy. It would be impossible not to notice them, for these covers and illustrations and ads were initially designed to stand out, to sell a magazine surrounded by dozens of similar magazines on a newsstand. They were designed to create desire: not only desire to buy the issue but to own the object depicted on the cover, whether the semi-nude pinup on the bachelor magazine, the physically perfect body of the triumphant male on the men's adventure magazine, or the glamorous lifestyle of the celebrity on the tabloid. They are paintings and photos in vibrant colors of explicit sexuality or extreme action. These magazines were intended to be visual lollipops, candy for men's eyes.

But counter to what Moskowitz foresaw, it is not the historians who have latched onto these magazines in recent years but collectors of pulp or fans of "low-brow" illustration. There has been a surge of interest in the cover art of pinup and men's adventure magazines, and numerous coffee table books, new lines of pulps-cover greeting and postcards, and the brisk trade of magazines on eBay attest to this.

On the one hand, our fascination with these illustrations—the pleasure we get from their campy sensation—is different from their appeal to that audience of men in the 1950s. It is obvious that for modern collectors, these magazines are kitschy, fun, pleasurable. It appeals to our senses of nostalgia and sophistication; they seem to tell us that we have come a long way.

Modern
MAN
THE ADULT PICTURE M

JUNE 1956 50c

HOW DUMB
ARE THOSE
HOLLYWOOD
BLONDES?

HEMINGWAY:
AMERICA'S
No. 1 HE-MAN

THE GIRL
WHO STRIPS FOR
CONVENTIONS

COUNTRY WITHOUT WOMEN

But there is an innate danger in this attitude. For, on the other hand, we really cannot separate ourselves and the appeal that these images have for us from the initial construction of masculine desire or violent sexism that these publications relied on. So, have we really come that far?

This idea of the construction of desire is similar to how a medium such as advertising creates desire in the consumer (telling us, "You need this product. You are not complete without this product"), but this is often gendered, playing off the unrealistic ideals that we are socialized to aim for, the unrealistic Barbie doll body of fashion models or the stoic toughness of the action hero. The fantasies of gender at work in these magazines and the construction of desire in the mass media are just as strong now as they were in the 1950s, the decade when modern advertising really came into its own. Today's mediated fantasies presented to us on television, online, and in print are just more sophisticated in their portrayal as compared to the sensational extremities of the men's magazines.

To understand this relationship with the past, I chose a representative of 1950s masculinity, one whose reputation as a "he-man" was forwarded in these magazines, but, at the same time, one whose reputation, both in popular culture and in the academy, was built by this media construction. Ernest Hemingway.

It would be difficult to overemphasize the popularity of Hemingway in the 1950s, and this celebrity is at its most extreme and sensational in these magazines. He appears as a blood-and-guts soldier in the adventure magazines and as an expert and lusty sportsman, drinker, and traveler in the bachelor magazines; and as a celebrity, he filled the pages of the tabloids. This popular representation of Hemingway as both serious author and public figure, sensitive artist and masculine ideal, has often been overlooked in both biographies and critical studies. But his reputation has as much, if not more, to do with the construction of Hemingway as a masculine role model in the popular press as it does with his work.

Therefore, this book is not about Hemingway's fiction but Hemingway himself as a fiction, as a popular representation, and as an innately visual image that grows out of twentieth-century mass media and the dynamics of midcentury gender. This image of Hemingway as he-man has proven resilient, continually seductive in the popular media. And like the pulp magazines in which it solidified, it is both fascinating and problematic. *All Man!* explores three interdependent manifestations of troubling masculinity in postwar America: the 1950s men's magazines as a text of masculinity,

Ernest Hemingway as the hero of that text, and the construction of that hero as a role model of the masculine persona.

As Moskowitz points out, magazines do indeed mirror their times. More than mere popular reading material, periodicals such as those listed above capture in amber the tensions, concerns, traumas, and fashions of a historic moment. Moskowitz's article, itself published in *The Nation* magazine, has written into it concerns of the time; he calls the "off-beat" irreverent tone of the bachelor magazines "a quality not easy to come by in the age of the packaged soul."[3] These magazines therefore offered some kind of antidote to the mass-marketed conformity of life and culture as portrayed in popular magazines such as *The Saturday Evening Post,* that Rockwellian slice of pure Americana.

Alternately, the extreme portrait of post-WWII America that the men's magazines paint is of a threatening and feminized world, where men had to learn to dominate and take back their own. If we were to judge the 1950s simply by the covers of these magazines, then men were attacked by wild animals (everything from piranhas and monkeys to spiders and Nazi-trained baboons), imprisoned by amazons and sadistic female SS guards, and spent all their leisure time either on safaris and deep-sea fishing or seducing semi-nude coeds. These magazines were fantasies of masculinity, tall sexist tales to bolster men's adequacy in the quickly shifting time after the war and before the cultural upheaval of the 1960s.

With the publication of Betty Freidan's *The Feminine Mystique* in 1963, scholars began examining the part that popular women's magazines had in proscribing gender roles in the middle decades of the twentieth century, especially those of housewife and homemaker.[4] Studies deemed the 1950s an age of conformity and as a time that enforced women's domestic roles as a way to, among other things, pressure women out of the WWII workforce.[5] An image of the 1950s as a homogenized culture of suburbanization—the "do nothing" generation or, alternately, the "golden age"—has been handed down through mass-culture nostalgia and is evident in reductive, very white, middle-class representations such as *The Donna Reed Show* and *Father Knows Best.* But lately this portrait has been questioned, for it is far from the way the decade really was. In reality, the postwar years were full of upheaval and social disparity, prejudice and race riots, Cold War containment and black-listing, juvenile rebellion and crime. Recent studies, such as Nancy Walker's *Shaping Our Mother's World,* have shown how women's magazines reflected the contrasts and complexity of 1950s culture and gender, how there were

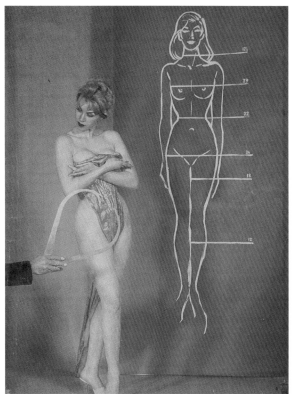

Left: One of the innumerable "man vs. killer animal" covers for the men's adventure magazines. Snakes, sharks, and piranhas were also favorites. If the reader was lucky, the action took place in a concentration camp and the animals were trained by Nazis, two favorite themes. *Man's Illustrated,* April 1956. ©1956 Hanro Corp.

Right: The illustration for Mel Bennett's November 1959 article "The Art of Selecting a Mistress" from *Monsieur* ("Entertainment for Men of the World") is introduced by a tagline that boasts: "Love has nothing to do with it, says this expert. You pick her like you pick a car—for performance."

more women in the workplace in the fifties than at the height of the Second World War, and how issues of race and class were navigated in magazines such as *Ebony* and *Ladies' Home Journal.* So our nostalgic vision of the 1950s is under revision, complication, and expansion, and we're beginning to see exactly how dysfunctional the Reeds and Cleavers really were.[6]

Men's periodicals, though, have been largely overlooked, despite the hundreds of titles produced between 1953 and 1961 and the millions of readers. Only recently have feminist and gender studies paved the way for the examination of the socialization (proscribing, shaping, or pressuring) of masculine gender roles in mass culture (media, entertainment, goods) produced for and consumed by the general population. Before the advent of cultural studies, these magazines were considered too low or trashy to be studied. Only *Playboy* has been regularly examined, having become accepted, even canonized, as compared with many of the magazines considered in these pages.[7] And these magazines' extreme misogyny points to the "crisis of masculinity" that scholars have identified at work in the post-WWII years—a series of crises, actually, that included postwar trauma, the rise of suburbanization and consumer-based conformity, the move from a Depression-era working-class ethos to white-collar corporate economy, and Cold War paranoia.[8] These magazines both embodied these fears for their popular male audience and attempted to navigate them, making them complicit in the sense of trauma and therefore creating a market for themselves.

One of the most extreme examples of the "petticoat scare"—the obviously false or constructed fear of a feminized, matriarchal America—from this age is the August 1958 issue of *Jem: The Magazine for Masterful Men,* which touts a kind of manifesto on its front cover that continues on the editorial page.

Men . . . THIS IS THE VOICE OF FREEDOM! . . . Freedom from the domination of Women! For generations we American males have been bullied, brow-beaten and neglected by the female sex . . . they have banded together to rob us of our independence, dominating qualities, muscularity and masculinity! WE ARE VIRTUAL SLAVES . . . and we must not allow it! IT'S TIME TO FIGHT BACK—and the editors of Jem herewith sound the rallying cry for the oppressed men of the nation. In these pages you will find advice and instructions on how to fight the battle! Yes, rally to us, fellow sufferers, and together we will win the FOUR FREEDOMS FOR MEN:

1. FREEDOM TO WANT . . . AND GET IT!

2. FREEDOM OF SPEECH . . . To say what we think, and mean what we say; viz.: "shut your flannel mouth before I drop you right in the middle of this supermarket!" Or, "No, we're not going to watch the Late, Late Show—we're going to *have* one! First, get my bath ready!"

3. FREEDOM OF WORSHIP . . . Whether it's Marilyn, Gina, Bridgitte, Sophia or any other Goddess of Sex.

[4.] Freedom from FEAR—the fear that we'll be deprived of the good things in life that should be free, unless we give up our time, paychecks, individuality—in fact, OURSELVES.

The battle is joined, men, and we have a real fight on our hands! Because if you think that the assorted wives mistresses, mates, fiancés, sweethearts and girl friends are going to give us these vital freedoms without a struggle—I can only say that ignorance is bliss. *Wedded* bliss! And serve you right, too!

No, this is going to be a matter of give and take: Either they give or we take. With the kind of editorial guts that harkens back to the era of Hearst, MacFadden, and Greely, JEM herewith throws down the gauntlet to the Women of the World:

You dames the world over!—you painted, tainted, tarnished, varnished, heat-treated, deep seated, pretty, giddy, half-witty, haughty, naughty, lustful, untrustful, neurotic, erotic and despotic dames!—*listen:* we're fighting back! After a half century of serfdom, we are getting a new grip on our destiny. From now on, we men are going to sit high in the saddle, apply the spurs deep and, when necessary, use the whip! All right, now—*back to your housework!*

There it is, fellows, a sample of what can be done. If you simply follow our lead—and read our special advice and instructions each month—then you will help us greet the dawn of a New Day for the American Male.

Remember—you have nothing to lose but your ball and chains!

This tirade appeared alongside the cover photo of a busty nude toweling off from the interior pictorial entitled "From Sink to Bed—(and Back Again)." The set for the pictorial features model Ann Peters doing domestic chores—vacuuming topless or ironing in lingerie—and captions such as "Make her keep it clean while you're gone . . . and have something nice and hot waiting for you when you get back." This photo spread embodies certain popular notions of 1950s gender roles: women as sex objects (Marilyn Monroe, Jayne Mansfield) or domestic role models (Doris Day, Donna Reed).

The dictation of women's roles through magazines such as *McCall's* and *Ladies' Home Journal* are echoed in the pressures on men to demand that women conform to these roles. *Jem's* plea for its reader to follow "our special advice and instructions each month" illustrates the role that such magazines played in socializing gender identity. Other articles in this same issue of *Jem* crudely convey the deep-rooted resentment and distrust at work in 1950s popular culture: "Slug 'em and leave 'em!" and "Steady Dating—Women's Ultimate Weapon." The misogyny of *Jem* would be less troubling if it were an isolated example; unfortunately, it is just one of hundreds such examples of magazines of that era that perpetuated these sexist dynamics. Obviously, *Jem's* manifesto supports the popular idea of the 1950s as being a decade during which women were kept in the kitchen yearning for no more than a brutish, gin-soaked husband and a dish soap that works. But more than "domestic containment," *Jem's* antiwomen hysteria, and the popularity of magazines like *Jem,* also points to the idealization of a hypermasculine persona, to the representation and acting out of extreme masculine gender traits.[9] There is a sense in these magazines that the suburban male was endangered by hordes of apron-wearing, vacuum-wielding feminine dictators. Jim Backus as James Dean's browbeaten milquetoast father in *Rebel Without a Cause* was a fate worse than death.

This misogyny stems in part from the wholesale trauma of the Second World War, when seven million American men had to repatriate into a society that could not imagine the trauma and horror of war. Graphic images of battle were kept out of the newspapers. No ideals of courage could prepare men for the horrible realities of D day, Wake Island, or Auschwitz. General repatriation was often inadequate in dealing with the kind of Post-traumatic Stress Disorder that plagued the veteran. Chapter 3 explores how men's adventure magazines created both a sense of camaraderie that was missing after decommission and supplied narratives of coping similar to the dynamics of vet support groups that became standard after Vietnam. But often these narratives took the form of hypermasculine performance, where men were tested and emerged triumphant. So not only were these magazines marketed to the veteran, but the covers often depicted themes of battle and other tests of manhood, of homosocial bonding that hearkened to military brotherhood such as prisoner of war camps or long tours at sea, or they depicted explicit fantasies of male dominance, such as the ubiquitous single male marooned on a desert island with numerous women.

This was also an age of economic prosperity, and part of this trauma stemmed from the pressures put on men to reenter the corporate workforce and conform to those American Dream ideals of family and success—much like the pressures placed on women to conform to ideals of domesticity and motherhood. The codes of conduct in the 1950s were as strict as those of the Victorian age and were manifested most often in the texts of mass culture: in books and articles on etiquette and dating, in children's games such as Mystery Date, in advertisements, and in magazines. Women's roles were in the home, confirmed by the pink-shaded domestic sphere of the kitchen replete with matching Frigidaire, range oven, and apron.[10] These may not have been the *actual* roles of the overall population, but this was the popular image as represented in mass culture, and one that was both homogenized and homogenizing, a perfect, crystallized picture of white, suburban America. Magazines like *True* and *Argosy* confirmed the father's role in

This July 1957 issue of *Man's Life* contains no fewer than five killer animal stories, including "Up to My Neck in Live Lobsters": "Claws clacked like giant shears slicing his flesh as he looked on." Such stories of survival play into masculine fears and triumph over them. ©1957 Crestwood Publishing Co.

Jem

A TREASURE CHEST OF RARE SPICE

AUG./50¢

MEN ...

THIS IS THE
VOICE OF FREEDOM!

. . . Freedom from the domination of women! For generations we American males have been bullied, browbeaten and neglected by the female sex . . . they have banded together to rob us of our independence, dominating qualities, muscularity and masculinity! WE ARE VIRTUAL SLAVES . . . and we must not allow it!

IT'S TIME TO FIGHT
BACK—

Continued on Page 4/

SLUG' EM and
LEAVE' EM!

FROM BED TO WORSE

Put her to work and she'll love it . . . and you.   Like Ann Peters – a dish drying a dish.

Left: *Jem* was the "magazine for masterful men," as articles such as "Slug 'em and leave 'em" illustrate. This August 1959 issue featured a call for action against domineering women. ©1959 Body Beautiful Corp.

Right: This August 1959 *Jem* spread featuring model Ann Peters cleaning and vacuuming was accompanied by captions such as "Make her keep it clean while you're gone . . . and have something nice and hot waiting for you when you get back." This pictorial not only plays off of the idealized roles of women in the 1950s, but the framing technique illustrates how voyeurism was integral to these magazines' success. ©1959 Body Beautiful Corp.

suburban leisure and home improvement. That idea, illustrated by *Jem*'s diatribe that the world was increasingly feminine, stems from these pressures of family, suburbanization, and domestication. Much has been written of the 1950s as an age of conformity, of being what Moskowitz labels the "age of the packaged soul." The bachelor magazines pandered to fantasies that opposed this. They relied on codes of behavior that were opposed to this domestic sphere by emulating the bachelor lifestyle defined by gadgets, style, and the bachelor pad itself. In this sense, the masculine persona was a commodity that was sold and bought: you are what you wear, where you live, how you relax.

The fantasies of desire—whether for a life of travel, economic independence, or irresponsible sex—that were constructed in these advertisements, magazines, and fiction of the time were dependent on a dynamic of removal that incorporated both lack of responsibility and an element of control. In other words, they were fantasies of voyeurism. These magazines both pandered to the need to escape and provided an avenue to do so through graphic representations, both on their covers and in their heavily illustrated contents. Adventure stories or exposés of masculine role models offered ways of looking in on another's life as a possibility for your own. In psy-

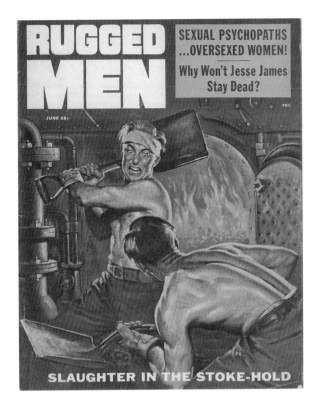

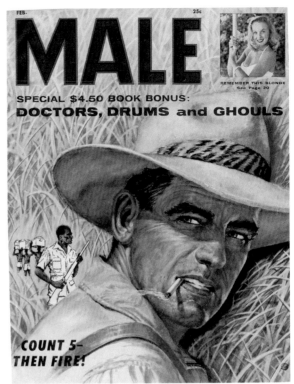

chological terms, the viewer identified with the object represented but is likewise conscious that he isn't that object (muscular or suave) or doesn't own that object (nude model, sports car, nude model in a sports car). This creates a desire for that object (or at least the representation of it on/in the magazine) and an urge to own it to make oneself complete.

Many of the 1950s men's magazines even accentuated the fetishism of this visually based ownership innate to voyeurism. This is most obvious in the fantasy of the pinup. Notice how the photos from the *Jem* pictorial, which are presented on the page in window frames, are of the idealized wife, both a domestic and sexual slave, thereby accentuating the passive woman in her subservient role and giving the male reader the role of active viewer but removed to the safety of fantasy, displaced just enough to allow fantasy to say "this could/should be mine."

There is a rich history of criticism about this male and voyeuristic gaze in film, some of which has been applied to the pinup magazine but little attached to the dynamics of male gender construction as dependent on a history of the marketplace: how men's magazines pioneered a masculine self-definition based on how and what they bought.[11] *Esquire* magazine made it okay for men to shop, to worry about fashion. It was developed

Left: The title of this men's adventure magazine says it all. ©1956 Stanley Publications

Right: *Male* is a typical example of the men's adventure magazine genre: women are either pinups, as in this issue's Russ Meyer pictorial, or portrayed as a threat. Not only is there a true crime article about a lady poisoner, but even one of the three hunting stories is about a killer female cougar, "She-Cat": "When she saw the Man-Animal, she dropped her kill." Many covers featured safari and other settings that excluded women. ©1956 Male Publishing Corp.

in 1933 as a male *Vogue.* And since fashion and the buying of clothes were historically thought to be effeminate or foppish, it succeeded by making itself unquestionably masculine by pioneering the pinup. Like extravagant Busby Berkeley musicals, *Esquire* was immensely popular in the years of the Great Depression, when most men couldn't afford the life advertised—further illustration of how fantasies of desire and consumption were integral to masculine identity.

The dynamics of voyeurism at work in these examples are dependent on a manner of audience creation through the construction of need as based on a cultural lack (i.e., you are not sophisticated or culturally savvy unless you buy x and y products). This kind of marketing, which both *Esquire* and, later, the 1950s bachelor magazines relied on, was pioneered in nonvisual ways by literary modernism, specifically that brand of modernism established (or marketed) in the mid-1910s by Ezra Pound, Wyndham Lewis, T. S. Eliot, and others. These "high modernists" sold the idea that it was necessary to be familiar with literary modernism if you were to be culturally savvy. One who read these authors and their avant-garde literary journals were arbiters of good taste. The tendencies toward artistic typography and visual writing (for example, Pound's use of Chinese symbols, Lewis's use of art and abrasive type fonts) would make modernism conducive to the blending of literature and visuality (painting, photos, typographic experimentation) in magazines.

To explore the dynamics of masculine fantasy more fully, it is important to look beyond voyeurism at the masculine tone of these modern writers and how it created a fantasy lifestyle of the modern artist. The marketing of modernist periodicals conveyed their sense of intellectual elitism through a misogynistic definition of popular literature as effeminate. This is why a lifestyle conducive to travel was often idealized in modernist expatriate literature, such as in work by Ernest Hemingway and John Dos Passos, for such a lifestyle means separation from the domestic and feminine world. Chapter 4 traces this strain from those modernists through *Vanity Fair* and *Esquire* to the 1950s bachelor magazines' fascination with modernist authors.

Finally, the element of voyeurism reemerges, in a less gendered sense, in the tabloid magazines of the day, what Moskowitz tellingly labels "Peeping-Toms," which were dedicated to sensational stories of celebrity scandal, vice trials, true crime, and movie star gossip—the grandparents of today's *National Enquirer* and *Weekly World News.* They had titles like *Confidential, On the QT, Exposed, Uncensored,* and *Whisper,* and most of this ilk were driven out of business by the continual barrage of libel suits. They are admirable, however, for the hubris of their sensational spins and their wholesale disregard for the truth. More important, they are purely a product, if not the epitome, of celebrity culture, particularly the public's fascination with the contrast between a celebrity's glamorous aura and his/her public life. Celebrity culture is a relatively new phenomenon, rising out of the consolidation of the entertainment industry (film, radio, publishing) in the 1910s and 1920s. The term means the popular or mass-cultural establishment and fascination of a celebrity through mass media attention. I discuss in Chapter 5 how modern celebrity arose when the public's fascination shifted from a public figure's work to his or her private life. And whereas scandal and fan magazines were instrumental in the rise of celebrity culture from the teens on, the 1950s tabloid magazines marked the collapse between private and public. These wildly popular tabloids, with circulations in the millions, relied on thinly veiled libel and celebrity sexploits, divorces, rumors, and alcoholism.

The reason for the tabloids popularity has much to do with that public image of the 1950s as one of cohesive prosperity: the more "proper" the decade seemed, the more fascinated the public with how improper it really was. This is the same conflict that creates celebrity fascination in the first place, but on a larger cultural scale, where the mass-mediated pressures of conformity or suburbanization fall apart. Though often heavily fictionalized, the tabloids illuminated real social tensions and problems that the mainstream media overlooked. In this sense, tabloid magazines act as a self-criticizing voice within the mass media that exposes its own shortcomings.

There is a fantasy of cohesion at work between the reader/voyeur and the fantasy/object in the adventure and bachelor magazines; they gave a feeling of reparation, an illusion of control to the reader. In other words, these magazines both created desire and fed that desire through fantasy: it is possible vicariously to own the object of desire, to travel the world, to control the traumatic situation by buying the magazine on the newsstand. But the tabloids fractured that illusion, accentuated the gap between the fantasy forwarded by mass media, which is embodied in the celebrity, and reality, which is embodied in scandal.

Similarly, much recent scholarship on the 1950s has been dedicated to separating its nostalgic image from the political, cultural, racial, and contradictory reality that was day-to-day life. As Stephanie Coontz has pointed out, "Contrary to popular opinion, 'Leave It to Beaver' was not a documentary."[12] Similarly, *All Man!* hopes to show our own complicity in that construction of desire, whether in the collector's buying of vintage

Hemingway wasn't the only modernist author to appear in the men's magazines that followed the *Playboy* formula, but he was by far the most prominent. This issue of *Dude* featured D. H. Lawrence. Other prominent modernist writers that appeared in the bachelor mags included William Faulkner and John Dos Passos. Notice also how the bachelor magazines pandered to the life of leisure. ©1956 Mystery Publishing Co., Inc.

pulps, the reader's appreciation of the kitsch of this book's illustrations, or even the modern television viewer's fascination with reality shows. The pleasure innate in viewing sensational and extreme media, so unavoidable in the pulp genre, can be enjoyed, but we must not forget its historic and troubling nature.

Many articles, like this one by Sam Boal, purported to find "the truth" under Hemingway's larger-than-life persona. Boal, a friend of Mary Hemingway, published three different versions of this in assorted popular magazines. This issue also included an editorial by Jack Kerouac. ©1959 Bruce Publishing Corp.

ERNEST HEMINGWAY AND THE MASCULINE PERSONA

What I have described above are the cultural dynamics that coalesce in the popular image or reputation of Ernest Hemingway. The construction of his reputation, his "masculine persona," is my central exploration. One thing that is necessary to convey, and which has been lost through the academic canonization and fascination with Hemingway, is both how popular he was in the decade before his death and how sensational this popularity was. The dozens of articles about him in the 1950s men's magazines illustrate this. Many of these articles blur Hemingway's characters' traits with Hemingway's own traits. And it is this blurring or misreading of the man with his fiction that needs to be examined, just as we need to ask to what extent has there been a misreading of his fictional works because of this public reputation, especially since his appearances in these magazines were not only ubiquitous but also so much a part of the dynamics of 1950s mass culture, gender, and celebrity. This confusion of the man and his fiction is obvious in how the many magazine articles and illustrations "pulp" him, make him into a sensational fiction of masculinity, an extreme example of the 1950s man.

Hemingway's rise to the position of America's most famous author started in the 1920s when he became the unofficial spokesman for the Lost Generation, that group of expatriated writers that emerged from the First World War and whose most distinctive trait was a wholesale pessimism, antiromanticism, and hardness. He was also leagued with other modernists such as Ezra Pound, Sherwood Anderson, and Gertrude Stein, whose stylistic experimentation set them apart from the formulaic writing of the popular Victorians. He broke onto the international scene with *The Sun Also Rises* (1926), the prototypical novel about Left Bank bohemianism and expatriation. His fame was confirmed with the best-selling *A Farewell to Arms* (1929), a novel about World War I. His sparse style, influenced by both journalism and modernism, was perfected in his short stories, most of which dealt with undeniably masculine themes such as war, fishing, and boxing. Hemingway was a strong believer in "write what you know," and he drew many of his plots and characters from his own life. For example, in the early decades of the century, it was a popular pastime among literary circles to identify the actual people on whom the characters of *The Sun Also Rises* were based. This was only strengthened by Hemingway's well-publicized lifestyle of travel and adventure and his strong personality and good looks. His exploits, such as marlin fishing, big-game hunting, and imbrications with critics, were often in the gossip columns. He was a public figure, but he was a literary figure rather than a full-blown celebrity; his work was still the central subject of scrutiny rather than his lifestyle.

This started to shift over the course of the 1930s due in part to his own journalism and nonfiction writing, such as his *Esquire* articles and *The Green*

Hills of Africa, where he became the subject of his own writing. His public image was furthered during the 1940s with his widely read war reporting, but it was also kept in check by the flourishing of his fiction, namely the best-selling *For Whom the Bell Tolls* (1940) and the republication of his earlier work in *The Portable Hemingway* (1944) and numerous paperback editions.

It was after the war that Hemingway's public image overshadowed his work, making him a celebrity on par with movie stars. Between 1952 and 1958, Ernest Hemingway was in two highly publicized plane crashes, won a Nobel Prize for literature, published a best-selling novel, and had five movies produced based on his work.[13] His fame rose to a level of celebrity never attained by a writer before or, arguably, since. At the height (or depth, depending on whom you ask) of this celebrity, Hemingway's image was sensationally and regularly splashed across the pages of men's magazines.

Hemingway was so emblematic of this type of publication that both were satirized in the spring 1957 issue of *Plowboy* magazine, a two-issue student-run humor lampoon out of the University of Michigan. The first issue was an on-campus publication; the second, the spring issue, was distributed nationally. Both issues are send-ups of the dozens of men's bachelor magazines that flooded the market in the wake of *Playboy*'s success. A slim volume, this issue must have been easy to miss among the many other men's magazines. The cover design is split between a slinky blonde in a see-through negligee and, next to her, a profile of a cartoon rabbit. At first glance, the cartoon seems to be a rip-off of the *Playboy* icon, but on a second look its satirical nature becomes clear. *Playboy*'s bunny, usually so smug and insouciant, is here degenerate and jaded. His ears are frayed, there are circles under his eyes, and a cigarette dangles from his mouth. High living seems to have taken its toll.

The first issue featured a biography of "Furnst Humway . . . the world's foremost blood, guts, and sex author." Besides tongue-in-cheek pictorials, ads, and articles, most of the space in the second, national issue of *Plowboy* was filled by pseudo-literary satires lampooning the common use of literary authors by the bachelor magazines. Of the three short stories in the national issue, "The Old, Old, Old Man and the Sea," which roasts Hemingway, is both the most prominent and the most cutting. It is full of lines like "'Tengo la pluma,' the Major said. 'I am very tired of simple declarative sentences'"; and "We went around a lot with girls from Passiac that winter or with nurses from Hackensack. It was very lovely but it did not mean anything to us." Clearly, Hemingway's popularity, as well as his idiosyncratic style, was ubiquitous enough in the men's mags to be lampooned.

STORIES BY MAX HEMINGWAY, MAX FAULKNER, MAX de MAUPASSANT

Above: The illustration for *Plowboy*'s Spring 1957 story "The Old, Old, Old Man and the Sea," by Max Hemingway.

Left: *Plowboy*, Spring 1957. ©1957 Bannister Publishing Co.

The illustration that accompanies the piece can be taken as an allegory of Hemingway in the 1950s. The most visible signifier of Hemingway's public persona since the mid-1940s, his close-cropped white beard, has symbolically grown so long as to be unwieldy, even dangerous to the man.[14] The shark could represent the dangers of the literary marketplace, either the critics or the specter of commercialism, of "selling out." The gin bottles allude to the author's legendary thirst, one of the integral components in the Hemingway legend. And when this appeared in 1957, Hemingway—or, to be more precise, his persona—was seemingly synonymous with tawdry and pulpy men's magazines, to which the inclusion of *True Confession*

Rogue for Men nominated Hemingway as a "Rogue of Distinction" in 1958. ©1958 Greenleaf Publishing

sardonically attests. This picture might be depicting Hemingway desperately struggling to stay in his (literary) craft while his reputation gets the best of him. But this is perhaps asking too much of the illustration and of the artist (and the reader). It is enough to point out that Hemingway's biography is so well-known and so identified with men's magazines that both could be parodied simultaneously.

The diverse types of 1950s men's magazines forwarded the idea that it was an era of middle-class martinis and lower-class adventure, and Hemingway became a hypermasculine ideal in all of them. Not only did *Modern Man* tout him as "America's No. 1 He-Man," but *Focus* labeled him one of the ten sexiest men alive (as did Zsa Zsa Gabor in *Show*), and *Rogue* gave him the honor of being a "Rogue of Distinction." Again and again Hemingway was held up as an example of manliness, a role model and tonic for the American male who was having trouble adjusting to a postwar suburbanization with its stress on domestic consumption. A *Man's Illustrated* article entitled "Ernest Hemingway's 5-War Saga" went so far as to state that "there aren't many men like Hemingway left in this soft-bellied world of ours. You may be one of them. If you are, then you belong to the select few who, along with Hemingway, are members of a vanishing breed of giants in a society dominated by women and women's ways."[15]

This image of Hemingway as he-man is what I call the masculine persona. In its most literate sense, "persona" is a writer's assumed voice or character and, in more philosophical terms, "the set of attitudes adopted by an individual to fit the social role which he sees as his."[16] The adoption of Hemingway as this idealized persona is indicative of a midcentury cultural need for establishing masculine attitudes in such mass media as television, film, and these magazines. "Persona," with its fictive and performative connotations, seems appropriate.

But Hemingway's persona is separate from Hemingway's fiction. Critics such as Carl Eby and Robert Scholes have discussed how Hemingway's fiction, from "Hills Like White Elephants" to *Garden of Eden,* explores complex issues of gender.[17] Much of it, such as "The Big Two-Hearted River," is about the limits of masculinity, about when masculine socialization falls apart. Yet the popular perception of Ernest Hemingway is almost the polar opposite, more akin to the headlines in the 1950s magazines, such as "Ernest Hemingway: Wars, Women, Wine, Words." So it is understandable that his literary reputation suffered in the gender wars of the late 1960s and 1970s in readings by feminist scholars.[18] In light of Hemingway's representation in these magazines, it is easy to understand why for decades his (and his fiction's) reputation was as a misogynist, an idea finally under revision. This popular reputation as a womanizer highlights the ways in which Hemingway has been misread because of his persona.

I am quick to point out, though, that this is not a book of Hemingway criticism. I am not as concerned with how Hemingway's reputation has affected the reception of his fiction as much as establishing a historical context for exploring how much of Hemingway's reputation stems from this constructed masculine persona or questioning how much his reputation stems from his popular celebrity rather than his fiction. There is a nostalgia, even myth making, around Hemingway that these magazines perpetuate and that still exists today in such events as the Hemingway Days in Key West, in the numerous restaurants and bars that market themselves through some kind of affiliation with the author, in the many one-man shows about him.

Before contextualizing these issues, I establish in Chapter 1 Hemingway's relationship with popular culture, especially with popular magazines. Hemingway's reputation as a high-brow modernist has been firmly established through the canonizing dynamics of academia that perpetuate the elitist idea that Hemingway, as a sophisticated author, is antagonistic to the popular marketplace. In truth, Hemingway not only sought out a popular audience but was himself heavily influenced by popular literature. Most critical biographies have explored Hemingway's modernist tutelage with Sherwood Anderson, Gertrude Stein, and Ezra Pound but have ignored his earlier attempts to break into the pulp fiction marketplace. The Hemingway Collection at the Kennedy Library contains unpublished manuscripts and rejection slips from pulp magazines, but few have been studied. This is not the conscious fault of scholars, for pulp magazines in general have never been considered worthy of study.

By pulp magazine I mean the popular American all-fiction magazines popular from the mid-1910s to the 1940s. Hundreds of titles published in the millions, these "pulps" were the reading material of the general populace, often sensational and often dedicated to genre fiction: romance, adventure, detective, western, and war. Hemingway read these as a child and submitted stories to them in the years between WWI and his leaving for Europe in December of 1921. Indeed, many of the topics of Hemingway's early and famous stories, such as boxing, soldiering, and horse racing, grew out of pulp conventions.

Concentrating on this unexamined shadow history of Hemingway and the pulps disrupts the academically defined reputation of Hemingway, paving the way for the later career of his persona in the 1950s men's magazines.

It is no coincidence that Hemingway's career, his rise to fame, parallels the evolution of the men's magazine. Both Hemingway's and the men's magazine evolution relies on the rise of visual culture, which I explore in Chapter 2. Visual culture is the evolution of a "visual fluency," the shift in popular culture from a purely literate, or written, language to media more dependent on images. Hemingway took full advantage of this in his journalism for *Esquire* and *Ken,* and his image appeared ubiquitously in the photo digests, sensational magazines that digested the news into photo narratives. This chapter also offers an overview of the spread of Hemingway's celebrity between the 1930s and the 1950s.

Chapters 3 and 4 offer not only rationales for the extent of Hemingway's popularity in the 1950s but reasons for the popular adoption of Hemingway's persona of masculinity. Hemingway's tendency to write about his own experiences in the First World War, specifically the aftereffects of battle trauma, guaranteed him a favorable audience among the soldiers and veterans who discovered his work in the widely distributed Armed Services Editions, abridged paperbacks that fit into a soldier's kit. Furthermore, his war journalism and books like *Men at War* (1942) established his reputation as a soldier, despite the fact that he never actually served in the army, only as a Red Cross volunteer and a war correspondent. Chapter 3 argues that Hemingway supplied a narrative of coping for veterans and, in expansion, appealed to a culture reeling from the instability of repatriation. Not only did men's adventure magazines—full of stories of battle, perseverance, and conquest—appeal to veterans and supply a sense of wartime camaraderie, but their adoption of Hemingway as the prototypical soldier in stories and interviews offered a role model for coping with the horrors of war.

Whereas the men's adventure magazines were geared toward a working-class readership, the bachelor magazines marketed themselves to the middle class, to the suburban male who looked to escapism from family and corporate pressures. The bachelor magazine defined itself against the ideals of mainstream America that grew out of the postwar pressures of rebuilding the American Dream so neatly embodied in the suburban ranch house and planned community. The bachelor lifestyle glorified the independence of the single male and success gauged by the consumption of stylish commodities and travel. Chapter 4 explores how Hemingway emerged in the pages of the bachelor magazines like *Playboy* and its dozens of imitators. But rather than the gruff soldier, here he was the savvy connoisseur, privy to the life of leisure. Hemingway's masculine persona in these pages emerged from the war

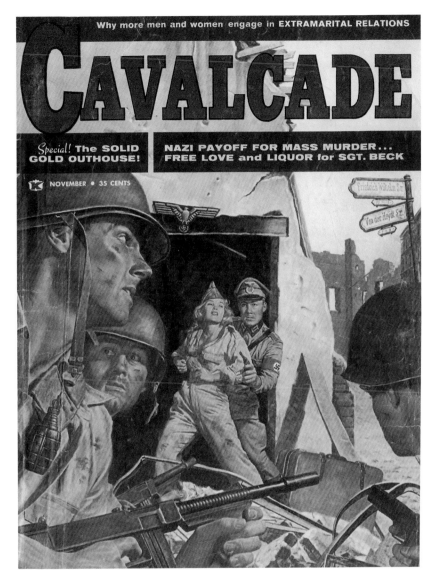

Why more men and women engage in EXTRAMARITAL RELATIONS

CAVALCADE

Special! The SOLID GOLD OUTHOUSE!

NAZI PAYOFF FOR MASS MURDER... FREE LOVE and LIQUOR for SGT. BECK

NOVEMBER • 35 CENTS

Left: Like many men's adventure magazines, this 1959 issue of *Cavalcade* was marketed to veterans of World War II. This issue had the added attraction of an article on Hemingway's son Patrick, a white hunter in Africa. ©1959 Skye Publishing Co., Inc.

Below: Photo digests like *Focus, See, Pic,* and *Show* were highly sensational, full of photos, and geared toward quick and easy consumption. ©1953 Leading Magazine Corp.

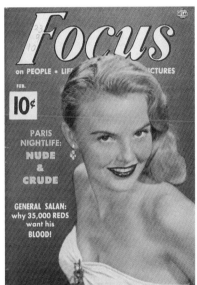

Focus
on PEOPLE • LIF[...] [...]ICTURES

10¢

PARIS NIGHTLIFE: **NUDE & CRUDE**

GENERAL SALAN: why 35,000 REDS want his BLOOD!

an expert in how to enjoy life and willing to let the reader in on his secrets. Hemingway, the soldier in the adventure mags, here was the expert lover, drinker, sportsman. In the bachelor magazines, the sense behind the "true gen," a Hemingwayesque military phrase that denoted reliable information, became the insider information of the cultural aficionado. Magazines such as *Playboy, Sir Knight,* and *Rogue* were full of compendiums of Hemingway's advice on how to hunt, fish, love, eat, and drink. Other magazines, such as *Sportsman* and *GunSport,* offered advice on the safari and what shotguns were

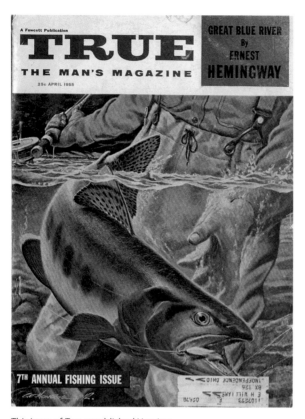

This issue of *True* republished Hemingway's "Great Blue River," which originally appeared in *Holiday*. *True* was the first to publish Hemingway's "The Shot" in 1951. ©1955 Fawcett Publications

best. Hemingway became the epitome of the male as savvy consumer, whether of culture, food, or women.

This chapter examines how male consumerism was integral to the bachelor magazine, which stood on the shoulders of *Esquire, Vanity Fair,* and, in general, the exclusionary dynamics of modernism. Hemingway, as the most famous and visible heir of modernism, was expert in audience construction, of privileging his readership through a sense of "the true gen," of cluing his audience in to elite knowledge. It is exactly this dynamic that informed his earlier work on the bullfight in *Death in the Afternoon* (1932), a book that is as much about modernist writing as the corrida. For him, both modern literature and the bullfight were insider sports. It is no coincidence that the bullfight was more popular in the men's magazines and American culture of the 1950s than either before or since, for modern advertising aspired to and was influenced by the masculine marketing techniques pioneered by the modernists. This is one of the reasons that the men's magazines were fascinated with the scene and authors of modernism, Hemingway being the prime example. The boy's club of advertising culture as a whole emulated and saw itself reflected in that modernist figure of the cultural aficionado. The culmination of this dynamic is the reoccurring blending of the figure of the advertising executive, or "man in the gray flannel suit," with the bullfighter in both fiction and ads found in the bachelor magazines.

Whereas Chapter 4 considers another reason behind the establishment of Hemingway as the masculine persona of the 1950s, Chapter 5 portrays both the extent of this persona and the negative ramifications of it by looking at Hemingway as a celebrity rather than as a literary figure. Hemingway's presence in the tabloid magazines, a venue reserved primarily for movie stars, illustrates the extent of his popularity. These articles do two things— conflate Hemingway with his characters and explore the gap between the constructed image and the real man. So functions celebrity in the media age, making apparent the ways that Hemingway's popularity is itself dependent on mass culture's creation of him as a masculine persona, how the 1950s image of masculinity and masculine desire fell short.

Gossip tabloids like *Whisper* flourished in the 1950s in response to a mass audience ready to believe sensational Hollywood innuendo. Hemingway's presence in them is indicative of his popularity throughout the decade. ©1955 Whisper Inc.

One of the most difficult aspects of Hemingway's fame to navigate is his own role in its development. One thing made clear by the tension between Hemingway's humanity and his larger-than-life persona in these tabloid articles is that the man was tortured by his own fame in the 1950s, even though he was complicit in its construction. There was obviously earlier self-promotion in his journalism, which I touch on in the second and fourth chapters, but there is something a bit more troubling at work in the 1950s

FOR MEN

REAL

THE EXCITING MAGAZINE

25c April

Jackie Robinson's Challenge to Baseball:
"WHY CAN'T I MANAGE IN THE MAJORS?"
Diary of a Combat Surgeon:
MY 57 BLOODY DAYS AT DIENBIENPHU

I SPY ON THE CALL GIRL RACKET

HEMINGWAY:
Wine, Women and War

and which becomes apparent in the interviews and articles in the men's magazines. That is the sense that as Hemingway aged, he put on a front, he acted a caricature of masculine bluster. In Hemingway's statements about his drinking, lovemaking, and fighting, there is an extreme bravado that these magazines latch onto and amplify. But just as often he would show his private face, balk at interviews, seem quiet and gentle, deplore the limelight. Sometimes "both Hemingways" emerged in the same interview. Was it because he felt that he had to live up to this ideal, to give the public what they wanted? Was it an element of the man's complexity or a defense against failing health? Or was it simply a construction of the media and just an aspect of this type of magazine? It is just possible that the Hemingway that has been passed down to us and that we have attempted to reconstruct in numerous biographies has been affected by the gravitational pull of Hemingway's masculine persona—that creation of midcentury mass media that rose not out of Hemingway's mind but our culture's own needs.

The tagline for "Hemingway: Wine, Women, War" in *Real* (April 1956) reads: "The world's greatest clutch writer is a standout wherever you find him—behind a gun, in a bedroom or leaning against a bar." If that isn't sensational enough, the article is also subtitled "The Hairy Chest of Hemingway." ©1956 Literary Enterprises

APRIL—TEN CENTS
PHYSICAL CULTURE

PHYSICAL CULTURE PUBLISHING CO., Main Office, Physical Culture City, Spotswood P. O., N. J.

Flatiron Bldg.
NEW YORK CITY

337 Marquette Bldg.
CHICAGO

10, Wine Office Court, Fleet St., E. C.
LONDON, ENGLAND

CHAPTER ONE

Hemingway in
The Pulp Milieu

In the 1890s, health guru Bernarr Macfadden was an impresario of inflated masculinity. He used his own muscular physique and talent for self-marketing to advertise his brand of exercise system, barbells, diets, Strengthos cereal, and penis pump. But it was as a publisher that he achieved real fame and success. In 1899 he started *Physical Culture* magazine, which was an instant sensation. Within a year it had an American circulation of 150,000.

Physical Culture embodied the ideals of turn-of-the-century masculinity even as it played a role in changing them. It was a product of the time's shifting technological, cultural, moral, and economic dynamics. Featuring "educational" articles about subjects sure to titillate the Victorian sensibility and profusely illustrated with early pinup and beefcake photography, it was a forerunner of the modern men's magazine. Macfadden saw his magazines as extensions of his own "improvement" mind-set. He was a presence in all his publications, appearing as the ideal man, a physical, moral, and entrepreneurial role model. Nominally, *Physical Culture* was for a progressive readership concerned with physical and mental health, but in reality it marketed itself through pure sensationalism. Many of the magazines Macfadden pioneered lasted through the 1950s and spawned numerous imitators and new genres of popular magazines that contributed to the explosion of men's magazines published after World War II.

It is telling that *Physical Culture* was launched the same year Ernest Hemingway was born, for the evolution of the popular men's magazine parallels Hemingway's own life and career. *Physical Culture* and Hemingway were

Opposite: *Physical Culture* (April 1907), edited by early bodybuilder Bernarr Macfadden, was a prototype for men's magazines.

more than just "products of their time," since they both "sold" the popular image of their generation, even defined it. Hemingway not only gave name to the Lost Generation, but his well-publicized lifestyle and writing projected the era's characteristic cynicism and restlessness. However, this is the *popular* or nostalgic version of the 1920s. In reality, the tensions that prompted the disillusionment of Hemingway and his fellow modernists also gave rise to active attempts to contain, control, and give structure to a quickly modernizing society. Alongside the riotous dynamics of the Jazz Age came a strengthening of religious conservatism, Prohibition, and the rise of the Ku Klux Klan. Yet what sticks in our collective memory of the 1920s are those indelible images of the thrill-seeking flapper and jaded vet.

So why does Hemingway so perfectly embody the character of his time? Is it because he consciously placed himself in the position to translate and represent it, first in journalism then in fiction (after all, his first book was titled *In Our Time*)? Or is it that he has come to be regarded as America's greatest novelist, and therefore his writing has been absorbed into our historical psyche across generations of readers, scholars, and cultural critics.[1] Reinforcing both suppositions is the fact that he came of age during the rise of twentieth-century magazine publishing; his fiction and persona are intrinsically bound with the evolution of the popular men's magazine.

GROWING UP HEMINGWAY

The decades flanking Hemingway's birth saw the rise of physical culture, the wave of fascination with well-being and exercise that Macfadden's publication rode. YMCAs grew in popularity. Exercise programs were implemented in public schools. Theodore Roosevelt called for boys and men to lead the "strenuous life," to be self-made, strong of body, and clean of mind. In speeches and articles aimed toward boys, the president conflated self-reliance and exercise with politics and imperialism, ideas that were spread through groups like the Boy Scouts of America and the Boone and Crocket Club. He was an advocate of natural parks, hunting, and fishing. As Michael Kimmel has pointed out, Roosevelt saw men as soldiers and women as mothers, and those that shirked their duties were traitors to their country.[2]

Hemingway's hometown of Oak Park, Illinois, embraced the movement, the Hemingway household included. In 1906 his mother, Grace Hall, was one of the first to join the new and controversial women's gymnasium class at the YMCA.[3] Hemingway emulated Roosevelt and regarded him as a life-

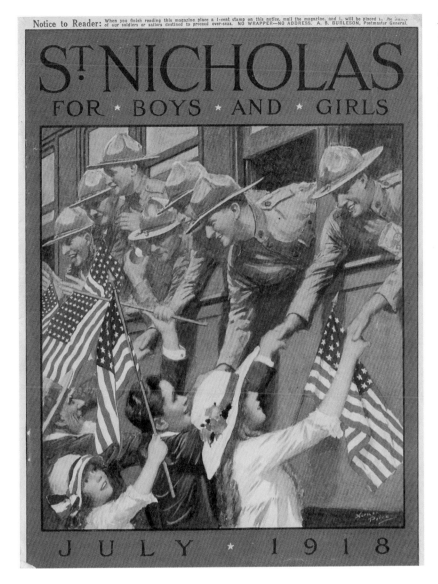

St. Nicholas magazine was a favorite in the Hemingway household. The nationalism of this July 1918 cover is even more fervent on the inside, with each article advancing the war effort in some way, either training boys to be soldiers or girls to be nurses.

long influence. Critics have even seen Hemingway's *Green Hills of Africa* as a recasting of Roosevelt's *African Game Trails* for the 1930s, with "the writer, not the politician, emerging as the key cultural icon."[4] Hemingway didn't have to join the Boy Scouts, since every summer he was living and learning his wood lore from his father, Dr. Clarence Hemingway, who taught his son the Latin names of plants and animals and tutored him in gun safety, hunting skills, and fishing. Hemingway would always conflate these skills with his father and fatherhood in general, and eventually he took on this same role of "Papa" in his *Esquire* articles of the 1930s.[5] Ernest's brother, Leicester, pointed out that Ernest "concentrated on learning thoroughly the

things Boy Scouts pride themselves on knowing." Notably, Ernest prided himself on boxing and swimming. In high school he practiced "the plunge, a dive in which the swimmer held his breath to see how far he could drift, which helped develop his extreme chest expansion."[6]

Hemingway was not unusual. It was part of growing up at the turn of the century. Physical culture was on the pulpit, in the classroom, and especially on the newsstand. It was part of an entirely normal midwestern middle-class childhood; it was the socialization of that generation of young men who flocked to enlist for World War I. Such ideals were widely spread through the books, magazines, and newspapers that young Hemingway devoured.

Besides Roosevelt and Macfadden, there was Horatio Alger, whom Marcelline Hemingway noted, "Ernest couldn't get enough of."[7]

This physical culture filled the pages of *St. Nicholas* magazine, which the Hemingways subscribed to and was Ernest's favorite.[8] *St. Nicholas* was famous for publishing *Little Lord Fauntleroy,* Kipling's "Just So Stories," and the nature stories of Ernest Thompson Seton, author of *Wild Animals I Have Known.* Ring Lardner, one of the most widely circulated sports columnists of his time and a big influence on the young Ernest, also got his start in that children's monthly.[9] Besides introducing America's youth to literature, *St. Nicholas* advocated the strenuous life that would train children to be upright contributors to society.

The July 1918 issue offers numerous examples—from the cover, which illustrates soldiers departing for war amid fanfare, to the ads that capitalize on the escalating patriotism of the day. One such ad for Bristol Steel Fishing Rods claims that "Fishing will do for you what the army does for the recruit. In bait casting, fly casting, or almost any kind of fishing, you get the same exercise of the muscles of the side, back, abdomen, legs, arms and neck that you get in the Army and Navy 'setting up' exercises. You also get the outdoor life. . . . You owe your country greatest efficiency. . . . Eat fish and save meat and wheat." The ad shows an army platoon exercising and a superimposed fisherman in the same pose—certainly a Hemingwayesque combination of images. Articles in this issue also equated the strenuous life with patriotism: how summer camp can make boys and girls fit "in body, mind, and spirit for any call Uncle Sam may have for them"; "How the boy scout winners sold liberty bonds"; and "Better Speech for Better Americans." Josephus Daniels, secretary of the navy, even wrote "A Message to the Boys of America" about how "American boys take to gunnery like ducks to water. . . . They go into it with the same vim and vigor that they display in baseball or gridiron contest, for this fighting the submarine they call 'the greatest game on earth.'" It was these same highly promoted ideals of physical culture and nationalism that sent Hemingway and millions of others to the front.

Hemingway's early attempts at commercial fiction writing soon after his wounding on the Italian front still smack of such guts-and-glory-filled melodrama. Later, after Hemingway's ideals of courage and honor gave way to disillusionment, he wrote about how exercise, sports, and the outdoors became a way to cope. In stories like "The Two Big Hearted River" and "Now I Lay Me," Nick Adams turns to fishing and camping to alleviate war trauma.

For his entire life, Hemingway held dear all those aspects of turn-of-the-century physical culture, fitness, and outdoor sports. In the 1950s, magazines such as *Modern Man* and *Illustrated Male* made much of Hemingway's physique, exercise regime, and expertise at sports. He was quoted in a 1956 issue of *Modern Man* as saying, "I think body and mind are closely coordinated. Fattening of the body can lead to fattening of the mind." Even as his health was failing in his late fifties, he bragged to reporters about his daily exercises. According to *Man's Illustrated* in 1960, "At 61, he's more of a man than most guys 20 years old. He still boxes, hunts big game, and can land a marlin without aid of a harness." And the men's magazines respected such values, for many of them were direct descendents of Macfadden's publications.

Not only did *Physical Culture* specialize in cheesecake and beefcake photography in its "Body Beautiful" section, but eventually it inspired a whole generation of confessional and "true" story genres of magazines that continued into the 1950s masculine pulps.[10] In its efforts to illustrate the threats to healthy manhood (and womanhood), *Physical Culture* took on subjects such as masturbation, prudery, and corsets in addition to the usual articles on men's diets, health, and exercise. It also featured ads for sex guides and diverse pamphlets on such topics as "spermatorrhea" and "night emissions." Not surprisingly, the magazine became a target for vice societies. The April 1907 issue ran an editorial against "Comstockery," moral- and religious-based censorship, in which Macfadden himself recounts how he was arrested for mailing "obscene material" from an earlier issue's article "Growing to Manhood." The same issue also printed a letter, with the header "Choosing Between Love and Duty," in which a reader asks advice about his fiancée, who is not a physical culturist and refuses to discuss "the duties of wifehood and motherhood. . . . She declares that such discussion is 'immodest,' and only fit for married people to indulge in."

The popularity of such features gave Macfadden an idea for a magazine dedicated to such confessions, one that was to become his most popular formula. The result, *True Story,* spawned a whole new type of magazine based on supposedly true and sensational experiences, and he quickly followed with *True Detective.* This populist realism was adopted by other Macfadden magazines, with other publishers also picking up on the trend. Magazines such as *True Marriage Stories, True Confessions, I Confess, True Love Stories,* and *Confession* were akin to today's reality television and garnered a huge audience of both men and women. Their tremendous popularity, according to one historian, was a result of as well as a contribution to the post-WWI upheaval in manners and mores.[11]

But *St. Nicholas* and *Physical Culture* were only two magazines that illustrated the popular ideals of masculinity during Hemingway's childhood.

As Hemingway grew into an aspiring writer, there were plenty of other magazines that, for a dime, would have given young men like him thrills, inspiration, and vicarious adventure.

HEMINGWAY AND THE EARLY PULPS

By the time Hemingway was in his early teens, pulp magazines were a presence on every newsstand. At this time they were evolving from general all-fiction magazines to ones dedicated to specific interests or genres of literature, the most popular of which were romance and adventure. Magazines like *Argosy, Blue Book,* and *Cavalier* were not yet the hypermasculine periodicals that they would later become, but with their exotic locales, fast-paced action, and exciting themes, they definitely appealed to a male audience. The September 1914 issue of *Short Stories* serves as an example. Besides the cover story, "The Claim Jumpers," a western by Stewart Edward White (a favorite author of the young Hemingway[12]), topics ranged from the navy, baseball, the circus, the sea, trapping, humor, and mystery. Authors included Sax Rohmer, creator of Fu Manchu; horror writer William Hope Hodgeson; and the prodigious H. Bedford Jones, known as the "King of the Pulps."

Hemingway was aware of these early pulps (few adolescents weren't), not only because of their sheer numbers and great popularity but also because one of the most famous pulp authors also lived in Hemingway's hometown. In 1912 Edgar Rice Burroughs published *Tarzan of the Apes* in *All-Story Magazine.* It was instantly successful, sparking reprints, sequels, pastiches, and films. Tarzan captured the public's imagination because he was the perfect embodiment of the physical culture masculine ideal. In a 1919 letter to friend Will Horne, Hemingway stated that Burroughs, who "perpetrated Tarzan & the Apes," was urging him to write a book: "If I do, I'll not send you one. You'll have to buy it 'cause the sales will need it."[13] Whether or not Burroughs really did ask Ernest to write a book, the letter to Horne shows that Ernest was versed in the world of pulp publishing and fully aware of how difficult it was to break into.

Many critics have noted that between 1918 and 1922 Hemingway unsuccessfully submitted short stories to *The Saturday Evening Post,* one of the most popular and successful magazines of its day. But what is not as well-known is that he also sent manuscripts to the nascent pulps: *Adventure, Everybody's* (a popular magazine that was something between the *Post* and the pulps), *Popular, Blue Book,* and *Argosy.*[14] These manuscripts reflect

Price 25 Cents

APRIL 1931

THE
BLUE BOOK
MAGAZINE
ILLUSTRATED

TARZAN
GUARD of the JUNGLE
By Edgar Rice Burroughs
▼
Captain Dingle – Arthur Akers
Clarence Herbert New – Henry
C. Rowland – Seven Anderton
Bertram Atkey – George Worts'
Great Detective Story — and others
$500 in CASH PRIZES FOR REAL EXPERIENCES

an important yet wholly unexamined stage in Hemingway's development as a writer. The Kennedy Library archives include drafts and fragments of manuscripts as well as rejection slips from pulp houses. Also, Hemingway's letters from that period include numerous references to pulp magazines and editors. Most significant, these early manuscripts are undeniably pulpish in both themes and style.

Writing for the pulps was referred to as "the Fiction Factory" or "the Grind," since authors were paid by the word and stories had to be written quickly. Successful authors usually shopped numerous stories at one time and could rarely afford to rewrite.[15] This resulted in clichéd themes, melodramatic situations, and formulaic plots (by the 1920s there were even "how to" books and quick systems for plot construction). Hemingway's early manuscripts keep to these conventions with situations and plots similar to countless other pulp stories. It is clear that he was trying to learn the "formula" by mimicry of the stories he read in magazines like *Adventure* and *Blue Book*. He even sought writing advice from successful pulp magazine editors.

Only biographer Peter Griffin has given extended attention to a few of these manuscripts, republishing five of them in his *Along with Youth* (1985), but he overlooks both the pulp influences and Hemingway's intended pulp market. Most of the manuscripts and fragments at the Kennedy were written by Hemingway between 1917 and 1922, when he was a reporter for the *Kansas City Star* or when he worked for the *Toronto Star*. It is hard to judge exactly when most of the pieces were written, however, since they are undated. Regardless, there are at least a dozen of these pulpish stories—war stories, boxing stories, gangster stories, romances, and at least one story told from the point of view of a dog. The writing is formulaic and melodramatic. It isn't the Hemingway we expect, that consummate craftsman sweating over every word. Rather, it represents the foundations of a popular writer. For decades, literary critics have stressed Hemingway's position as literary modernist over his popular appeal. So this pulp influence and early writing divulge the popular foundations of his writing sensibility, which predate and undermine his modernist reputation and training.

Purely escapist, the general fiction pulps included stories about boxing, horse racing, gangsters, hunting, logging, adventures, and soldiering. Hemingway's earliest existing stories, published in his Oak Park High School literary magazine, aspired to pulp themes, locales, and topics, especially those from magazines such as *Adventure* and *Popular*. Stories like "The Judgment of Manitou" and "Sepi Jingen," both written when Hemingway was sixteen, are similar to the stories of the northern wilderness made popular

Opposite: *Blue Book* was one of the longest lived and most respected pulps. Hemingway sent early stories to the *Blue Book/Red Book* magazine combination only to have them rejected. This cover features a story by fellow Oak Park author Edgar Rice Burroughs, who first published Tarzan in *All-Story Magazine* in 1912. It also captures the type of story that Hemingway's early work aspired to, such as "The Mercenaries." ©1931 The McCall Company

Started as another early general fiction pulp magazine, by 1926 *Popular* was featuring more masculine fiction, as illustrated by this issue. Hemingway submitted his story "The Woppian Way," about an Italian American boxer who joins the Arditi, to *Popular* in 1919. It was rejected. ©1926 Street and Smith

by author and conservationist Stewart Edward White, whose adventures of hunters, lumberjacks, and trappers made him a favorite of young Hemingway.[16] *Adventure Magazine* from April 1918, for example, has a story about a hard-nosed game warden who catches a young man poaching deer to sell to the lumber camps in order to earn money for his ex-showgirl-wife's medical expenses. But when a big-city gangster comes to town to get even with the young man for taking away the showgirl, the game warden redeems himself by setting the gangster up to get shot for trespassing. The plot, locale, and themes of vengeance—all pulp conventions—are reminiscent of Hemingway's juvenile writing and foreshadow stories like "The Killers," a frequently anthologized 1927 Nick Adams story about Chicago gangsters gunning down an ex-boxer in a small rural town.

Also, war and aviation stories were popular before, during, and immediately after the war, and most were highly romanticized. While the number of war stories diminished and their melodramatic tone faded as real-life experiences came home with the returning soldiers, by the mid-1920s these same soldiers craved novels, stories, and histories to help explain what they had been a part of. Magazines like *War Stories* and *Battle Stories* became especially popular due in part to ex-soldiers turned writers, such as Arthur Guy Empey, who wrote the 1917 best-selling memoir *Over the Top* before turning to the pulps in the mid-1920s.

Of the dozen or so surviving pulp fragments and stories Hemingway wrote during this period, five of them are war stories or have heroes who are ex-soldiers. A far cry from the cynical disillusionment of *A Farewell to Arms,* these stories often exalt those same ideas of "glory" and "honor" that so disgust Frederick Henry. Three of Hemingway's unpublished manuscripts written immediately after WWI forwarded the clichéd idea of war as sport. "The Woppian Way," "The Visiting Team," and an untitled fragment about a fighter named John Wesley Marvin conflate boxing and football with a romanticized and immature sense of soldiering. "The Woppian Way" (also known as "The Passing of Pickles McCarthy"), the most polished of these pieces, tells the story of boxer Pickles McCarthy (actually Piccolo Neroni), who suddenly leaves boxing on his way to the championship in order to join the Arditi, one of Italy's elite fighting corps. The story, which opens on a hijacked freighter, is told by a reporter who runs into the ex-boxer, now either a mercenary or revolutionary—which is unclear—and recounts how McCarthy's Arditi battalion took Arsino against the Austrian army. The story is badly constructed, never concluding the action of the initial time frame (i.e., the hijacking of the freighter). It is also marked by a romanticized portrait of battle and retreat that is the total opposite of the horrific retreat from Caporetto as described later in *A Farewell to Arms.* Clearly, McCarthy's admiration of the Arditi reflects Hemingway's own, an esteem even more evident in the complete short story "How Death Sought Out the Town Major of Roncade" (very likely a slightly later effort), which is about an Arditi soldier who takes vengeance on the cowardly and pedophilic town major by tying him down and putting an unpinned grenade in his shirt pocket. The soldier is the epitome of both swift justice and stoic courage as he tells the major of those "good men who have spilled out their guts" while the major has "made love in Roncade."

The boxing fragment about John Wesley Marvin again establishes the connections of boxing, bravery, and fighting in the war. Marvin is labeled a coward by his father, a former middle-weight champion, because he doesn't have the killer instinct despite the fact he was awarded war medals for his valor as an aviator. As his father says, "You were quicker than the other birds and a better flyer and could shoot better and so you killed some of 'em. . . . But that ain't what you're doing now. Now you're fighting and you're yellow as they make 'em. You was just boxing in the air. . . . You're good at that but you ain't got the fighting instinct." Even Hemingway's attempts at irony, such as in "The Visiting Team," fall into melodramatic cliché. At the end of this story, the brave and dying ambulance driver mutters, "Only the good die young."[17] But the height of pulpish melodrama is the vignette told from the viewpoint of Piet, the pet dog of an Austrian soldier. Set in the trenches during a battle, the unusually perceptive dog knows that his dying master is thinking of "the days they had spent together lying in the shade along the stream. Piet dozing with his nose between his paws and the Master lying face down on the grass reading." This is a prime example of the animal narrator, a Victorian and pulp literary convention.

Clearly, these war stories are preludes, however distant, to Hemingway's later fiction and are easier to categorize as such. But others, especially those Robert Paul Smith refers to as the "Chicago stories," stories about boxers or gangsters, are harder to ignore as being pulp fiction; they are flawed examples of the stories that made up magazines like *Top-Notch* and *Adventure.* Boxing stories make up about half a dozen of the early manuscripts in the Kennedy Library's Hemingway collection. These include "The Current" (reprinted by Griffin), "The Woppian Way," and numerous fragments. If not war or boxing themed, the other pulp manuscripts are gang or crime related, most likely stemming from Hemingway's experiences as a reporter in Kansas City. These include "The Mercenaries" and "Ash Heel's Tendon," both reprinted by Griffin. "The Mercenaries" is about three soldiers of fortune in a Chicago barroom who are drinking and trading tales while waiting for a job. Critics have examined the themes of bravery in this story as a precursor to later Hemingway work. "Ash Heels Tendon," however, has received little attention because it is so much more pulpish. It deals with a Chicago hit man who cannot be captured because he always has his eyes open and his hands on his two guns. A police detective finally gets him by distracting him with a recording of Caruso, apparently his Achilles' heel. The narrative relies on the same ethnic stereotyping that marks most pulp fiction, a result of the need for quick characterization. But even more astounding than these

contrived stories is the untitled mystery about reporter Punk Alford, who solves the murder of a Jewish curio dealer who was slashed to death by an antiquarian weapons collector who fell in love with his prized long sword: "'I never fooled much with women and lately this old girl has taken their place.' He ran a blunt amorous forefinger along the shining blade. Punk shivered." This was obviously a bit much, even for the pulp magazines of the day.

Another tried-and-true pulp formula involved boxing stories. Rarely did an issue of *Popular, Blue Book,* or *Top-Notch* hit the stands without at least one boxing story. And by the mid-1920s, pulps like *Fight Stories* and *Knockout* were dedicated to nothing else. Hemingway's story "The Current," about a handsome young socialite who takes up boxing to prove his worth to his doubting fiancée, is standard pulp fare with its cliché-ridden prose and hyper-romanticism. (The story was rejected by *Red Book/Blue Book.*[18]) The popular and formulaic nature of "The Current" is reminiscent of another pulp story published around that time, William Sebelle's "Black Butterfly,"

Left: From 1926 on, war stories were a favorite topic of the pulps. Besides *Battle Stories* other titles included *War Stories, Air Trails, Battle Birds, War Birds,* and *War Novels.* Always timely, many of these war-themed pulps started up in the latter half of the 1920s in an effort to cash in on a resurgence of interest in WWI. ©1935 Fawcett Publications

Right: The stories in this issue of *Top-Notch* ranged from westerns to war to tennis, but the cover illustrates the popularity of tales about trapping and the northwest. ©Street and Smith

Boxing stories were popular in the pulps for decades. ©1938 Street and Smith

which is about a poor boxer who ultimately has to choose between fighting for the championship and his girl and a steady job.[19]

Both George McClelland, Sebelle's hero, and Stuyvesant Bing, Hemingway's hero, question why they box, and both remind themselves that it is for the love of a woman, for "You know how women are," says McClelland, they "want a man that's a fighter." And both, of course, choose the girl over the fight racket. "Black Butterfly" also has similarities to the original opening of Hemingway's later boxing story "Fifty Grand" that was edited out (or, as Hemingway puts it in a typescript note, "mutilated") by F. Scott Fitzgerald, where a boxer leaves the ring to become an actor. The same happens in "Black Butterfly." While it is impossible to know if Hemingway read the earlier story, it is evident that boxers becoming actors was a trope in the pulp fight story.[20] Also, the formulas and tones are certainly similar, even if the plots are not. And each has a happy ending and a "heart interest"— two elements different pulp editors advised Hemingway to have if he were to succeed at writing.

In an early study of Hemingway's boxing stories, Charles Fenton wrote about one of his first short stories, "A Matter of Colour" (1916): "It was a very slick story—slick, that is, in the sense that its plot was an O'Henry twist and its punch line an old vaudeville gag."[21] Fenton's "slick" here refers to the sort of material that would appear in magazines printed on slick paper, such as *The Saturday Evening Post,* as opposed to the stuff printed on wood-pulp paper. But he overlooks the fact that the subject of the story is much more the stuff of pulp.

The fact that Hemingway submitted these early stories to both pulp magazines and mainstream ones like *The Saturday Evening Post* is in keeping with the submission practices of most pulps writers. In submitting stories for publication, pulp authors usually sent their work to the better magazines in hopes of breaking into the slicks; then, if rejected, they sent it on to the better pulps, persevering down the levels of pulp until some editor—any editor—accepted the story. In describing his own writing history, pulp writer Frank Gruber said, "I wrote stories and submitted them to magazines like the old *Smart*

Set, Atlantic Monthly, and *Scribner's Magazine.* They were all rejected and I thought that I would lower my sights and try the more popular magazines, *The Saturday Evening Post, Collier's,* that type of trash. They wanted none of me and I found myself, at the age of twenty-two, with the ambition to write burning more brightly than ever, but nowhere to go" except the pulps.[22]

Similarly, a December 1919 letter Hemingway wrote to his friend Bill Smith describes a similar process. After "The Mercenaries" is declined by *The Saturday Evening Post,* Hemingway sends it off the next day to *Adventure.* Hemingway then "hope[s] to God" that another story will be bought by *Popular Magazine* (another general fiction pulp) editor Charles Agnew McLean.[23]

In general, these early works are pretty bad, not even good enough for the pulps. But they show how Hemingway was trying to pin down the formula, how he was trying to write to the genre. In just a few years, by 1922, he was working on more cynical stories in a style that blended the leanness of newspaper journalism and the experimentation of modernist stylistics in addressing the stereotypical themes of pulp stories. Hemingway's growth as a writer from unsuccessful pulp hack to virtuoso modernist minimalist in the matter of only a few years points to both his drive and ability. Yet still, the role popular literature and magazines played in this growth is almost entirely overlooked.

Whereas it would be fruitful to hunt for such Hemingwayesque themes as grace under pressure in the early and unpublished manuscripts (as many critics have already done), it would be more interesting to consider canonized and famous early stories like "The Killers," "Fifty Grand," "The Battler," and "My Old Man" in relation to the pulps and popular culture.[24] These stories are about gambling, gangsters, and boxers and are working off of or influenced by the pulp milieu, if not stylistically then at least thematically. "My Old Man," for example, a widely anthologized story about gambling, gangsters, and fixed horse races, is usually regarded as being inspired by Sherwood Anderson's racing stories, though Hemingway denied this in an early letter to Edmund Wilson. But considering the stories that directly preceded it, including "Ash Heels Tendon" and "A Matter of Colour" (written years before Hemingway read Anderson), it can just as easily be seen as a continuation of the pulp influence, given its popular "underworld" themes.[25]

Indeed, Hemingway's evolution from "The Current" to "The Killers" parallels the movement in pulp writing from melodramatic romantic adventure to cynical hard-boiled themes and stylistics. Though Hemingway is often credited with its invention, the hard-boiled style is a product of the pulp magazines, specifically the writing of John Carrol Daly and Dashiell Hammett in *Black Mask*. Critics who contend that Hemingway significantly influenced or even invented the hard-boiled style do not take into account that both Daly and Hammett were perfecting the style as early as 1922 and 1923, respectively, and that Hemingway's first widely read hard-boiled works—"The Battler" and especially "The Killers," which was Hemingway's first major periodical publication—were not published until 1925 and 1927.[26] Whereas Hemingway's style influenced later generations of hard-

Dashiell Hammett's second appearance was in this issue of *Black Mask* from 1923. Even though the hard-boiled tone was being perfected in these issues, *Black Mask* was still publishing "Romantic Adventure" as well as mystery and detective stories. ©1923 Pro-Distributers Publishing Co.

boiled writers (and writers in general, especially those after World War II), his themes grew out of the same conflation of popular literary topics and modernist postwar cynicism. And just as Hemingway's writing can be seen as a response to masculine trauma—whether his war injury, his jilted love affair with Agnes von Kurowsky, or his overbearing mother—the masculine pulp genre, especially the hard-boiled variety, is seen as a reaction to the traumas of the war, the Depression, or new woman feminism.

Whether or not Hemingway was an influence on or was influenced by the hard-boiled genre, it is clear that many of the settings, types, and topics were shared by the pulp magazines. The themes he explored in his early fiction reflect the trauma of what happens when youthful myths and preconceptions are shattered—a tone that is certainly hard, if not hard boiled. Also, stories such as "The Mercenaries" foreshadow many themes and tropes of his later fiction, such as impartial narrator with inside access, male bonding based on war and drinking, political cynicism, and a deflation of courage. But it is just as true that these stories also reflect aspects of the masculine pulp milieu, especially the detective and crime magazines, which evinced this same urban pessimism.

HEMINGWAY'S MODERNISM AND THE PULPS

Embedding early Hemingway into the milieu of the popular magazines illustrates that the demarcation between popular and early modernist fiction was not so easy to see. It is no coincidence, for example, that *Black Mask* was started by cultural impresarios H. L. Mencken and George Jean Nathan as a means to pay for their more "literary" magazine *The Smart Set,* which published the likes of James Joyce, F. Scott Fitzgerald, and Ezra Pound. But, mixing the "high brow" and "low brow," *The Smart Set,* like other early fiction publications, also featured stories by pulp writers such as Achmed Abdullah and Dashiell Hammett. Though the traditions of literary criticism would shy away from seeing pulp fiction among canonical works, many of the historical foundations are the same. And evidence of the pulp influence in modernist works or on modernist authors, such as Hemingway, underscores the popular and the accessible in "quality" high-brow literature of this era.[27]

While it would be a stretch to label modernist poetry like T. S. Eliot's *The Waste Land* "popular," it does rely on popular allusions as well as erudite ones (especially the footnotes), and it's worth acknowledging that Eliot also wrote "Old Possum's Book of Practical Cats" as well as an introduction to

Pierre Louys' racy *Bubu of Montparnasse.* Remember, too, that James Joyce's *Ulysses* was read as much as a sensational book as a masterful one. And whereas Hemingway's early pulpish stories are a far cry from the stylistic mastery of his later prose, he tellingly wrote to his publisher Horace Liveright that "my book will be praised by highbrows and can be read by lowbrows. There is no writing in it that anybody with a high-school education cannot read."[28] In this letter he acknowledges the influence of the mass market and makes clear his early desire to reach a popular audience.

Even what is arguably Hemingway's most literary work, *The Sun Also Rises,* is akin to contemporary and sensational risqué pulp magazines. Like F. Scott Fitzgerald's novels and stories of the Jazz Age a few years before, Hemingway's popular 1926 novel captured the imagination of his generation. Whereas it was lauded for its original style, it was decried for the sensationalism of alcohol, travel, and sex that covered an existential emptiness. Reviewers dwelled on how the book was "about utterly degraded people . . . sensationalism and triviality" and how "the characters, both men and women, . . . are so consistently soaking themselves with alcohol as to lose all human interest. . . . O that wearisome, drenching deluge of drink!"[29] But based on the sales of the book, the reading public was undeterred by the negative critical reviews. In 1926 and 1927 the novel sold almost 28,000 copies and, as its editor Max Perkins had hoped it would, effectively dispelled Scribners' reputation as a conservative publishing house. In an effort to appeal to the youth culture of the day, Scribners' marketing campaign made full use of the book's cynical tone, Parisian locale, and "literary revolt."[30] It obviously worked, since contemporary accounts tell of college students emulating its characters—dropping out of college, running to Paris, and "talking in tough understatements from the sides of their mouths."[31]

No doubt part of the novel's success could be attributed to its bohemian, Left Bank setting, which featured a life that was romantic to Prohibition-era America. The mid-1920s explosion of French-themed girlie pulps onto the American magazine market further illustrates the popular, if lurid, fascination with risqué booze-and-flapper-laden fiction. Sparked by the success of what pulp historian Douglas Ellis calls the first true girlie pulp, *Paris Nights,* in 1925, numerous knock-offs appeared, including *Gay Parisienne, La Paree Stories, Paris Frolics, Parisian Life, French Follies, Streets of Paris, French Stories, French Nightlife Stories*—all of which featured nude or semi-nude cover art. And like the hard-boiled pulps, these also had modernist foundations.[32]

In 1914 and 1915, Mencken and Nathan started *The Parisienne* and *Saucy Stories Magazine* using manuscripts not included in *The Smart Set.* After the war, these two magazines, along with their competitor, *Snappy Stories,*

Above: Fiction pulps, such as *Saucy Stories, Snappy Stories, Telling Tales,* and the later *Smart Set,* played off the early- to mid-1920s fascination with modernism, especially flappers testing the boundaries of morality and propriety. Later-generation modernists such as Dawn Powell and Robert Coates got their start in such magazines as these. ©1924 The New Fiction Publishing Corp.

Below: The popularity of the Left Bank scene, which Hemingway used in *The Sun Also Rises* gave rise to a myriad of racy pulps such as *La Paree, French Follies,* and *Gay Parisienne.* ©1933 Merwil Publishing Co.

became increasingly sensational, reflecting the postwar generation's rebellion against Victorian moral codes and challenge of cultural complacency (albeit with a creeping misogyny). Their innate modernist trappings, such as bohemian locales and glamorized flappers on the covers, brought modernism into a visual and popular sphere. For example, *The Parisienne* (and its ensuing imitators) cashed in on the sensual promise that bohemian Paris held in provincial America. It abounded with stories about art models, free-loving musettes, and the notorious Moulin Rouge. *The Parisienne* was even successful enough to be noticed by John Saxton Sumner, head of the New York Society for the Suppression of Vice, who brought publisher Eltinge Warner up on obscenity charges in 1915.[33] This was just a single instance of where the battleground of the "loosening" morals of the post-WWI years would become a meeting place for both pulps and modernist literature.

That testing of and pushing against the boundaries of taste and "decency" done in popular magazines of the day, among them *The Smart Set, The Parisienne,* and Macfadden's *True Story,* was exactly what modernists writers were doing in their fiction—and one reason for their early popularity. Like much of the work of the modernists, including Fitzgerald and Hemingway, these magazines tapped into the popularity of flapper youth culture, especially their attitudes toward drinking, smoking, and, above all, sex. According to historian Ronald Allen Goldberg, "The breakdown of the Victorian code, with its emphasis on feminine purity . . . accelerated during the 1920s. There was greater sexual freedom during the decade, reflecting the influence of Freud, the automobile, and the 'sex and confess' magazines."[34]

In January 1922, the story "The Art of Ki-Ki" appeared in *Snappy Stories.* About a French model/cabaret singer in London who is engaged to a penniless modern artist estranged from his millionaire father because he won't go into business, the story is based on the real Kiki, Alice Prin, the most famous muse of the Paris avant-garde, the lover of Man Ray, friend of Hemingway, and a frequent model for Picasso. Kiki, with her famous pageboy haircut, embodied modernism. In 1930 Hemingway would write the introduction to her memoirs.

In popular magazines like *Snappy,* the flapper became the most ubiquitous representation of the "new woman" of the 1920s, young women who challenged the conventions with liberal attitudes toward gender roles, sex, fashion, and careers. Liz Conor points out that "she was both indulged and made deviant by magazines that assumed a male readership, and she was at once a darling and the disdained of women's print media."[35] Not merely commodified or objectified by the men, the flapper figures in these magazine stories were often sexually open and independent women who usually outsmarted erring husbands or confirmed bachelors. For example, the *Snappy* short story about Ki-Ki has the model ingeniously making both herself and her fiancé famous while paving the way for their marriage by teaching the boy's father to respect modern art.

Similarly, with *The Sun Also Rises* reviewers saw Lady Brett Ashley as "a perfect product of that postwar world of which Mr. Hemingway is the brilliant chronicler. After all we have suffered from novelists intent on describing hard-boiled flappers, Ernest Hemingway comes along with this modern version of *la femme de trente ans,* and we know more about the eternal feminine, model 1926, than ever before."[36] But Lady Brett also suffered the vicissitudes of such readings, being both demonized as a femme fatale and lauded as a proto-feminist figure. Either way, the popularity of *The Sun Also Rises* and Brett's fierce independence and open attitude toward drinking and sex made her a figure of emulation for college girls.

This public fascination with Hemingway's characters was extended to the author himself. It was during the mid-1920s that Hemingway's true or imagined drinking, brawling, or bullfighting exploits became newsworthy. His popularity became a story itself, as Guy Hickok's *Brooklyn Daily* article of March 4, 1928, "Paris Won't Let Hemingway Live a Private Life" illustrates. The rise of Hemingway's public persona had begun.

HEMINGWAY, *TO HAVE AND HAVE NOT,* AND THE DEPRESSION-ERA PULPS

By the mid-1930s, it was clear that Hemingway had fulfilled his early promise as the voice of his generation. The success of *The Sun Also Rises* was quickly followed by the much-lauded short story collection *Men Without Women* (1927) and the best-selling *A Farewell to Arms* (1929), which cemented his position as an established literary celebrity. But this fame also opened Hemingway up to derision. In the mid-1930s he published two works of nonfiction: *Death in the Afternoon,* a voluminous reflection on bullfighting, writing, and art; and *Green Hills of Africa,* a memoir of big-game hunting. As America suffered through the Great Depression, numerous literary critics thought that Hemingway had sold out, that he was wasting his talent writing about such banal and privileged pursuits. He answered that criticism with *To Have and Have Not,* a novel that not only contains working-class sympathy but is both influenced by and comments on commercial pulp writing.

Pulp magazines flourished during the Depression; they not only offered inexpensive escapism for millions, but they also gave the working class a

Many pulps illustrated and pandered to populist fears surrounding the Great Depression and the Spanish Civil War—*Operator #5* more so than most. The magazine featured a long-running story line about a foreign fascist takeover of America: "Civilization, already weakened by months of bloody conflict, begins to crumble."
©1937 Popular Publications

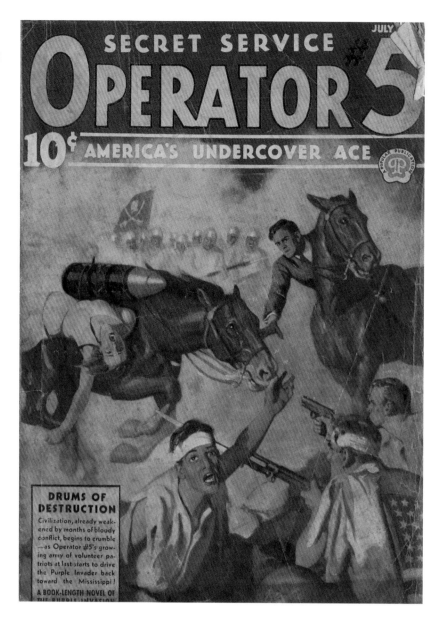

venue for social criticism. Pulps like *Operator #5*, with its long-running story line about the military and economic downfall of America at the hands of a ruthless dictator, created a cynical vision of a disintegrating society that reflected the bleak economic scene and the rising threat of fascism. In the gangster and detective pulps, heroes inhabited a space somewhere beyond pure good and evil, since in Depression-era America the traditional good guys—policemen and government officials—were often portrayed as corrupt. Science fiction pulps frequently used fantastic utopian and dystopian settings as parables for modern society. And authors of hard-boiled fiction, most famously Dashiell Hammett, Raymond Chandler, and Horace Mc-Coy, injected political and class commentary into their stories, but in ways that were neither overt nor preachy.[37] Other authors, among them Milton Lowe and Bruno Fischer (former editor of the *Socialist Call*), looked to the pulps as a way to reach a wider, working-class readership and specialized in proletariat heroes such as hobos and even handicapped detectives.

The attitude of the leftist avant-garde and intelligentsia during the Depression, which had criticized Hemingway, called for novels of blatant socialism. Hemingway's own politics at this time were sympathetic enough to socialism and communism that he rescinded his "editorship" of the antifascist magazine *Ken* when it was critical of communism. He was also working hard for the republican cause in the Spanish Civil War, donating time, money, articles, and narrating the propaganda film *The Spanish Earth*. Yet rather than pandering to the critics' call for an overtly political novel, Hemingway offered a pulp novel with a true hard-boiled, working-class hero in *To Have and Have Not*'s rum-running Harry Morgan. Like many Depression-era pulp heroes, Morgan blurs the line between good and bad, and throughout the novel he struggles to make a living in increasingly dire and illegal circumstances, from deep-sea fishing charters to rum-running to smuggling illegal aliens. In the novel Hemingway also paints politicians and the wealthy as petty and corrupt. At one point one of the "three most important men in the administration" out on a fishing cruise sees Morgan dumping alcohol and wants to arrest him as a bootlegger. The charter boat captain tells him that Morgan has "got a family and he's got to eat and feed them. Who the hell do you eat off of with people working here in Key West for the government for six dollars and a half a week?" Morgan's own social commentary is even more explicit; his last words are "a man alone ain't got no bloody fucking chance."[38]

But more than this, in the novel Hemingway criticizes his critics by damning literature that panders to the current fashion for overt political content over realistic and working-class practicality. Richard Gordon, the writer figure in the book, provides juxtaposition with Morgan's Depression-era struggle. Gordon's pretentious and vicarious "socialist" novels are contrasted with stark reality when he encounters a group of WWI vets, shell-shocked and brutal, the government's forgotten men. He "feels a little sick" at their unromantic tales of life. After Gordon brags that he has written three books and is currently working on one about the 1929 Gastonia labor strikes, one vet, a true radical, recognizes Gordon's name and refuses to accept drinks from him because his books are "shit." Hemingway's portrayal of Gordon is highly unsympathetic: his marriage falls apart because of his philandering, his pandering to people, and, as his wife accuses, his changing "politics to suit the fashion."[39]

Harry Morgan, however, is the prototypical Hemingway hero, a man defined by his ethical workmanlike attitude, whether fishing or smuggling, whether inside or outside of the law. This is made apparent in the original title of one of the short stories that made up *To Have and Have Not:* "The Tradesman's Return." The proletariat practicality of Morgan, in contrast to Gordon's empty "work," reflects the working-class attitude toward the pulps versus "high-brow" literary output. In a 1933 letter to the *New York Times,* pulp writer Will McMorrow claimed that pulps were unlike "the Brahman type of [magazine] to be found on the library table of every cultured home. With the pages uncut. Wood-pulp magazines are not bought for ornamental purposes. They are read."[40] In a similar parallel, Hemingway contrasts the vapidity of the Key West tourists like Gordon with the hardworking "Conchs" like Morgan. The book's final line reaffirms this working-class practicality: "A large white yacht was coming into the harbor and seven miles out on the horizon you could see a tanker, small and neat in profile against the blue sea, hugging the reef as she made way westward to keep from wasting fuel against the stream."[41]

A work of fiction reflects its time, its writer's concern, and the concerns of his generation. In *To Have and Have Not,* Hemingway portrays the situation of the working class, of WWI vets quietly struggling below the radar of acceptable literature. At one point in the book, one of the vets—shell-shocked, brutal, forgotten by society—asks, "You haven't got a book with you? . . . Pal, I'd like to read one. Did you ever write for *Western Stories,* or *War Aces*? I could read that *War Aces* every day." With that allusion, Hemingway acknowledges how the pulps, like forgotten vets of literature, reflect the modern condition, the empty violence and struggle in Depression-era America. *To Have and Have Not* is Hemingway's most extended work of pulp themes, his most hard-boiled work and the sparse, workmanlike modernist culmination of his own pulp tutelage, his early emulation of and aspirations to the pulp genre.

The following interview from *Bluebook* is the first of many that appeared in the fifties men's magazines, and its circumstances are typical: a noticeably star-struck young reporter hunts down the author in Cuba—in this instance at the Floridita bar—becomes drinking buddies and fast friends and relates the "inside scoop" on the famous author to the reader. But in another sense this interview is atypical. In comparison to later interviews, the mythologizing is relatively staid and contains insight into Hemingway's political shift during the Cold War and his attitude on violence, popular literature, and the 1950s best-selling author Mickey Spillane.

By the late 1950s, *Bluebook* declined into pure sensationalism, often featuring military action or sadistic torture covers. But at the time of this interview, it was still one of the three most respected men's magazines, along with *Argosy* and *True,* all of which pandered to the fatherly, suburban adventurer. *Bluebook* was the kind of magazine that you could find at the family barbershop, as you can tell by the humorous Norman Rockwell–like cover. Besides the interview, this issue also featured stories about Olympic weightlifter Bob Hoffman, vending machines, living in a trailer, escaping from Devil's Island, as well as the usual sports, crime, and western fiction. *Blue Book,* one of the most respected adventure pulps for almost fifty years, became *Bluebook* in 1951, marking the magazine's final years of respectability. Ironically, Hemingway had stories rejected from them in the late teens.

Little is known of the interviewer, Jackson Burke, beside other stories that he published in the men's magazines. It could very well be a pen name, which was a pretty standard convention for the men's magazines. His other stories include an interview with Mickey Spillane in the April 1955 issue of *Man's Conquest,* which quotes Hemingway's thoughts on Spillane, and "Matadors Die Rich" for the June 1953 issue of *Bluebook,* which he alludes to in this interview. Interestingly he also published a different version of this same interview twice, first in *Conquest* (April 1955) and then in *Man's Illustrated* (September 1958). Whereas the setting and situation is the same— reporter finds Hemingway in bar and they proceed to get sloshed together—this second interview goes on to tell how the reporter "discovers" the original Santiago, inspiration for *The Old Man and the Sea.* But in this fisherman's version, it all happened during a hurricane. In general, these latter interviews are much more sensational, more fictionalized than the earlier *Bluebook* interview, which stands on its own merit due, in part, to *Bluebook*'s higher quality.

The portrait of Hemingway that Burke paints is of a gruff, knowledgeable father figure shelling out advice as fast as he sucks down daiquiris, jumping from topic to topic. Boxing, fishing, writing, drinking—an expert in them all. It is summed up in the final lines of the later version of this interview published in *Man's Illustrated,* "He was real. He had truth in him. The old master knew some smart things." It is this portrait that epitomized Hemingway's "Papa" persona from the mid-1940s on.

Whether you like him or not, you have to admit that "Papa" Hemingway is a terrific hunk of man. And a terrific hunk of writer. Witness his recent Pulitzer Prize.

The old maestro sat at the end of the bar in the Cafe Floridita, with an eight-ounce frozen daiquiri in his hand. I sat near him and started the conversation. Three hours later he had put away seven more of the outsized daiquiris, and when he left he carried one away with him. By that time we had talked about Mickey Spillane, bullfighting, drinking, writing, and hunting.

It was the typical Cuban way of spending the midday, when the tropical sun is blazing outside, and within the saloons it's cool. And the Cafe Floridita is where Hemingway always hangs out when he's in Havana. He always sits on the same bar stool, too, and drinks the same drink—tall frozen daiquiris in large amounts, made by Pedrito, the Spanish expert on this drink.

The old man of the sea looked pretty rugged—tall, over six feet, around 220 pounds of fighting muscle. He doesn't shave often because of a skin ailment, and his white, stubbled beard gives him the look of an ancient mariner. But those merry brown eyes and that broad grin remind you that the ageing [sic] Hemingway is still all man—and more man than anyone else in his class.

Naturally I wanted to know his opinion of Spillane. So I asked him about it, point-blank: "What do you think of America's latest literary sensation, Mickey Spillane?"

"Why ask *me?*" His deep, rumbling voice was friendly but challenging.

"Because you're the man who started this school of writing—tough writing about hard guys."

This struck Hemingway as funny. He laughed loudly and slapped the bar. Then he said, "And you

think Spillane writes that way? Well, you're wrong. Spillane doesn't even understand his own subject. He thinks he's writing about crime. He isn't. I'll give you facts. Remember my story 'The Short Happy Life of Francis Macomber'?[1] Francis' wife hates him because he's a coward. But when he gets his guts back, she fears him so much she has to kill him—shoots him in the back of the head. That's crime. If she had shot him when he was a coward, that's one thing. But shooting a brave man because he is brave—*that's* crime. The Spillane type wouldn't understand this if they broke their brains trying. So don't tell me they belong in my school. They belong with the comic books."

"When I came into the bar I noticed you were reading a comic book yourself."

"Sure. But I don't call it literature. Spillane started out as a comic-book writer, and he's still one, to my way of thinking. He even admits it himself. People who read him, [sic] don't read me. They couldn't."

"He's very popular."

"Naturally. There are lots of scared little bank clerks and office boys.[2] They read stuff like 'I the Jury.' But they couldn't read 'The Old Man and the Sea.' I don't break a man's arm just to hear the bones crack or shoot a woman in the belly when there are lots of better things to do with her. Spillane's violence is for its own sake and means nothing. But if you find violence in good literature, it's only because violence is a natural condition of human life—except for bank clerks and office boys. Don't talk to me about Spillane."

He called the bartender. "*Hola,* Pedrito! Set 'em up in the other alley!"

We started on a couple more of frozen daiquiris. The drink was invented at the Floridita, and they still make the best ones in Cuba—or anywhere else, for that matter. Pedrito keeps plenty of bitter green olives and cold fried fish in front of you, so there's not so much danger of falling on your face from an overload of daiquiris. It's important to eat when you drink.

Hemingway consumed a lot of these hors d'oeuvres with his drinks. He's a big man, and he needs a lot.

As we talked, various persons known to Hemingway would come through from time to time and greet him. He always had a smile and shake of the hand ready for his friends. When they saw he was there, they brightened up as if they had seen a long lost friend. His popularity was amazing. And he was popular with everyone.

Pedrito, Hemingway's special bartender, kept one eye on the old maestro's glass as he worked. And usually there was a fresh drink ready before Hemingway had to ask for it.

Hemingway is easy to find in Havana. Just ask anyone and you'll get an answer like this: "Hemingway? The American writer? When he comes to town he always goes to the Cafe Floridita. You will find him there around eleven o'clock in the morning." That's how I found him.

There are many ways to interview a famous person. Sometimes it's in his office or in his home. Usually it is not in a bar. And in only one case is it in such a bar as the Floridita. As Hemingway remarked during the course of our long talk, "I like to come here and meet my friends. The frozen daiquiri oils the wheels of social progress."

I was glad he had said what he did about the

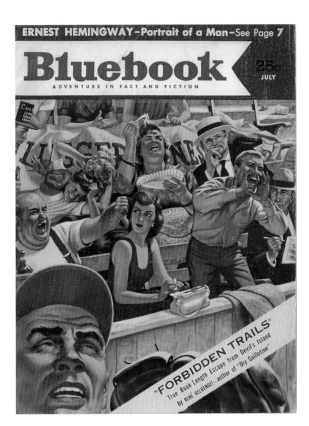

The first issue of *Conquest* (July 1955) published another version of Burke's interview. The teaser on the contents page brags, "Conquest interviews Ernest Hemingway. He's hard drinking, hard loving, hard writing." ©1955 Hanro Corp.

The July 1953 *Bluebook* published Jackson Burke's interview with Hemingway. ©McCall Corp.

Spillane school of writing, that weird phenomenon in American publishing. Practically everyone in the trade agrees that the new school hasn't taken a single reader away from writers like Hemingway, and it was good to hear Hemingway express himself on this matter.

But there was something else I wanted to ask him. I didn't quite know how to go about it. A few months ago, *Life* published a so-called expose on Spanish bullfighting. According to *Life,* an old matador named Bienvenida complained that bullfighting in Spain had gone to hell because everywhere the bulls' horns were being sawed off, thus taking the risk and danger out of the sport. *Life* showed a set of photographs as proof.

We were having another daiquiri and rolling the poker dice when I figured I'd better just up and ask. He was in thick with *Life,* true enough, and had got several dollars from them for "The Old Man and the Sea," and maybe he wouldn't want to bite the hand that fed him. But I figured the old maestro would come out with the truth regardless.

"How about that *Life* magazine expose?" I asked. "What do you think?"

"Come again?"

"As the man who introduced bullfighting to American readers with 'Death in the Afternoon,' what do you think of *Life's* story?"

"It's all true, of course. What did you expect me to say?" Those sharp brown eyes peered at me quizzically from beneath the shaggy brows.

"Did Manolete get gored by a sawed-off horn?"

"Now, step down. I didn't say it was the whole truth. I just said it was all true—which it is. Do you know anything about bullfighting?"

"A little. I gave it a whirl down in Mexico last year."

"Good. Did you get next to any bulls?"

"A couple."

"And did they have sawed-off horns?"

"Not hardly. I've got a scar on my forehead from a horn that had a damned sharp point."

Hemingway peered at the small scar just under the hairline. He said, "Good. Now, did you ever see bulls with sawed-off horns in the arenas?"

"Twice. Pat McCormick's first fight at Juarez, and one Sunday when Juanita Aparicio appeared at Guadalajara."

"Lady bullfighters, both of them. Well, the McCormick girl no longer fights sawed-off horns. She's really in there now. That goring she got at Aguascalientes proves it. Now, sometimes you'll see men fighting blunted horns. But these are sawed-off *men,* if you get me."

A Cuban woman, no longer in the first bloom of youth but still retaining some of her former beauty, came into the Floridita. Hemingway stood up and spoke to her in Spanish. They conversed for a short while, then she left.

Looking after her, he grinned and said to me; "I've stood up for that woman many years now, and I'll still stand up for her. Now what were we saying about bullfighting?"

"We'd just about agreed that sawed-off horns do sometimes happen, but no good *torero* ever does it. What about Bienvenida? Did you know him in Spain?"

"Bienvenida? Sure. Toward the end of 1936, he and some other bullfighters joined up with Franco's forces. Bienvenida and Maravilla followed Marcial Lalanda into battle."

"On the side of Franco?"

"That's right."

"Fascists, eh?" I commented.

Hemingway took a deep pull at his daiquiri and said in a deep growl, "Now, look here. I don't know whether you were in Spain at that time, but I was, and I know that you can't say fascist and anti-fascist the way you say black and white. Sure, Franco was a fascist. But the government he was fighting against was controlled by Communists.

"Let me tell you something not everybody knows. During the night of October 18, 1936, 1,000 women from the aristocratic Salamanca quarter of Valencia were arrested by government troops and bundled into two mansions that had been commandeered for this purpose. Mind you, their men were not seized. And all night long, fathers and husbands and sons and brothers stood helplessly outside those two mansions, calling to their women. That's one thing.

"But there's something else. No one knows how many thousands of priests and nuns were murdered by the so-called Loyalist government. Franco was a fascist. Well, Spain needed a strong man to protect the women, the homes and families, the Church. Now I'll tell you something else. Marcial Lalanda, at that time, was one of the greatest of Spain's matadors. He was also President of the Spanish Socialist Bullfighters' Union. The Communist government wrecked his union. Marcial Lalanda, *matador de toros,* took up arms as a captain of artillery, fighting the men who had done these things. With him went Bienvenida and Maravilla. Soon the great Belmonte himself joined Franco.

"And there were other *toreros,* too, who joined Franco not because they were fascists (for many were socialists) but because they knew the greater enemy was their own government, run by a Communist clique.

"And along with these bullfighters went such famous ones as Chicuelo, Torerito, Sanchez Mejia, Curro Cairo, Gitanillo.

"Bienvenida, who was *Life*'s informant on the sawing of the horns, told a true story. But *Life* itself didn't tell the whole story. And part of it is that Bienvenida himself was always too fine a man of honor ever to fight blunted horns."

Cuba is, of course, run by a dictatorship, too. I asked Hemingway what he thought of Batista, the strong man of Cuba.

He frowned and said, "I don't mix into politics. I like the Cubans, and they don't like Batista. Maybe they'll do something about him. But I'm a foreigner here, you know. I can't go butting in. Well, I did give some rights to 'The Old Man and the Sea' to *Bohemia* magazine."[3] (This is an anti-Batista review.) "No, I just live my own life and mind my own business. I'm a beat-up old bird. I can't go joining revolutions when I have other books to write. That's for younger men. There shall be wars and rumors of wars. Might as well enjoy it. Go find yourself a revolution, young fellow. Try Cuba, maybe."

"What are you writing now?"

"Can't tell you. I don't want to talk it all away. And I don't want any publicity about it. When I write, I try to avoid publicity. A man needs a private life to write, and sometimes he has to seem a bit rude to keep his private life. Now I have to work like hell to write a better book than my last one, which I had a lot of luck with, and I am laying off all publicity until I have done something that's worth talking about. And until then all I can do is to hope I'll be able to keep my mouth shut as tight as possible."

I asked him for just a hint of what his new book will be about, but he wouldn't crack. It's a safe guess, though, that it will be about one of the sports of death, or maybe about the tragic things that happen to those engaged in the sports of love. He probably will not write a war book. I asked him if he had thought of doing a bullfight novel, since several already have been successful and the men's magazines all have run bullfight articles.

"Maybe some day; not now. I liked Tom Lea's book all right, but these magazine articles on bullfighting are the most ignorant damn things I ever read."[4]

"I had one in last month's *Bluebook.*"[5]

"Well, I hope it was better than the others. You say you studied bullfighting in Mexico? Did you write about how the young men have to buy their own bulls?"

"Yes, all that."

"You probably wrote it all right, then. Ever go hunting?"

"No. I never did. Are you planning a trip?"

"I'd like to finish this new book first and then go to Africa again. If you don't hunt every so often you get fat—fat in the head and fat in the heart. Hunting keeps your brains where they belong and your heart in the right place.

"And there's something about Africa. I don't know what it is, but when you go there you feel it. It's big and exciting. Make some money, young man, and go hunting in Africa."

"Ever hear of Alex Montani?"

"No. Who's he?"

"A South American bullfighter who went hunting in Africa armed with nothing but his fighting cape."

"You know him?" he asked.

"I've talked with him," I said.

"What animals did he find with the cape?"

"I can't remember all of them, but I've got the notes written down somewhere. The buffalo was one of them—and the rhinoceros, too. He'd pass the animal with the cape a few times and then his hunter would shoot the beast."

Hemingway frowned and said, "I wonder what he was trying to do. Did he say?"

"Sure. He just wondered whether some of this African big game would run like the fighting bull—straight for the cape, not at the man. Of course, he'd never know until it was over. By then, it would have been too late. But luck was with him."

Hemingway pondered this awhile. Then he said, "I'll stick to guns."

I offered him a good Cuban cigar, but he refused, saying, "I don't smoke any more. Used to, though; but it makes you feel bad in the morning, so I quit it. Liquor is another matter. Only thing wrong with rum is the cost. I'll sign the tab here for about $15. Every nine months I go broke."

"But you made a lot on 'The Old Man and the Sea,' didn't you?"

"What's 'a lot,' young man?"

"*Life* said $30,000."

"I know. And someone else guessed $50,000 and another one $65,000. What I got was $40,000. Ever figure out the tax on that? Besides, I have heavy expenses. My wife doesn't spend anything; she's a fine girl, and she saves dough for me. But I have a house, a car, a boat, servants, cats, dogs, pigeons, cows—out there at Finca Vigia. You ought to see that place."

"I'd like to, but I go back to the States tomorrow morning early."

"Well, I'm busy on this new book until June, anyway."

"Working on it every day?"

"Can't work days. I write at night. Bad for the eyes, but that can't be helped."

"How are your eyes now?" I noticed he wore steel-rimmed spectacles when reading.

"Not bad. I've got one bad eye and one good one. Some son-of-a-bitch poked his finger in my eye one time, and I can't see out of it ever since. But the other one is fine."

"You've had a lot of trouble that way, haven't you?"

"Some. Seven concussions, six broken ribs. . . ." He ordered another round of daiquiris. "Well, we can't worry about a few little accidents. They're bound to happen if we don't hide in bed. Matter of fact, some of the worst accidents of all can happen to you right in your own bed."

He chuckled quietly over that one.

Hemingway's white hair might deceive the casual onlooker, but actually he still is in fine shape.

I wondered how he managed to keep fit. So I asked him about boxing, knowing he always liked to work out. Some say he could fell a horse with his fist.

"I don't do much any more," he said. "Game fishing and fooling around the farm keep me in shape. I still like to see a good prizefight, though."

"Do you know Kid Gavilan?" I asked.[6]

"Sure thing. The greatest little welterweight in the world. Know him?"

"I've talked with him out at his farm."

"Ever notice his hands?" Hemingway asked.

"What do you mean?"

"His hands. They're murderous in the ring, but when he touches the faces of his children, or his pretty wife, those powerful hands open like delicate flowers and you see long slender artistic fingers. The guy is as gentle as a lamb. A clean fighter, too."

"You must be pretty happy in Cuba," I remarked. "Here you have a highly sporting country—baseball, boxing, horse-racing, fishing—"

"Well, considering the size of this little island," he answered, "I guess we have as good baseball as in the States. And you're right about the Cubans: they're a very sporting people. Like the Spanish and the Mexicans. You know Spain?"

"Never been there," I replied. "But I hear it's wonderful."

"Yes, the bullfights, the wonderful wines, the spirit of the people. It's one of the poorest countries in Europe, but the people still have that terrific spirit of *alegria*. I don't know what that word is in English, but it means a deep-going happiness that nothing can kill."

He had said that game fishing helped him to keep in shape, and I wondered about "The Old Man and the Sea"—whether Hemingway himself had ever caught a marlin like the one in the book. In the novel, an old Cuban fisherman hooks an 18-foot, 1500-pound blue marlin which drags him on a wild two-day ride. This fish breaks records. The world's record for black marlin (the Pacific counterpart of the blue marlin found in the Caribbean) is a 1095-pound fish caught on August 23,

1952, by Alfred C. Glassell, Jr., of Houston, Texas, at Cabo Blanco, Peru. This is the largest fish which has ever been taken by rod and reel.

"Well," Hemingway said, "that's hard to answer. Maybe I did, and maybe I didn't. We've got bigger ones in these Caribbean waters. The commercial fishermen along the waterfront of Havana often bring in blues weighing 1500 pounds or more. Personally, I've hooked some damn big ones, but I never brought in a fish that big. There's a long time between hooking one of those giants and bringing him in. Lots of them get away. But I guess I've fought the big ones." He handed me another daiquiri and asked, "Do you fish?"

"Not lately. Used to fish a little around Catalina—yellowtail, albacore, tuna, barracuda."

"Tuna and barracuda with light tackle can be fun," Hemingway said. "But hunting's the thing. I'm impatient to get back to Africa—maybe this summer after I finish the new book, if I can get it done that fast. My wife keeps after me to work harder on it. From Africa I want to go up to Venice and shoot ducks. My wife is good with the shotgun, too. Once a party of six of us downed 331 ducks in one afternoon near Venice. And then, maybe we'll get up to Paris again." His eyes took on a dreamy look. "I like to go back to Paris," he said. "We were all young there and worked hard and played harder. I got started there."

A party of American tourists came into the bar then, and I observed that the women looked cold, compared with the Cuban girls.

Hemingway had a good laugh over that and said, "So you know the difference, eh? Walk down the street and look into the black eyes of these Cuban girls and you'll see hot sunlight in them—fierce and wild, but friendly, too. No doubt you've noticed the difference in the way they walk. Our girls come down here on a trip, and they're still wearing girdles, so they walk stiffly and coldly. But these Cubans! . . . A girdle manufacturer would die of starvation down here. Yeah, you can always tell a Cuban girl by the way she walks—free and easy and unashamed. But of course, I'm a married man. I live down here because of the climate and the fishing. And because I like Spanish people."

Hemingway spoke in Spanish from time to time, mixing up the two languages. His Spanish was very good.

I asked him if he would compete in the big Cuban shoot that was scheduled for the near future. Antonio Solar, of the Cuban government, had purchased around 4,000 live pigeons from the States for the big shoot. But Hemingway said that, no, what with a flock of pigeons of his own, and the need to work hard on the new book, he just didn't think he'd be able to enter the competition. Besides, with Africa maybe coming up very soon, he would wait.

So with plenty of tall frozen daiquiris and smooth Cuban cigars (the latter for me only) and talk about this and that, we spent a very pleasant three hours. In fact, after a few of those oversized daiquiris the Floridita bar seemed just about the finest saloon in the Western hemisphere. Which it may be. They also serve a filet mignon that can't be beaten even at Antoine's, and a lobster with mayonnaise that will make small men grow strong. Hemingway is right in picking the Floridita as his headquarters. But the prices are a trifle high. I saw one customer sign a three months' bar bill for $1,500.

I asked Hemingway about his standing with the literary critics, because he doesn't draw a very good press. His answer was typical.

"Well, now, would you worry a damn about the critics when your books sell? I'll really start worrying when those pantywaists write good reviews about my work."

There's a rumor that he has on occasion taken a poke or two at some of the literary reviewers. He didn't say no.

The thing that makes him not too popular with the critics, but very popular with the general reader, may be that Hemingway strikes the interviewer as a decent man—a man of decent feeling, as Evelyn Waugh (wasn't it?) once pointed out. Also, Ernest Hemingway frequently makes fools of the critics, showing up their confusion, as in "For Whom the Bell Tolls"; their cowardice, as in "The Sun Also Rises"; ridiculing their prissiness, as in "Across the River and into the Trees." I suggested these reasons to him, and again he didn't say no.

Nor would he say yes. Hemingway is a modest man, contrary to popular belief. Not backward, but modest. For example, he does not boast; he just tells the facts. It's hard for him to explain himself except in the simplest terms. I asked him if he could put into words his theory of the novel.

He said, "Hell, no. I don't make theories. I write books. My books are about people doing real things. I write about lovers and cowards and brave men and fools, showing acts of love, cowardice, bravery, foolishness."

"Like Robert Browning?" I asked.

"He's one of the greatest poets in the English language. I wouldn't say I write like him, but he did write about the same things I do."

"Who would you say is the best younger novelist in America right now?"

"There may be several good ones. There's one I like very much. Have you read Nelson Algren?"

"The Man with a Golden Arm"?

"Damn fine novel! That boy Algren has really got it."

"Do you think he has learned from Hemingway?"

"That's hard to say. Maybe he learned most of all from himself. One writer can be influenced by another, of course, but if he's any damn good at all he learns mostly from himself, and his material."

It was time to go. He had to leave before two o'clock. As he left, he carried another big frozen daiquiri with him, to keep him cool during the hot ride from Havana to his farm. A chauffeur was waiting for him outside in a Buick station wagon.

I was waiting for a parting word, hoping he would sum things up somehow.

He did.

"As one writer to another," he said slowly, and very quietly, with absolute conviction, "I can tell you something: Know your work. And do it. And live with your material."

When the station wagon had pulled out of sight, I looked around me at the hot streets of Havana and the good-natured Cuban people. These were the common people, the real ones, the ones to write about. Hemingway was to be written about, too, in a different way. For he was real. He was the truth. The old master of us all knew some pretty smart answers.

CHAPTER TWO

Pinup Papa:
Hemingway and the
Rise of Visual Culture

The premiere issue of *Esquire* (Autumn 1933) featured as its lead article "Marlin off the Morro," a "Cuban Letter" by Ernest Hemingway. The account of deep-sea fishing is illustrated with sixteen photographs, many of them featuring the proud and beaming author alongside his record-setting catches. Without the photos, the article still makes apparent Hemingway's expertise through his abundant advice on and exhaustive knowledge of the subject; but with the photos the article becomes as much about Hemingway as about fishing. This article set a trend. From the mid-1930s on, and with ever-greater frequency, photos of Hemingway at play would accompany his journalism, articles about him, even book reviews. The growth of Hemingway's public image paralleled the rise of the photo magazine genre, until both realized their most extreme form in the sensational men's pictorial magazines of the 1950s, in which Hemingway's image and presence were used again and again as a symbol of virile masculinity. It was Papa as pinup.

FROM *ESQUIRE* TO *ROGUE:* THE SHIFT FROM GRAPHIC PROPAGANDA TO POPULAR IMAGE

As critic John Raeburn states, "The importance of photographs to [Hemingway's] public reputation cannot be overemphasized."[1] Whereas many of Hemingway's articles have been collected and republished, none have included the original illustrations, so Hemingway's photogenic presence has been noted but largely overlooked in the analysis of his textual presence.

Opposite: This is one of seventeen photos that accompanied "Marlin off the Morro," Hemingway's "Cuban Letter" in the first issue of *Esquire* (Autumn 1933).

This complementary relationship between fame, photography, and persona that explains Hemingway's great popularity also reflects the general dynamic of celebrity culture, that often ghoulish fascination of ours with public personalities. The rise of celebrity culture in print media stems from the early-twentieth-century improvement of visual media (such as new photo reproduction techniques), the rise of the photo digest magazines, and the consolidation of publishing, radio, and the Hollywood studio system. Cultural critics refer to this as a shift in fluency from a written media to a more visual media.

Both this shift to visual media and the rise of celebrity culture in America stem from the growth and consolidation of modern media: popular magazines, cheap reprint book houses, movie studios, radio. As historian Amy Henderson puts it, after 1922, "the machinery providing mass information—the new broker network [of agents] and the flourishing print, broadcasting, recording, and film industries—created a ravenous market for celebrity culture. Media-generated fame became a raging popular vogue."[2]

The construction of celebrity—and especially literary celebrity—in the twenty-first century is intrinsically different from that of 1955. The dynamics of literary biography were just coming into their own then. Richard Ellman's pioneering biography on Joyce, which is still considered the high-watermark of modern literary biographies, was published in 1959, but Ellman did not quite have the maddening task that Hemingway biographers from Carlos Baker to Michael Reynolds have had. Whereas Joyce's reputation was built on works defined by their nonmarketability (seven years to write *Ulysses,* seventeen years to write *Finnegan's Wake*), Hemingway's reputation was built on literary merit, his modernist affiliation, *and* on public celebrity. Perhaps the reason there is an inordinate mass (critical or not) of Hemingway biographies is because of the difficulty disentangling the two, made all the more impossible when literary history ignores the more sensational aspects of media-based myth making in the age of the image. The many articles on Hemingway in these magazines are perfect examples of popular legend making, and, considering Hemingway's often scandalous reputation, it is important to reembed them in their original visual surroundings. But it is also important to note how Hemingway used visuality toward his own ends, either politically or in furthering his own reputation.

An example of this shift to visual storytelling as linked to Hemingway is evident in his article "Dying, Well or Badly," which appeared in the second issue of *Ken* magazine, a brother publication of *Esquire.* Sparked by the shadow of growing fascism in Europe, *Esquire*'s publishers, Arnold Gingrich

APRIL 7TH
VOL.1. NO.1 1938
THE COMING MOROCCAN REVOLT
PRICE 25¢ PER COPY
EVERY OTHER THURSDAY

The striking cover of the first issue of *Ken,* the oversized, profusely illustrated political brother publication to *Esquire.* Hemingway was a regular contributor. ©1938 Ken, Inc.

and David Smart, started *Ken* in April 1938 as a political forum. Hemingway was originally listed as an editor but rescinded when he found out about the magazine's anticommunist stance (which again illustrates his populist leaning during the 1930s). The large, oversized format of the early issues sported idiosyncratic and visually stunning caricatures, ominous extreme close-ups of a face, usually an exotic ethnic staring out at the reader. The magazine was equally visual and unflinching on the inside, and nowhere more so than in Hemingway's article.

"Dying, Well or Badly" is illustrated with extremely graphic photos of Italian dead participating in the Spanish Civil War. Shocking in their explicitness, the photos, taken by Hemingway, show soldiers hit by bombs

and tank shells, limbs or heads blown off, stiff and bloated corpses. In the short article (one page of text, four pages of photos), Hemingway details how the men died and what they carried with them. Clearly, it is a call to arms for the fight against Franco and fascism, and it ends with the statement that "people who do not have to go hungry, fight and die . . . get tired of the whole thing. They do not even want to hear about it. Perhaps these pictures will make it seem a little more real. Because those pictures are what you will look like if we let the next war come."[3] In many ways, the article is reminiscent of Hemingway's fiction, especially "A Way You'll Never Be," in which Hemingway, in much the same matter-of-fact tone, unabashedly relates postbattle scenes. The prose has been described as cinematic: the way he constructs a scene, not offering commentary but describing it almost like a photo or painting, "making it clear so the reader will see it too and have the same feeling you [the author] had."[4] But, working as he was for the Spanish cause and in a political venue not always available to him, Hemingway is editorializing with these photos in a manner similar to famous war photographer Robert Capa, whom he had become close friends with only the year before.

Unlike much of his journalism, this article in *Ken* relies on an unavoidable visuality; the photos are central to its message rather than merely decorative. In using these graphic photos, he forces the reader out of complacency. "Dying, Well or Badly," as well as the antifascist film *The Spanish Earth,* which he was narrating and filming at the same time, demonstrates how Hemingway used the visual for propagandistic means. This article, alongside those that promote his persona or lifestyle, such as "Marlin off the Morro," points toward Hemingway's awareness of the public's growing appreciation for visual storytelling, a dynamic he used in constructing and furthering his reputation.

In the same issue of *Ken* are two other examples of this shift in 1930s magazines toward the visual "language" of journalism. First is an ad for the newly launched *Look,* a magazine that celebrates the new visual language that features word balloons added to photos. The copy reads:

This is SEE-READING . . . The new editorial technique created by Look to make all subjects interesting to millions. Many is the dusty tome that cloaks an important subject with impenetrable words. The pity is that only scholars and specialists have the time and training to ferret out the facts. To the millions whom these subjects concern the most, they remain unfamiliar hearsay. But now, something has happened to change all that. A new editorial technique has been invented. It is

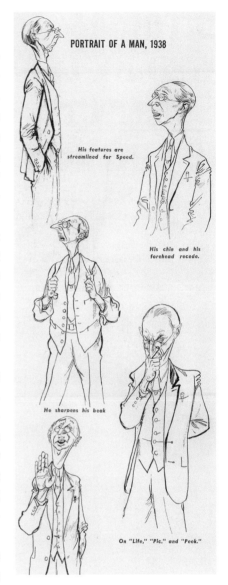

Opposite: This ad for *Look Magazine* appeared in the second issue of *Ken,* which also featured Hemingway's graphically illustrated article "Dying, Well or Badly"—both of which illustrate a conscious appeal to the new tendency for illustrated magazines . . . which *Ken* then snobbishly (and ironically) took to task on the very next page with the above cartoon.

called SEE-READING . . . a new *picture-language* that makes possible a new kind of magazine . . . LOOK. LOOK takes wordy subjects and transforms them through picture-language into fascinating SEE-READING. Today, thanks to LOOK, millions are now well informed on such various subjects as medicine, facial-makeup, child-care, slum clearance, war propaganda, religion, eye-beauty and taxes, to mention just a few. Each and every one presented in interesting picture-article form. In SEE-READING no subject is too involved or weighty to interest every member of the family.[5]

Hemingway's reliance on photos in the same issue points to not only an awareness but also a use of this visual language. And, being a voracious magazine reader, he could not help but be aware of this new fad in journalism, one popular enough to warrant a cartoon lampooning it on the very next page from the *Look* ad: "Portrait of a Man, 1938: His features are streamlined for speed. His chin and his forehead recede. He sharpens his beak on 'Life,' 'Pic,' and 'Peek.' He'd waste too much time if he'd read!"[6] The cartoon is snobbishly taking to task the middle-class American love for this new format of the news and entertainment magazine, the photo digest. "Digest" is an apt description, since they digested the news for you, condensing it into short, accessible articles. This was the idea behind *Reader's Digest, Time,* and *Newsweek.* Magazines such as *Life* and *Look* just added photographs to allow the stories to be shorter and more descriptive. It wasn't long before imitators appeared, photo magazines like *Click, Pic,* and *See,* and digest magazines like *Coronet* and *Pageant,* each increasingly sensational. In 1947 Harris Shevelson, editor of *Pageant,* stated, *"Reader's Digest* is sort of the old senator with the long beards, *Coronet* the middle-aged prosperous businessman, and we the youngster. We'll have to be more electrifying, more shocking, and perhaps brasher."[7]

Pocket photo digest magazines, such as *Show* and *Focus,* became increasingly popular in the 1950s due to the increased demand for speedy consumption. They were small, thin, pocket-sized magazines about five-by-three inches that "carried the conciseness of the news magazines almost to the point of absurdity."[8] The first such magazine was *Quick,* soon to be followed by *Tempo, Focus,* and *Point.* They were low on facts and high on movie star gossip and sensational photos; they were the slick, slightly more respectable little brothers of gossip magazines like *Confidential* and *Hush-Hush* (which isn't saying much). They illustrated the gossip and comings and goings of the illuminati.

Even the titles of magazines like *See, Foto-Rama, Focus, Show, Peek,* and *Peep Show* point to the newly entrenched visuality of American periodicals of the time. The need for speedy consumption in a popular market, which gave rise to the digest magazine, spawned *Tempo, Quick,* and *Brief.* Almost all of these were sex or gossip magazines, and all of them, whether geared toward men or a more general audience, featured pinup models. This trend contributed to, and then was energized by, the huge success of *Playboy* and its imitators.

Men's magazines of the 1950s were especially reliant on, and exemplary of, printed and popular visual culture. There were men's adventure magazines with graphic photos and covers, gossip magazines with semi-nude actresses and true crime photos, and bachelor mags, which were both the most popular and the most overtly visual. Indeed, bachelor magazines even reflexively made their visuality a selling point by making the idea of voyeurism the subject of their covers and pictorials: the May 1957 *Bachelor Magazine,* for example, which features the article "A Crazy Afternoon with Papa Hemingway," has a man in a lawn chair leisurely smoking a pipe and looking at numerous television screens, each one with a different semi-nude girl. Many magazines, like *Jem* or the 1961 *Playboy,* which publishes "Hemingway Speaks His Mind," feature nude women in picture frames or, most famously, seen through keyholes, like the pinup covers of the early *Whisper Magazine.* Between the 1930s and the 1950s, visual fluency changed popular magazine publishing. It also made Hemingway's image a nationally recognizable icon.

These three covers illustrate explicitly the element of voyeurism innate to both men's magazines and celebrity culture of the 1950s. ©1957 Official Magazine Co.; ©1961 HMH Publishing; ©1952 Whisper Inc.

HEMINGWAY AS IMAGE: THE EXTENT OF CELEBRITY

During the 1940s Hemingway's presence filled such magazines, fueled partly by the sales of *For Whom the Bell Tolls* (it being a Book-of-the-Month Club title helped) as well as his vivid and popular wartime articles that appeared in *Collier's Weekly* in 1944. And many of the most enduring, almost cinematic, Hemingway legends come out of publications of this period: his submarine chasing aboard the *Pilar*, his mixing martinis in foxholes, his "liberating" the Hotel Ritz in Paris. If Hemingway and his publishers had worked to build an image as part of a marketing ploy, this was no longer necessary by the 1950s. Now "others were ready to produce his publicity for him."[9] Pictorials of Hemingway appeared in pocket digests next to stories such as "A British Father Tells 'How Surgery Made Me a Woman'" and "The House that Marilyn Haunts." Photos of him dining out at popular nightclubs appeared in "Pictures of the Week" sections alongside photos of Ann Miller and Groucho Marx. This decade following the war saw the development of Hemingway as masculine instructor and father figure, which he encouraged years before in his *Esquire* letters as "Papa."

Numerous feature articles about Hemingway, all profusely illustrated, ran throughout the 1940s in magazines such as *Town and Country, Life, Time, Holiday,* and *Pageant;* photos accompanied book reviews, cocktail recipes, gossip columns, and travel guides.[10] Articles like "A Portrait of Mister Papa"

Tempo was one of the more popular of the dozens of photo digests. As in this issue, Hemingway often appeared in the gossip column, and just as often alongside some Hollywood celebrity, here Ann Miller. ©Pocket Magazine, Inc.

It Was Awful: Novelist Ernest Hemingway, in Genoa restaurant, relating vivid description of his recent Africa plane crashes, grimaces at memory. He and wife are scheduled to sail to Havana.
10

Marathon Of Legs: Saucy Ann Miller, estimated to have danced more miles than any Hollywood star, takes a moment off to explain: "It's all in the legs."
11

HOW WOULD YOU put a glass of
Ballantine Ale into words?

Here—Ernest Hemingway
turns his famous hand to it...

Ernest Hemingway
FINCA VIGIA, SAN FRANCISCO DE PAULA, CUBA

Bob Benchley first introduced me to
Ballantine Ale. It has been a good companion
ever since.

You have to work hard to deserve to drink
it. But I would rather have a bottle of Ballantine Ale than any other drink after fighting
a really big fish. When something has been
taken out of you by strenuous exercise Ballantine puts it back in.

We keep it iced in the bait box with chunks
of ice packed around it. And you ought to taste
it on a hot day when you have worked a
marlin fast because there were sharks after him.

You are tired all the way through. The fish
is landed untouched by sharks and you have a
bottle of Ballantine cold in your hand and drink
it cool, light, and full-bodied, so it tastes
good long after you have swallowed it. That's the
test of an ale with me; whether it tastes as good
afterwards as when it's going down. Ballantine
does.

In every refreshing glass... Purity, Body and Flavor — **BALLANTINE**
America's largest selling ALE

One of two advertisements that featured Hemingway at this time (*Life,* November 1951). The other was for Parker Pens.

(1949) in *Life* and "Giant of the Storytellers" (1949) in *Coronet* gave over more space to photos than text. But more illustrative of this commodification of Hemingway is his 1951 ad for Ballantine Beer that appeared twice in *Life* in the form of a letter to readers, stating, "You ought to taste it on a hot day when you have worked a big marlin fast because there were sharks after him."

Over the next decade, Hemingway appeared with more and more frequency in increasingly sensational magazines. By the early 1950s, his image had permeated the popular extremes of publishing, and the media came to use him as an example of masculinity, as "America's No. 1 He-Man" or "Rogue of Distinction." In August 1952, *Focus* photo digest even named him one of the "Ten Sexiest Men in the World," stating "Literary Sexiness is ably represented by famed Ernest Hemingway, whose physique is as tough as his stories (According to *New Yorker* magazine, he invites people to test his physical fitness by punching him in the stomach). He now lives in Cuba with wife, admiring Mary Welsh, works on 'the big novel.'" And in *Show* Zsa Zsa Gabor listed him at number four of the "10 Most Sexciting Men," stating that "Hemingway's such an outdoor man! So different in every way from women. . . . He's more masculine than anyone he's ever written about. If you could be with him, you'd never want to read a book."[11]

Hemingway's many appearances in the photo digests illustrate how photography and photojournalism facilitated his transition from private writer to public figure, a transition that was ultimately *sensational*—as in

In 1952, *Focus* voted Hemingway one of the sexiest men in the world.

Literary Sexiness is ably represented by famed Ernest Hemingway, whose physique is as tough as his stories (According to *New Yorker* magazine, he invites people to test his physical fitness by punching him in stomach). He now lives in Cuba with wife, admiring Mary Welch (above), works on "the big novel."

"of the senses" as well as the brand of yellow journalism. Since the articles in these magazines devoted the majority of space to photographs rather than prose, the Hemingway being "sold" is not the great writer but the great adventurer, drinker, lover, and fighter.[12]

A CELEBRITY NOT HIS OWN

The extent of Hemingway's celebrity is most evident in the articles that presented him as a male role model, a concept that emerged in social scientific research of the 1950s. His image, with its instant recognition value, exemplified the meanings of "role model" as both mentor and hero—mentor in his Papa persona's mantle of expertise on hunting, fishing, sports, writing, food, and travel (most explicit in his nonfiction) and how his fictional heroes are always conflated with his own larger-than-life exploits.[13] An excellent example of this hyperbolic buildup is a profile of Hemingway published in *Man's Illustrated* (1960), which ends by stating, "When Ernest Hemingway fights his last fight, no matter when or how he goes, we'll be able to say of him: 'There went one of us—perhaps the best of us. There went a man—*a real man!*'" Similarly, the byline for a *Modern Man* (1956) article that consists of the usual stories about Hemingway's exploits and injuries, gossip and apocrypha states that Hemingway "has lived and enjoyed life as powerfully as he has written about it." Certainly, Hemingway's own role in constructing this image, as evidenced in numerous interviews, is impossible to overlook. *Rogue*'s profile (1958) of him ends:

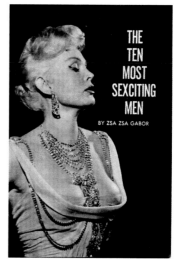

Starlet Zsa Zsa Gabor did as well, in *Show,* stating in a 1957 feature, "Hemingway's such an outdoor man! So different in every way from women. . . . He's more masculine than anyone he's ever written about." ©1957 Show Magazine, Inc

> Speaking from his deep chair in the central living room of *Finca Vigia,* ringed by the heads of numerous animals he has slain and by some 5,000 scattered volumes embracing every conceivable subject, Papa will tell you exactly what he wants to do and see when he grows old.
>
> "I'd like to see all the new fighters, horses, ballets, bike riders, dames, bull-fighters, painters, airplanes, sons of bitches, big international whores, restaurants, wine cellars and newsreels and never have to write a line about any of them." And then he will grin broadly, like a wicked, short-bearded Santa Claus. "And I would like to be able to make love good until I am 85."
>
> Truly, if you talk to Papa, this is what he will tell you.

For years, Hemingway both fought and nurtured his image as a larger-than-life character. In 1930 he made Grosset and Dunlap destroy dust jackets that claimed he had joined the Arditi in the First World War; later he had his editor, Maxwell Perkins, send a letter to correct this information in Paramount studios' press about him for the upcoming *A Farewell to Arms.*[14] Yet thirty years later these myths were still appearing in interviews and profiles of the author, as were those that he had been a bullfighter and a professional boxer. Whereas these "facts" dogged and bothered him, the image that he put forward in interviews with his quips about meeting international whores and making love until age eighty-five were just as extreme—not so much masculine as a caricature of hypermasculine proportions. In his interviews, "the Hemingway who emerges . . . is a man living life to the hilt" yet also "a dedicated careerist who skillfully nurtured an heroic public image until the vainglorious role took over the man and it became necessary for him to live up to it."[15]

It wasn't unusual for articles in photo digests, such as the oversized, *Life*-like *See Magazine,* to sensationally blur the line between Hemingway's fiction and his biography, taking an already eventful and romantic lifestyle and fictionalizing it. In *See*'s "Inside Hemingway: His Strange Search for Love and Death," published in the May 1956 issue, author John Owen unreservedly lifts details out of the Nick Adams stories and ascribes them to Hemingway. According to the article, Hemingway experienced firsthand the experiences described in his short stories "The Killers," "The Battler," and "The Light of the World." For example: "There were no saloons in Oak Park, Illinois, where Hemingway was born, and when he ran away from the respectable woman's world of his mother to become a boy hobo, it must have been a little like going for a stiff drink after church on Sunday." Of course, he never "hoboed" and actually led a pretty sheltered, normal midwestern boyhood until the war. What is even more insidious in this article is how the author describes Hemingway's love life as a sadistic blending of war, violence, romance, and eroticism. For Owen, it seems that the answer to the question posed in the article's tagline, "Why Does America's Greatest Writer Carry on His Never-ending Flirtation with Destruction?" is that it turns him on.

Many of the articles on Hemingway smack of voyeurism: the author at home, the author in private moments. Readers of fan magazines demanded personal information on celebrities, which added to, rather than detracted from, their aura. The tension between intimate and public empowers an audience by giving "the inside track." Interviewers made much of being able to break into the domestic life of the author, of breaching his well-known privacy, and defying his dislike of interviews—giving an air of having the "true gen" (a military term for reliable information) on the man. Milt Machlin, whose biography *The Private Hell of Ernest Hemingway* (1961) grew out of his articles in numerous men's magazines, recounts how he jumped a fence at Hemingway's Cuban villa and almost got shot. Yet other articles profess to find the real man under the persona, such as the *Modern Man* article (1956), which said, "Much has been written by Hemingway, much has been written about his adventures, but little has been written about the loquacious, cranky, wound-scarred, pain-wracked individual that is the human Hemingway." Likewise, Sam Boal's interview from *Escapade* (1959), "The Old Man and the Truth," which Boal attests Hemingway called "the best thing ever written about me" because it gets across the truth, the real man, states, "Lots of words about Hemingway have been put on paper, largely by people who have never met him." Again, Boal's role as expert on Hemingway both draws from and parallels Hemingway's own role in

SEE

15¢ MAY 1956

Runaway Husbands– A National Epidemic

INSIDE HEMINGWAY:
The Wounds of Love and War

EXCLUSIVE PHOTO REPORT:
The Wildest Street in Dixie

JOAN COLLINS
Global Glamor Girl
SEE PAGE 6

the interview as an expert on dozens of topics. Even more telling are the photos that accompany these articles, especially in the gossip magazines, which catch Hemingway in awkward or embarrassing personal moments, usually guzzling from a bottle. This sort of publicity, both the positive and the negative, illustrates Hemingway's status as a full-fledged celebrity.

Star Ascending: Hemingway in the Digest Magazines

"The Duel Hemingway Didn't Fight" in this issue of *Picture Week* became the popular fodder for multiple other gossip articles. This issue pairs him and Marilyn Monroe again. ©1955 Popular Magazines, Inc.

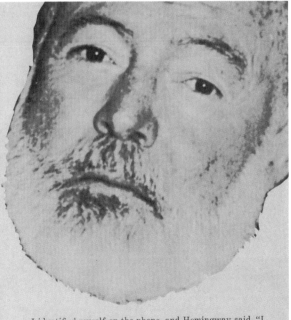

The newspaperman who made the challenge tells the startling story of—

the duel
HEMINGWAY
didn't fight

The twentieth century almost lost one of its greatest men recently—in a decidedly nineteenth century way. Ernest Hemingway—Nobel prize-winning writer, war correspondent, adventurer, and authority on courage—and Ted Scott, a journalist, exchanged heated phone calls over a column Scott had written in the Havana Post. The column was decidedly uncomplimentary toward Hemingway's wife, Mary, and stemmed from a cocktail party argument the two had had over the succulent qualities of lion steaks (she liked them; he didn't). The phone calls ended in Scott challenging Hemingway to meet him in a duel with .45 caliber pistols.

Strangely enough, there was nothing said in the press about the incident when it occurred, and it would have been lost completely if the research staff of NBC radio's Biographies in Sound hadn't unearthed it. They could only get one man's version of the duel; Hemingway was, apparently, not talking. But one version is better than none, and so PICTURE WEEK presents, in journalist Ted Scott's own words, the story of the duel Hemingway didn't fight. Scott's story starts with Hemingway's first phone call to him:

I identified myself on the phone, and Hemingway said, "I want to know if you're going to apologize to my wife for the things you've been writing about her."

I replied that I did not intend to apologize in a situation in which I clearly was the offended party.

Hemingway isn't as handy with a telephone as he is with a pen or a typewriter, but this day he was in good form. "Well," he said, "you said in your column that if I had said to you what my wife said to you, you would do this and that and so to me. Well, I think you are ———"

(cont'd)

Challenger Ted Scott

And then Mr. Hemingway went down the list of names—none of them of honorable connotation — which he thought should be applied to me. At the conclusion, he said that he was waiting for me out at his residence, that I should go out there alone, and he would be alone, and we would settle our differences man to man.

I told Mr. Hemingway that a meeting would have to take place in some mutual spot, certainly not at his house. I then wrote him a formal letter in which I told him that "I consider myself grievously offended by his language and conduct as he made it clear he intended me to be." I now challenged him to meet me with .45 caliber pistols, the other details to be arranged by the respective gentlemen serving as seconds.

On the evening of August the 21st, following his several telephone calls in the afternoon, Mr. Hemingway again telephoned me. I told him that if he were looking for trouble, he could set his mind at ease, because trouble he was about to have. I then assured him that he would be hearing from my seconds within 24 hours. "Oh," Hemingway said, "you're challenging me to a phony duel."

I replied that if he thought there was anything phony about .45 automatics, it was not my idea of phoniness.

Hemingway then said that he did not want to kill me, and I replied that that was a task which lay ahead of him.

When we talked in the evening, which was the last time I spoke to him, he suggested, several times, that I intended to make a front page story about the difficulties existing between us. I then told him that I had no hope or intention of riding to fame on his shirt tail or his shroud. All I wanted was an apology, or for Mr. Hemingway to give me satisfaction at a shooting party. He could take his choice.

Well, on Sunday—that is to say the following day—my representative went out to San Francisco de Paul to see Mr. Hemingway at his house. He was received courteously, and apparently a lengthy conversation took place. The relevant part of it is summed up in my representative's letter to me, in which he said that Hemingway manifested no intention whatsoever of apologizing to me. At the same time, according to the letter, Mr. Hemingway said he had no desire to fight a duel with me, and further stated he did not consider me to have the qualifications to duel with him.

I pressed the matter in a subsequent letter to my representative and insisted that he challenge Mr. Hemingway formally to meet me and give me satisfaction.

To the challenge, Mr. Hemingway replied by registered letter, the relevant part of which reads as follows:

"For good and sufficient reasons, I do not choose to meet Mr. Edward Scott on the so-called field of honor nor anywhere else. I will answer no challenge from him, and will send no friends of mine to meet with his friends. If any tribunal interprets this as being motivated by cowardice, I believe they would be in error. I am not a publicity seeker, and I will not be provoked into something which can only lead to the worst form of publicity.

"Aside from other considerations, my obligation at this time is to continue my writing and regain my health. At the present time, I am fighting no duels with anyone. If any friends of Mr. Scott's consider that to be an act of cowardice, they are at liberty to think so. But it is a decision made by a man who has served in war with honor, and is fully conscious of his obligations.

"Since I have rested on my decisions, reached after mature consideration and after talking with you, there is little point in explaining further. Signed, Ernest Hemingway."

Hemingway undoubtedly believed that his desire to continue writing was ample reason, and to a great many, it was. But to those who might regard this as a rationalization, as early as 1923, while he was in Paris, Hemingway wrote an article on that great braggart and dueller of the twentieth century, Benito Mussolini. In his conclusion to that piece, there is a line that bears on his answer to Scott: 'Really brave men do not have to fight duels.'

END

The featured "Hemingway Shows You How to Hunt" (*Focus,* February 1955) was merely a collection of excerpts from the author's writing paired with some sensational photographs, such as a leopard attacking a man. The tagline reads: "When Papa Bagged the Nobel Prize, It Was Just Another Big Kill for a Wise Old Hunter." ©1955 Leading Magazine Corp.

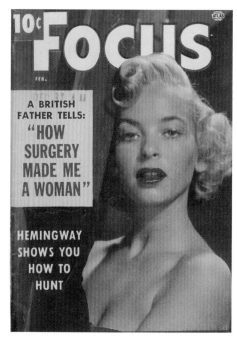

DUCK HUNTING WITH ERNEST HEMINGWAY

EXCLUSIVE

He-man Hemingway hits the target with gun and typewriter. His recent return to Italian haunts saw the author shooting for birds along an historic route as he tried the centuries-old lagoon hunt.

IT'S never farewell to arms where Ernest Hemingway is concerned for the Nobel prize winner glories in the hunt and can match his characters shot for shot. He ran true to type on his latest jaunt to Italy, scene of the World War I novel he rode to riches and renown.

As expected, "Papa" scorned

Known as a terrific worker, the author has taken time to hunt the world over.

As the boatman poles out into the lagoon, hunter Hemingway scans the sky ready to get a shot off.

The writer tracks a duck in his sights before bringing it down.

54

Tab, the "Pocket Picture Magazine," promised "Action! Beauty! Exposés! Thrills!" in each issue. Tucked between the nineteen pinup pictorials in this issue is a story on Hemingway duck hunting. © Carnival Magazine Corp.

CHAPTER THREE

Adventure Magazines and the Narrative of Coping

MEN'S ADVENTURE MAGAZINES AND THE POST-TRAUMATIC HERO

Audie Murphy didn't look like a war hero. Soft-spoken, 5' 5", barely 150 pounds, and boyishly handsome, he looked like the kid next door, not someone who could single-handedly knock out a German pillbox or hold off an entire platoon. Yet in his two years of infantry service, Murphy was awarded thirty-three medals for such bravery, including the Medal of Honor and the Croix de Guerre. And perhaps it was this contrast between Main Street normality and such extremes of action that captured the public's fancy—and Hollywood's. A legend in his own time, Murphy went on to star in more than thirty films, even playing himself in the adaption of his autobiography *To Hell and Back* (1949).

Yet demons hid beneath Murphy's unassuming grin and shy demeanor: he was plagued by depression, insomnia, nightmares, addiction. He broke down on the set of the radio show *This Is Your Life* when meeting his best friend's daughter, a best friend whom he saw gunned down in a German foxhole. His first marriage, to a Hollywood actress, quickly failed because she couldn't come to terms with her husband's mental state. Signs of what troubled Murphy can be found in his 1956 article for *Battle Cry* magazine, "The Day I Cried," the tagline for which stated, "There is a great gulf between those who fought and those who didn't. Unless you were there, you cannot understand. In this story, written by our most-decorated GI, that gulf is bridged."[1] The reintroduction of the battle-scarred vet into a society largely unaware of or unwilling to accept the horrors of war augments the displacement felt by war trauma. Soldiers returned to an America that only saw a white-washed version in magazines, newsreels, and films since,

Opposite: Soldiers and vets made up most of the audience for men's adventure magazines, many of which featured recently released photos from WWII, like "The Hell of Battle" feature in this June 1956 issue of *Man's True Action*. ©1956 Star Editions

in what Christina Jarvis calls "sanitized death" on the home front, images and information on American dead were controlled by the war department and the Office on War Information.[2] Seemingly for Murphy and others, you really couldn't return home.

It is clear that Murphy was suffering from what we now know as Post-Traumatic Stress Disorder (PTSD), as were millions of other veterans. What is uncommon for the time is how Murphy learned to cope: he narrated his experiences. In this article, he confesses to "brooding" about that disjunction between himself and those who hadn't participated, about how "war makes an uncommon person" of participants. He admits that his writing *To Hell and Back* was a way to explain the life of an infantryman, to aid in the civilian's understanding of the horrors of war, the experience of the solider. Murphy's notoriety and public image gave him both a platform and a responsibility to help others, either by making war experience known to the general populous so as to aid in better understanding the plight of the veteran or by explicitly talking about postwar mental illness, which he did with more and more frequency during the Korean and Vietnam wars. He was instrumental in breaking the taboo about discussing war-related mental problems.

Such men's adventure magazines as *Battle Cry* offered a venue for shared experiences to America's veterans, as in this August 1956 story "The Day I Cried," by Audie Murphy, who was instrumental in making shell shock a national topic.

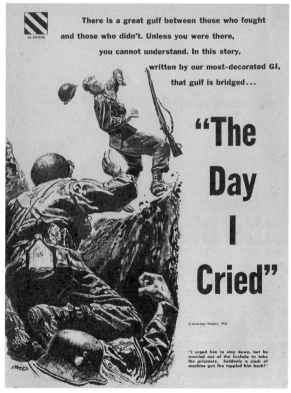

As Murphy's case exemplifies, the promise of the new decade didn't mean the end of difficulties for the 17 million servicemen who had survived the unimaginable horrors of the Second World War. Repatriation wasn't easy. Besides that "great gulf" between vets and their families, servicemen also returned to increasing social pressure placed on conformity and corporate growth. Soldiers were expected to trade the battlefields of the Pacific for those of Madison Avenue. Beneath the cultural image forwarded by mainstream film and television—that of *Father Knows Best* and *Mr. Blanding Builds His Dream House*—there was deep-rooted social upheaval: African American soldiers returned to Jim Crow laws and heightened racial tension due to northern migration, and women were expected to leave the newfound respect and freedom of wartime jobs and return to the role of obedient wife and mother.

The result was that once-entrenched ideas of gender and masculinity came into question. Kaja Silverman describes this as "historical trauma" and "ideological fatigue," a specific cultural moment where there is a "loss of belief not only in the adequacy of the male subject, but in the family and small town life," where the "dominant narrative" of society is disrupted[3]—where there is a gap between constructed or expected identity and the real world. After World War II, the socialization of stoic masculinity faltered. Murphy's 'The Day I Cried,' for example, describes unashamedly the moment when the soldier's conditioning, his necessary stoic reserve, breaks: "When I went into the Army, I swore to myself that the war would never make me cry. But when Tipton died I sat at his side and bawled like a baby."

Psychologists found that war trauma was widespread. During battle many were too scared to even fire their weapons, and no one could stand the strain of prolonged warfare without crippling emotional effect. As J. W. Appel and G. W. Beebe pointed out in 1946, "There is no such thing as 'getting used to combat.' . . . Each moment of combat imposes a strain so great that men will break down in direct relation to the intensity and duration of their exposure. These psychiatric casualties are as inevitable as gunshot and shrapnel wounds in warfare."[4] With the end of the war, the crutches of coping, such as the regimentation, hierarchy, and the brotherhood of the battalion, were suddenly removed and replaced with unemployment and/or a family that had no idea of the horrors of warfare.

Reading about the war and sharing experiences returned men to the camaraderie of the service, which, according to psychiatrists who worked with trauma victims, was one of the defenses against shell shock. As Judith Lewis Herman points out, "The strongest protection against overwhelming terror was the degree of relatedness between the soldier, his immediate fighting unit, and their leader. . . . The situation of constant danger led soldiers to develop extreme emotional dependency upon their peer group and leader." This dependency made the transition to civilian life all the more traumatic, especially when the majority of the population at home had been spared the horrors of war evident in graphic photographs and realistic accounts and presented with only a white-washed and propagandistic version of events.[5]

This need for sharing experiences explains Murphy's need to tell his story in his biography; the need for others to hear war experiences in order to reconnect to the familial fighting unit explains Murphy's popularity, how *To Hell and Back* became a best-seller and a hit movie. It also explains both Murphy's choice of publishing "The Day I Cried" in *Battle Cry* and the general popularity of men's adventure magazines, which were generally geared to veterans of WWII and soldiers in Korea. Titles like *True War, Battle Cry, Combat, Battlefield,* and *Men in Combat* were centered around the wartime experience. *Man's Illustrated* featured a "Military Memo" column of news and advice for servicemen on anything from new weapon technology to how to get lucky with Japanese women, and *Battle Cry* featured a "Whatever Happened to . . . ?" column for the reader who was "still trying to find that joker who shared your foxhole at Heartbreak Ridge?" or for parents who were "trying to find out the names of some of your son's buddies . . . the ones who can tell you what really happened that dark day at Iwo Jima."[6] Articles recounted battles, gave profiles of platoons, and told personal experiences.

The popularity of "true" stories of the war, which relied heavily on recently declassified and uncensored war photos, rose out of the need to relive the experience, to put it into a narrative that aided in the healing of wartime trauma. This search for a common narrative is evident in many of the classified ads in men's magazines. *Battle Cry,* for example, featured ads like "HAROLD EMMIS, of Kent, England, now living in Canada, would love to hear from his friend 'CHUCK,' a Texan, whom he was with in Stalag XIB, Fallingboftel, Germany." Kirby Farrell points out that repeatedly revisiting the wartime experience is an attempt at healing.[7] Since the Vietnam War, the creation of a narrative of trauma by a patient suffering from PTSD has become a standard treatment. Psychologist Robert Neborsky writes, "I want the patient to leave the initial interview with a coherent narrative of the origin of his or her psychopathology. By a coherent narrative, I mean an understanding of the origins of the difficulties that includes the unconscious perspective. The patient will understand the dynamic origin of his or her anxiety, and will understand the role of anger, guilt and/or shame,

Left: Many men's adventure magazines, like *Battle Cry* (August 1956), had classified sections where veterans could get in touch with each other. To a certain degree, magazines like *Battle Cry* and *Stag* were literary counterpoints to the social aspects of army life: camaraderie, shared stories of military life, and racy barracks anecdotes.

©1952 Official Magazine Co.

in depression or self-abuse."[8] This is the same reason why support groups and rap sessions were implemented after the Vietnam War, to help vets deal with PTSD.

Of course the audience for men's magazines included more than just soldiers and vets; the postwar ideological fatigue was more widespread than just those returning from the front. Farrell identifies the society-wide, midcentury neurosis as a "post-traumatic culture" stemming from the contagious quality of post–traumatic stress: "Because of our capacity for suggestibility, post–traumatic stress can be seen as a category of experience between a specific individual's injury and a group or even a culture. An extreme example is the way Hitler, who was nearly killed in World War I, infected an entire nation with his post-traumatic symptoms. In a sense, all his policies obsessively attempted to undo that earlier calamity through fantastic aggression."[9] Therefore, PTSD can have a snowball effect on society at large. This idea surfaces in the popular fiction of the day. In Robert Finnegan's novel *The Bandaged Nude* (first published in 1946), the main character moves from town to town after his decommission: "He'd have to settle down sooner or later. Maybe it was just a world without Ethel that got on his nerves. His wife died while he was in the army, and it made a particularly empty home-coming. But probably it was more than that. Other people felt it too. He could see it in their eyes and sense it in their conversation. Restlessness. Dissatisfaction. An uncertainty about the world and about themselves. The war left everybody on edge."[10] There are many similar examples of repatriation and dissatisfaction in fiction and film of the time—too many to be ignored. This was especially so in hard-boiled fiction and film noir, arguably the most popular genres after the war, such as the Raymond Chandler scripted film *The Blue Dahlia* (1945), Humphrey Bogart's *Dark Passage* (1947), and even as late as Donald Hamilton's Matt Helm series in 1960.

If one of the ways to cope with a society "on edge" was to read literature that dealt openly with facing traumatic experiences, then men's adventure magazines were the perfect venue. After the war their popularity exploded and lasted for over two decades. There were more than 150 different magazine titles, such as *Man's Magazine, Man's Conquest, True Action, Real For Men,* and *Man's Illustrated,* all of which specialized in sensational covers and "true" adventures that were not confined to war experiences and espionage stories but included any conflict where man was challenged and triumphed, where masculinity was reestablished and confirmed. There were man versus nature articles, sex exposés, pseudo-medical advice columns, and, of course, the ubiquitous pinup pictorials.

The fact that for years these magazines continued wartime propaganda with stories about WWII concentration camp torture or escape stories, even during new conflicts such as the Korean War and Vietnam, is evidence of these magazines' foundations in postwar trauma. Sometimes these topics were combined in eaten-alive-by-creatures stories, another favorite (again, usually featuring a semi-nude female victim), as in "Hitler's Baboon Tortures in Mabuti" and "The Nazi Madhouse of Zoo Ravaged Women."[11]

Postwar men's magazines also aided in the general resocialization, or "remasculization," of society. The wartime pinup, which emerged as idealized propagandistic inspiration for the lonely GI, became the raison d'être for a whole genre of girlie mags, nullifying the so-called threat of a female wartime workforce and the latent feminist movement that would rise up a generation later. Within a decade of the end of the war, the newsstands were selling hundreds of different men's magazines, all of which promoted the idea of male domination through pinup objectification and those sensational stories of man victorious against man, animal, nature, and, especially, woman.

The September 1958 issue of *Man's Illustrated,* with its "exclusive interview" with Ernest Hemingway, also features the hunting story of aging tracker and hunter Ben Lilly, an actual woodsman of the southwest who, when surprised by a mountain lion, led the cat into a bear cave, there pitting the two animals against each other. The story tells both a "true adventure" of wilderness survival and an animal-amok story with the theme of masculine ingenuity and grace under pressure. In that same issue there is another hunting story, "Hell Is a Hog with Tusks," and an article on "How and Where to Get a Job That Takes You Adventuring: For bold men everywhere, *Man's Illustrated* presents a practical plan for you to travel around the world—and make some money while doing it." "What You Should Know About Sex Stimulants," another feature, provides clues about shoring up flagging potency and/or secrets of seduction. Next to this article is an ad for "The Pleasure Primer," which claims that "NO WOMAN IS SAFE . . . (*or really wants to be*) when a man's mind is in the bedroom. . . . Here's entertainment for open minds and ticklish spines."

Postwar men's magazines (like hard-boiled fiction's femme fatale) mark a shift in the portrayal of women. During the war, the men's mag embodied an American ideal of women. If we are to believe many pictorials, the pinup did as much to win the war as any GI. As Maria Elena Buszek notes, "Swept up in the 'good fight,' the [prototypical pinup] Varga Girls [became] a liaison to the home front and a metaphor for the American girl."[12] Magazines such as *Titter, Pic,* and *Beauty Parade* featured photo essays with models wrapped in flags, saluting aircraft, and womping cartoonish Japs and Jerries. *Thrill* featured stories on "What Women Can Do to Win the War." Purely American and marketed for the soldier overseas, the idealized pinup embodied what the troops were fighting for. So as not to worry the absent boyfriends and husbands, the 1930s spicy pulps' stories of free love and wife-swapping gave way to a patriotic, wholesome sexiness. But after the war the tone of these magazines changed, becoming more sensationalized and more, if possible, aggressively masculine to meet the reconstitutive needs of the male psyche. The 1950s men's magazines became the propaganda of what feminist critic Susan Faludi called the "undeclared war against American women."[13]

Such adventure magazines as *Man's Illustrated* (September 1958) pandered to male fantasies of all kinds, from an adventurous life away from the world of women to explicit sexual fantasies about possessing women, as evident in this ad for "The Pleasure Primer" that appears beside an article about sexual stimulants. ©Sterling Publications

However, the brutish patriarchy and misogyny perpetuated in 1950s men's magazines and 1950s gender roles cannot be attributed solely to a large number of traumatized soldiers who needed to bolster a collective bruised masculine ego. These men did not make up the entire culture, but, as Farrell points out, "In cultural applications, then, it is useful to see post-traumatic experience as a sort of critically responsive interface between people: a space in which patterns of supremely important, often dangerous symbols and emotions may reinforce one another, gaining momentum, confirmation, and force when particular social conditions and historical pressures intersect."[14]

BLOOD AND GUTS HEMINGWAY

And Ernest Hemingway, with his personal larger-than-life exploits and his writings' undeniably masculine topics that scrutinized man under pressure, made good copy for these postwar magazines. The degree with which he was present as a model for postwar masculinity is evident in how his image was shown to be a tonic for encroaching femininity. *Man's Illustrated*'s article "Ernest Hemingway's 5-War Saga" states that "there aren't many men like Hemingway left in this soft-bellied world of ours. You may be one of them. If you are, then you belong to the select few who, along with Hemingway, are members of a vanishing breed of giants in a society dominated by women and women's ways."[15] Seemingly, Hemingway was a five-star general in the war against women. But judging from the article that this appears in, an overview of Hemingway's battle experience, he was also a role model for the perfect soldier in general.

This role is ironic, for he never actually served in the army. He was an ambulance driver for the Red Cross in WWI, and when his wounds were sustained, he was not in combat but distributing chocolate to Italian soldiers. And in the Spanish Civil War and WWII he was a journalist.

Yet again and again he appears in the men's magazines as a participant in and even an expert on war. In addition to *Man's Illustrated*'s "Ernest Hemingway's 5-War Saga," there is *Man's Magazine*'s "Hemingway's Private War with Adolf Hitler," *Bluebook*'s "Ernest Hemingway's Lust for War," and *True*'s "Hemingway's Longest Day," which recounts Hemingway's unlikely landing on Omaha Beach on D day.[16] More than simple popularity, Hemingway's ubiquitous presence in these magazines—and, more important, its *extremity*—hints at a cultural fascination, an adoption and elevation of his image.

This can be seen in *Man's Magazine*'s 1959 article "Ernest Hemingway's Private War with Adolf Hitler," which reads like a firsthand account of Hemingway's wartime exploits after D day.[17] The article's author takes liberties, adds dialogue, and combines Hemingway's experiences on the German Siegfried line and his march to Paris into a single narrative. His "liberation of Paris" is one of the most persistent of Hemingway legends, one repeated by artist John Groth, photographer Robert Capa, and many biographers, including Carlos Baker and Kenneth Lynn. But nowhere is the story told with as much gusto as in this article. The information is culled from Groth, Capa, and Hemingway's own dispatches. More fiction than fact, it is the epitome of Hemingway's larger-than-life persona. The cover of the magazine—a close-up painting of Papa, who is looking directly at the reader, surrounded by explosions and soldiers—portrays Hemingway's fame and reputation in the 1950s: not only a writer but a soldier, a celebrity, and a he-man extraordinaire. This article illustrates a hero worship dynamic where the author, the heroes of his work, and his personal legend all meld into fiction: Hemingway becomes the kind of hero that peopled his own juvenile pulp stories.

Why exactly was Hemingway adopted as the premier soldier of the mid-century? A very good question, especially since Hemingway never actually participated in combat.[18] The Second World War offered plenty of other heroes who had proven themselves under fire, among them musicians and

The wartime pinup embodied everything "our boys" were fighting for. This would quickly change after the war. ©1942 Crestwood Publishing

MAN'S MAGAZINE

PDC

SEPTEMBER 35¢

HEMINGWAY'S PRIVATE WAR WITH ADOLF HITLER

BOOZE HELL
MY SIX NIGHTMARE DAYS IN BELLEVUE'S ALCOHOLIC WARD

HOW TO PROLONG YOUR SEX LIFE

ERNEST HEMINGWAY

THE MAN WHO DEFIED CHICAGO'S MOBSTERS | **THE DAY CUBA EXECUTED 25 AMERICAN CITIZENS!**

movie stars, but none appeared with as much frequency or sensation as Hemingway. In interviews and biographical articles in these magazines, his most common guise was soldier rather than writer, hunter, fisherman, journalist, or traveler. The many articles detailed his war wounds and recounted his experiences. For example, *Rogue Magazine's* 1958 profile "Ernest Hemingway: A Rogue of Distinction" repeats and confirms the myths and misinformation, such as how his kneecap was blown off by machine gun fire while he was carrying a wounded Italian soldier and how he "suffered ten brain concussions in combat."[19] (Of those many concussions, at least two were driving accidents, two plane accidents, and one from a skylight he inadvertently yanked down on himself in a Parisian attic loft while reaching for the chain to flush the toilet.) Despite this myth making, Hemingway was a highly visible figure who represented the battle wizened.

That Hemingway was adopted into this role points to a cultural need in the 1950s for a masculine role model. He met this need for an extreme model of masculinity due to a number of interrelated reasons: he had been in the limelight with growing frequency since the beginning of the war; he established himself as a role model by taking a position of expertise in his own writing on travel, culture, and, especially, war; since the 1920s on he had written narratives about coping with the trauma of war; and this work was more available in the 1950s than ever before.

During WWII Hemingway's assignment as a correspondent for *Collier's Weekly* gained him an audience of 2.5 million, his biggest readership ever, and his presence in the European Theater established his role as "Papa" to the servicemen around him. His first dispatch, on July 22, 1944, "Voyage to Victory," prominently featured a half-page photograph of him surrounded by soldiers. In the photo he is bearded, vital, comfortable with the attention he is receiving. The accompanying caption reads, "Ernest Hemingway, who gained his first fame as a war reporter in 1918, chats with G.I.s before leaving to cover the biggest action yet."[20] It didn't matter to readers that Hemingway was an ambulance driver in WWI, not a reporter; what mattered was that America's No. 1 man of letters was at the front and, as the story contends, in the middle of the D day action.

Between July and November 1944, Hemingway wrote six articles for *Collier's.* In these pieces his tone is knowledgeable, humorously self-deprecating, and self-referential almost to the point of self-promotion. Critics have pointed out that Hemingway's reporting often seems to be about himself and only tangentially about whatever the subject happened to be. Historian Stephen Ambrose harshly stated about Hemingway's WWII

Opposite: These magazines furthered Hemingway's reputation as a soldier, despite the fact that he had never actually served in the military. ©1959 Almat Publishing Corp.

Again, Hemingway's reputation as a soldier is played up in the popular masculine press. Notice the Cold War paranoia evident in the other featured articles of this 1960 issue of *Man's Illustrated*. Seemingly, Hemingway was a safe role model in McCarthy's America. ©Hanro Publications

This lead photo from Hemingway's article "Voyage to Victory" in *Collier's* captures his avuncular "Papa" persona. ©1944 Crowell-Collier Publishing Co.

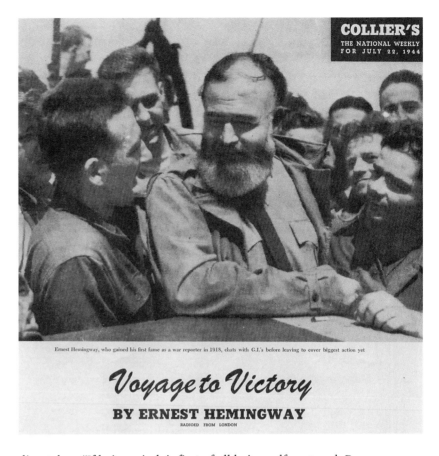

Ernest Hemingway, who gained his first fame as a war reporter in 1918, chats with G.I.'s before leaving to cover biggest action yet

Voyage to Victory

BY ERNEST HEMINGWAY
RADIOED FROM LONDON

dispatches, "If being a jerk is first of all being self-centered, Papa was one. When Hemingway sat down to write, he was the only person in view."[21] Indeed, throughout his wartime articles, readers were repeatedly apprised of the author's expertise, his jaunty familiarity with the theater of war. Hemingway's closing paragraph from "How We Came to Paris," for example, illustrates not so much how and why the American army was over there and how it came to Paris, but, with its repetitive use of the first-person pronoun, why Hemingway was over there: "'Yeah' I said. I couldn't say anything more then, because I had a funny choke in my throat and I had to clean my glasses because there now, below, gray and always beautiful, was spread the city I love best in the world."[22]

Even if his first-person narration does seem a bit self-serving, its emotional nature is undeniably powerful, and it is this balance of self-reference, personal insight, and celebrity that fuels the Hemingway legend, the popular accounts of the man that live beyond his action. This is illustrated in not only the semi-fictional account in *Man's Illustrated,* which forwards the idea that Hemingway was personally out to win the war ("Hemingway's *Private*

War with Adolf Hitler"), but also in the popular accounts of Hemingway's liberation of Paris that the article relies on. After the action of "How We Came to Paris" ends, he supposedly entered the city ahead of U.S. forces, stopped briefly to hang a sign reading "Property of Ernest Hemingway" on a cathedral door, and then proceeded to liberate the Ritz Hotel—more specifically the bar.

His legend's postwar popularity relied on a foundation of popularity stemming from 1940's publication of *For Whom the Bell Tolls,* which was a best-seller and a top pick for the Book-of-the-Month Club. During the war, Hemingway's work was available to soldiers and vets in vast numbers. Hemingway didn't just infiltrate 1940s popular culture, he bombarded it. Copies numbering 155,000 each of *To Have and Have Not* and *Selected Short Stories* were distributed to soldiers in Armed Service Editions. Malcolm Cowley's edited *The Viking Portable Hemingway* really was portable and, published in 1944, had sold 30,000 copies in its first year, and many of these found their way into soldier's kits.[23] Author and WWII veteran Robert Emmett Ginna first encountered Hemingway "while serving in the navy in the South Pacific," where he "read and reread" "The Big Two-Hearted River" in *The Fifth Column and First Forty-Nine Stories* so many times that he would dream about "the dark and quiet waters of the Michigan north country and young Nick Adams, alone, fishing for trout."[24]

Hemingway's editing of *Men at War* (1942), a 1,072-page anthology of war fiction, cemented his reputation as a military expert, an identity he cultivated and one that certainly blossomed in the 1950s men's magazines. According to Hemingway, *Men at War* defended against trauma; the purpose of the book, he said, was to let "you know that there are no worse things to be gone through than men have been through before."[25] His tone throughout the introduction is avuncular as he writes of his own wounding, giving advice on how to cope with the calls of war and bravery. Again, here he was Papa to the thousands of young men fighting in and returning from war.

Tellingly, in 1952 the pseudo-news/adventure/pinup magazine *Sir!* broke its "no book review" policy to include a piece on Avon's paperback edition of *Men at War.* Reviewer Thorp McClusky emphasized the rarity of the review (hence its worthiness) since *Sir!* is usually "so specialized—slanted at the he-men of above average intelligence—that a continuing search for books that the editors know would appeal to most of its readers would be a costly and generally disappointed task." (Worth noting is that the discriminating editors of *Sir!* surrounded the book review with articles such as "The Man

Who Collects Circus Freaks," "The Secret Love Life of Stalin's Daughter," and "Ten Ways to Increase Sex Power.") McClusky established *Men at War*'s credibility based not on the book's content but on Hemingway's expertise:

> Whether you like Ernest Hemingway's writing or not, you must admit that Gray Whiskers knows a lot about war. In addition to seeing plenty of action (he was wounded in World War I), he's written more than half a hundred short stories, several novels, and a play, most of them dealing with conflict of some sort or other—whether it is men against men, men against animals, or men against something they want to conquer in themselves. Gray Whiskers has also studied war—as a science, art, political device *in extremis,* and cauldron in which some men are refined, others fused into slag.[26]

McClusky's description of Hemingway's themes of conflict just as easily describes those of the men's magazines. And seemingly for both, war is the industry of manhood, the site where men are "refined" or made worthless. Men's magazines' articles were not limited to the modern memories of WWII but included any type of combat, ranging from "the Mongol raids of Genghis Khan to the most obscure conflicts of the twentieth century," just as *Men at War* featured stories from Thermopylae to Midway.[27] The book appealed to the editors of *Sir!* because, like Hemingway, it was a template for 1950s manhood. Aggressive statements in the book review—"If you are a wishy-washy guy, a mama's boy, a sentimentalist, you will not like this book"—point to the deeper affirmation and socialization of masculinity, which in turn points to the era's deep-rooted crisis of gender, exactly what the proliferation of these magazines is symptomatic of.

PAPA HEMINGWAY AND THE NARRATIVE OF COPING

Hemingway's popularity both in these magazines and in general in the 1950s builds on those themes of camaraderie of war, since his fiction navigated the trauma of war and repatriation decades before. His writing, stoically hinting at depths of emotion, dealing with issues of masculinity under duress, appealed to the soldier. After WWI, *A Farewell to Arms* captured the public imagination because it exposed the nineteenth-century idea of masculinity as a faulty "fiction": "the things that were glorious had no glory and the sacrifices were like the stockyards of Chicago. . . . Abstract words such as glory, honor, courage, or hallow are obscene," states Lt. Henry in *A*

Farewell to Arms, encapsulating the disillusionment of a code and war that had ultimately proved hollow, pointless.[28] But for the WWII generation, involved in a righteous war against fascism and holocaust, the tensions arose from how masculinity falls apart or is maintained under pressure. So stories like "Big Two-Hearted River" and "The Killers" become Hemingway's most reprinted works, especially in paperback anthologies and magazines such as *Field and Stream* and *Ellery Queen's Mystery Magazine.*

Resultantly, as stories like "Soldier's Home" became more widely available in wartime and popular editions, they took on a whole new resonance for readers in the late 1940s and early 1950s. Philip Young, who wrote one of the earliest and most important critical explorations of Hemingway's work, is a perfect example.[29] Young's psychological study of Hemingway's fiction tags the WWI wound as *the* key to understanding Hemingway and his text, as if the entire oeuvre was a roman à clef. Young saw Hemingway writing and rewriting the incident of his first wounding. It is telling that Young finds Hemingway's wound so central at just the time, 1952, when thousands of young men were dealing with similar experiences. (And it is worth noting that Young himself "discovered" Hemingway as a soldier during the war.)

Such threats to the cultural construction of masculinity after the Second World War parallel the experiences of Hemingway's generation. Malingering,

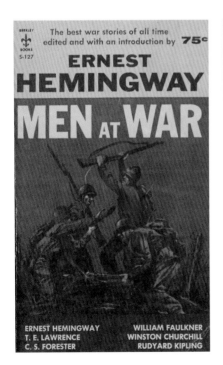
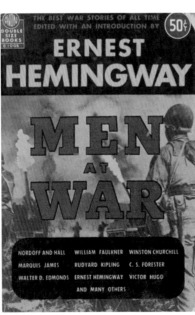

Hemingway reached a larger audience than ever in the 1950s through paperback sales. Two popular editions of *Men at War* (1942) were published in 1952 (left) and 1958.

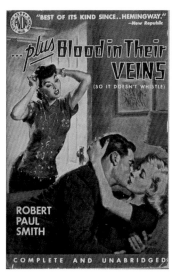

During the 1950s, Hemingway was used as a high-watermark of excellence for the male reader, as illustrated by the marketing copy on these paperbacks. This was especially true for hard-boiled literature, such as Wade Miller's *The Big Guy*.

dismemberment, and male neurasthenia (shell shock) were widespread and argued about in the popular press.[30] For example, shell shock during WWI was considered a form of malingering or the manifestation of psychopathic tendencies.[31] In reality, these were just symptoms of the gap between reality and the romantic ideals of masculinity constructed in popular culture (such as in *St. Nicholas*). Hemingway's fiction that deals with war trauma and healing, such as "The Big Two-Hearted River" and "A Way You'll Never Be," makes explicit these issues, especially for the generation of veterans returning from WWII. These stories both feature a fractured main character tenuously grasping sanity after physical and mental wounding. As Hemingway's name, persona, and fiction became increasingly popular and available during the war years, his WWI stories prepared and offered narrative frameworks for the men of WWII. For example, Hemingway's short story "Soldier's Home" perfectly illustrates the returning veterans' feeling of disenfranchisement. In it, Harold Krebs returns home to Kansas from the front, cynical and world-weary enough that he just wants to "live along without consequences." But the complications and politics of domestic and family life eventually get to him. In response to his mother's statement, "I pray for you all day long, Harold," Krebs just "looked at the bacon fat hardening on his plate."[32] In a wonderful bit of domestic imagery, Krebs's heart, like the bacon fat, becomes hardened to his old family ideals, religion, prewar morality, and parental expectations.

Hemingway's fiction returns again and again to the themes of disillusionment and loss of innocence. Stories such as "The Battler," "My Old Man," and "The Killers" center around events that shatter young men's idealistic views of the world, a father, and rural innocence. The terse prose and hard-boiled settings and themes reflect a generation's disillusionment after the seemingly needless losses and violence of WWI. This parallels the situation of returning vets in the 1940s. Just as the war experiences of Krebs in "Soldier's Home" clash with his family's white-washed concept of the war, so did the experiences of the later generation of veterans with the "sanitized death" seen in newsreels and newspapers. There were similar reactions in the popular fiction of the time as well. The rise of such cynical fiction in the 1920s, whether in high-brow modernism or in hard-boiled pulp magazines, parallels the popularity of film noir in the 1940s and 1950s. In both cases, popular culture reflects the inadequate ideals of slipping masculine socialization. It is telling that Hemingway's works were easily adapted to noir stylistics in the films *To Have and Have Not* (1944) and *The Killers* (1946).

We can further detect his influence on popular fiction in the 1950s and the aura that his name held by the large number of gaudy paperbacks that used Hemingway for promotional purposes: John Thomason Jr.'s *Texas Rebel* (a blurb by Hemingway stating "it is a fine story"); *The Last Party* and *New York Call Girl* by Robert Lowry (compared to and praised by Hemingway); *. . . Plus Blood in Their Veins* by Robert Paul Smith ("the best of its kind since Hemingway"); Alan Kapelner's *Lonely Boy Blues* ("reminds one of Farrell and Hemingway . . . Startling Fresh and Original"); Elio Bartolini's *La Signora* ("Winner of the Ernest Hemingway Prize"); and the "Hemingway of Suspense" Wade Miller's *The Big Guy*.[33]

Just as his name recognition was used as a marketing tool and logo for sensational or masculine fiction, the presence of Hemingway's *persona* in men's magazines—as distinct from Hemingway and his fiction in its hypermasculinity—and the sensational manner in which the men's magazines constructed him reflect the extent to which the cultural unconscious needed to rebuild itself.

While Hemingway—the man as well as his work—was available to soldiers, and these soldiers made up much of the market for the postwar men's magazines, this audience cannot account entirely for his popularity in the 1950s and early 1960s. Thanks to the GI Bill, this huge captive audience of servicemen became the writers and teachers of the following generations, and they read Hemingway in a new way because of their own wartime experience. Hemingway offered a narrative that was adopted by returning vets, who absorbed it and made it the narrative of their generation.

Just one of many examples of shirtless men in peril. ©1956 Hanro Publications

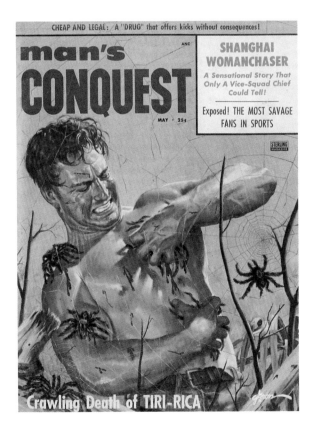

H emingway's Longest Day," published in *True* in 1963, exemplifies the continued fascination with Hemingway and his wartime exploits, even after his death. Charles Whiting, in his book *Hemingway Goes to War* (which is quite sensationally written in its own right), identifies the author, William Van Dusen, as the aide to Admiral Lovette who was in charge of public relations for the U.S. Navy.[1] He was often with Hemingway in London, and his account of how Hemingway finagled his way onto a landing ship of the seventh wave of attack on Omaha Beach is true, but Whiting casts doubt on the possibility that Hemingway ever touched the sand of Omaha Beach and ascribes Van Dusen's information to Hemingway himself. This is in all probability the truth; very few correspondents were allowed on the beachhead. Regardless, the article does capture the brave and/or foolhardiness of Hemingway's action that marks his experience at the front. As Michael Reynolds points out, he was either testing himself or just didn't care if he died.[2] Either way, the anecdotes that marked Hemingway's role in WWII, imagined or not—such as the canteens of cognac, leading rag-tag irregulars, and liberating Paris—became part of his legend, and most have some foundation in truth. There are very few popular articles on Hemingway in the 1950s that do not allude to one of these anecdotes. Also, note that this article, published a year and a half after Hemingway's death, illustrates the continued fascination with Hemingway and how the myth kept growing even after the man was gone.

❖　❖　❖

Everyone knows that the invasion of Normandy went through beaches called Utah and Omaha. Actually, they should have named another one Hemingway—for his hilarious D-Day heroics.

The problem of what to do with Ernest Hemingway when the invasion of Normandy began was, for those entrusted with his safety, a delicate one. Until 1944 the old literary warrior hadn't appeared particularly interested in claiming a combat correspondent's berth. But now that the Allies had finally decided to march straight across the Channel and punch Hitler in the nose, Papa was really ready to go to war.

Understandably, neither publishers nor the military wanted to be held responsible for exposing such valuable literary property to any lethal line of fire. But, because he was a bona fide war correspondent, they couldn't keep him out of the war entirely. The plot, then, was to let Hemingway go swimming—but not in deep water.

"Ernest Hemingway's Private War with Adolf Hitler," from *Man's Magazine* (September 1959), is an excellent example of how Hemingway was adopted as a war hero and role model for soldiers as well as how he became more of a fictional character than a real man in these adventure magazines. ©Almat Publishing Co.

Task Force Hemingway wine, women and songed its way through France—occupying towns 30 miles in front of the nearest GI units. And when the Allies first marched into Paris, they found a sign reading: "PROPERTY OF ERNEST HEMINGWAY." It was all part of . . .

ERNEST HEMINGWAY'S PRIVATE WAR WITH ADOLF HITLER

by PAUL DITZEL

continued on page 20

Papa knew nothing of his upcoming troubles when he went storming out of New York early in May any more than I could have known, when I caught up with him at the bar in Botwood, Newfoundland, that I was witnessing the birth of another one of those rare Hemingway legends.

While Hemingway and I—and our flying boats—tanked up for the long overnight grind from Newfoundland to Ireland, we renewed an earlier acquaintanceship, compared prospects. My story, what I could tell of it was quickly told: I had talked my doctor into postponing a date to carve me up for ulcers so that I could take on a classified Navy mission of small consequence involved with the invasion. Hemingway, of course, was on a secret mission of his own. There was still a chance to make some sense out of this war, he confided, but the stratagem was beyond the comprehension of brass-headed generals. He knew just how it could be done. Once a beachhead was established, the thing to do, instead of parading our own armor across France, was to funnel it into the hands of his friends in the French underground and let the Maquis liberate their own beloved country.

Twenty-four hours later when we checked into the Dorchester Hotel, off London's Hyde Park, I was thoroughly briefed on the Master Plan. Hemingway couldn't wait to get started. Before he even got his bag unpacked, he was talking code into the telephone, lining up his "contacts."

When I got back from a trip to a staging area on the Cornwall coast a few nights later, Hemingway and an air raid arrived simultaneously. He had by then discovered that, combat correspondent or not, he probably wasn't going to make the first wave onto the beach. The spectacular fireworks of pounding antiaircraft batteries and thudding Nazi bombs dropping on the blacked-out city formed a fitting Wagnerian background for Papa's fury. Waving a can of beef broth in one hand and a bag of butter in the other,

This was the illustration for William Van Dusen's "Hemingway's Longest Day," published in *True*, February 1963. There were numerous articles after Hemingway's death that added to his larger-than-life legend.

he ran his vocabulary of four-letter words into three languages to describe the depth of the "double-cross" that would keep him from being first onto the beaches. By the end of his recital the beef broth was foaming, the butter almost churned to cheese. I had never seen the normally soft-spoken Hemingway so explosive.

Although he was chief of *Collier's* European bureau, his D-day credentials carried a relatively low priority. The press controllers had accredited him, not to an American combat team but to what Hemingway considered some panty-waist operation with the British fly boys. Papa was convinced he would not get to the battle beaches until about D-plus-17 unless those credentials were changed. And changed, by God, they would be!

When I returned to the hotel about a week before the big day, Hemingway had his campaign all mapped out. He had just gotten out of the hospital, where he had been incarcerated while they sewed the top of his head back on, a matter requiring some 50-odd stitches, made necessary after his car careened into a water tank in the black-out. This fortuitous circumstance, he explained, "attracts all kinds of flies to my web."

Between my trips to his command post for Scotch and bitters, which he stored and prescribed in large quantities for my stomach ailment, I got to watch Papa's whole counterplot unfold. It was as subtly contrived as any the master ever devised for his best novels. And in the end it was as successful. A small but highly select claque of recently uniformed and highly impressionable reservists were attracted to The Great Man like bees to honeysuckle. Before he was through he had commanders of D-day units vying for the privilege of escorting him to the beaches of France. Others might arrive at the gates of Hitler's fortress on D-plus-17, but not Papa!

Nor was Hemingway one to be bound by the "no arms" rule of the Geneva Convention which vouched that correspondents were innocent non-combatants. Battle-blooded on the Piave in the first World War and a veteran of the Spanish Civil War, he considered himself a tactician—with seniority. Once within range of shots being fired in anger he felt duty-bound to take command. And he was prepared. When Papa went into battle he carried enough armor for four men. His usual equipment included bandoleers of various types of ammunition crossed over his chest, a blouse-full of hand grenades, at least one pistol and a knife tucked into his waist and a rifle hanging from his broad back.

It wasn't until he was well on his way that the

cautious types back in London discovered that the code number of Hemingway's invasion ship indicated it was an Attack Transport—which meant he would hit the beach with one of the early assault waves! But it was too late to panic. There wasn't a way in the world he could have been intercepted without halting the whole invasion. Papa had got away!

I wasn't there for his return and didn't catch up with Hemingway again until some time later. One of his co-conspirators, however, reported that faithful to his pledge, Papa was back in London within 48 hours, smoke-grimy, his baggy trousers and jacket caked with dried mud, but all in one piece, thirsty, of course, and hungry.

And what had happened to our hero in those 48 hours?

A few days later I was tracing the invasion course inland from the American beaches and tallying up on commanding officers missing in action. Along the road to St. Lo I came on a D-day combat team that had come ashore on one of the hottest points on Omaha. I put my questions to them.

"Our C.O.? Hell, we've had a dozen in the last four days. They keep gettin' killed."

"Tell him about that wild man that dumped us on the beach."

"Who? Ernest Hemingway? Aw, he'd never believe that. I don't think it's true myself—and I was there."

"Go ahead. Tell him anyway."

"Well, as I said, you won't believe it . . ."

As they explained it, when they went over the side of the Attack Transport and into the LCVP for the run in to the beach there was this extra guy along. The men didn't know who he was at first or even what army he belonged to. No sign of rank or anything. He was just a big guy with a bushy beard and one of those Hindu towels wrapped around his head—like a rajah or something. After that lousy crossing of the Channel they were too seasick to pay much attention, anyway. It was worse in the LCVP: the wind was blowing up the cold spray and the waves kept sloshing over the side until they were soaked to the skin. All those big guns firing behind them didn't help, either, but they were better than those shells from the beach that kept exploding all around in the water. They couldn't see anything ahead except mist and smoke and a long hill burning and all kinds of murderous looking things in the water that their coxswain was trying to steer around.

Finally, this guy with the beard spotted the place they were supposed to go in and told the coxswain how to head.

The beach was full of little rocks. It wasn't easy to run on but they made it. Only lost two men. When they stopped behind a sea wall to catch their breath the Jerries got three more of them. Machine gun bullets were ricochetting [*sic*] off the stone wall and digging up rows of little dust clouds all around and every once in a while a mortar shell would pop over the wall and somebody else would get killed. Hemingway started routing them out again.

"Listen to me," he yells. "They've got us zeroed in with those mortars. They'll get us all in another minute or two. We've got to get out of here. See that hill? It's only about 150 yards away—50 steps. That fire you see up there won't hurt you. It's only grass burning. They've got a couple of machine guns planted at the corner of that hill. Don't run that way. Keep straight ahead. Now, get out of here. Keep down low—and don't stop running."

When they got to the hill and looked back they saw they were a lot better off than the guys trying to hide behind those steel things in the water and that sea wall. Those poor dog-faces were getting knocked off like sitting ducks. But under the hill they were safe. When the Jerries stopped shooting at them from the machine gun pit around the corner they knocked it out with a couple of grenades. Then things quieted down some.

"By about noon this Hemingway guy had us dug into the hill pretty good and said for us to sit tight and get ready to move up the draw as soon as the tanks got there. He told us to wait for them. We ate chocolate out of our K rations and settled back.

"About that time he left us and started to crawl back over the beach toward the water. We figured he was going to get somebody to do something about that big German gun up on the hill that was blasting our landing ships apart. Don't know what happened to him after that. The Krauts started lobbin' some stuff down the hill just about then and we got pretty busy for a few minutes. When things quieted down he wasn't in sight any more. Never did see him again. He must have got it before he could get back.

"You think that was really Ernest Hemingway?"

"Could be," I answered. "Could well be!"

When the American attack finally got rolling down the Cherbourg Peninsula, Hemingway was with it. Or rather, he was ahead of it—with his friends from the French underground. The war had gotten half way to the Rhine before the cautious types finally shot him down—with a court martial for field generalling his own private army of Maquis too far out in advance of the Allied attacking forces. Fifty-five miles in advance, as a matter of fact.

Papa was holed up in the Ritz Bar in Paris, under house arrest, when I finally caught up with him again. I told him what the GI's from Omaha beach had said about the guy with the Hindu towel around his head.

He just kind of laughed with his eyes and ordered up another bottle.

CHAPTER FOUR

Consuming Masculinity in the Bachelor Magazines

I n 1953, editor and publisher Hugh Hefner described *Playboy,* his new magazine, as "an entertainment magazine for the indoor man . . . a pleasure-primer for the sophisticated, city-bred male. . . . We hoped that it would be welcomed by that select group of urbane fellows who were less concerned with hunting, fishing, and climbing mountains than good food, drink, proper dress, and the pleasure of female company."[1] And thus was launched a thousand nudie mags, all trying to outdo Hefner's how-to manual for the midcentury male. The newsstands were rife with magazines featuring mascots aspiring to the bunny's insouciant hipness: Tigers, Tikis, Knights, and Dudes. These magazines purported to have the "inside track" for the worldly male. They were devoted to a flashy lifestyle based on toys and travel, music and food. They said that men could be consumers as long as it was for pleasure, as long as it advanced "the bachelor cause": *Jem,* "the magazine for the playful man"; *Dude,* "the magazine devoted to pleasure"; *Monsieur,* "sophisticated entertainment for men" and "entertainment for men of the World"; *Ace,* "the Magazine for men of distinction"; *High* and *Adam,* "The Man's Home Companion."

Hefner's introduction to *Playboy* illustrates how it and its ilk defined themselves against the decade's popular men's adventure magazines, which catered to the suburban male who wanted to define his masculinity as rugged and outdoorsy. The bachelor magazine gave off the odor of cologne, vermouth, and Turkish tobacco, but the smell of sweat and wood smoke wafted from such adventure magazines as *Argosy, True, Man's Illustrated,* and *Peril,* and Hemingway stalked through their pages in stories about

MALE

IS THERE A
LESBIAN
IN YOUR TOWN?

25 QUESTIONS
ANSWERED

BY DR. SHAILER
UPTON LAWTON

bullfights, safaris, and deep-sea fishing, just as Hemingwayesque characters appeared in the true adventures, the fictional or fictionalized accounts, the how-to articles.

Hemingway is just as much a presence in the bachelor magazines that modeled themselves after *Playboy*. These magazines forwarded the idea of Hemingway as a world-wise traveler and gourmet, an expert on food and cocktails, on women and culture, even offering advice directly from the man himself.[2] They "sold" the Hemingwayesque idea of masculinity, expertise, consumption, and travel. The May 1961 issue of *The Vagabond* (for "The Man of the World") offers an excellent example of this type of conspicuous consumerism in its feature "The Vagabond in Sevilla," a firsthand account of the *feria*—a guide on where to go in Seville to "meet" women. In the same issue there is also the "Vagabond 4 Month Vacation Guide," which includes Mexico City's bullring as one site; an "International Datebook," a selection of beautiful pinups from around the world; and "Death in the Afternoon," a depiction of the mano a mano between Domínguin and Ordóñez at Bayonne, "The Last Bullfight Seen by Author Hemingway." Similarly, *Carnival,* which dedicated itself to reporting on travel, carnivals, burlesque, and fiestas worldwide, featured "The Old Man and the Spree," a long article about Hemingway in Pamplona in its second issue. Again and again, articles appeared in these magazines on Hemingway, travel, and the bullfight, all of which captured the tone and lifestyle these magazines were selling to the American male.

But what is common to both the adventure and bachelor magazines is this selling of a strain of masculinity dependent on consumerism and leisure—whether which shotgun or rod was better for hunting or fishing, or where to drink, what to drive, what jazz was best for seduction. A man's outfit for the Serengeti was on par with a man's outfit for a summer cruise. In general, the clothes made the man, the pad made the bachelor.

The postwar baby boom is popularly seen as an age defined by advertising and heightened consumption at a time when growing suburbanization stressed conformity. The huge economic growth after the Second World War ensured the fulfillment of the white middle-class suburban ideal. Spurred on by the GI Bill and government stimuli for more housing and growing families, millions of veterans married and moved into suburban ranch houses, which became the symbol for America's prosperity. According to Warren Susman, "One can represent the new affluent society [of the 1950s] collectively in the image of the happy suburban home."[3] But this suburban prosperity wasn't without its drawbacks. Steven Gelber points

Opposite: *Male Magazine* boasted "Tough, Shocking Features!"—among them a letter from Hemingway (April 1954).

Many of the bachelor magazines used gimmicks to stand out among the dozens of rival publications on the newsstand. *Cocktail* featured drink recipes with each pinup.

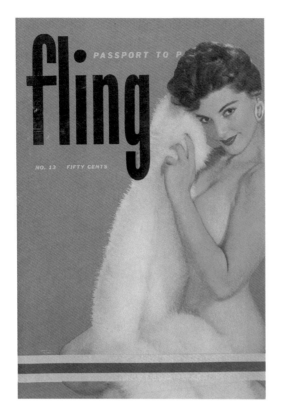

Top left: *Fling Magazine,* a "Passport to Leisure," was one of the slicker *Playboy* knockoffs, though it was digest size. Such magazines defined men's role not as father but as bachelor. This 1959 issue published the portrait "Hemingway—Some Notes on a Legend." ©1959 Relim Publishing Co.

Top right: One of the many *Playboy* copycats, *Satan* only lasted for a few issues. This April 1957 issue, *Satan*'s second, features prototypical pinup girl Bettie Page. Such magazines tried to capture the public's fancy with their own mascot in the mode of *Playboy*'s bunny. ©1957 Stanley Publications

Left: In comparison to the bachelor magazines, *Argosy* and *True* were much tamer in playing into the suburban dream of postwar America, though they still pandered to the 1950s fascination with safaris and bullfights. This issue of *Argosy* republished excerpts of *The Green Hills of Africa* in June 1954.

out that the postwar years were not only a return to the "neo-Victorian" family roles of father as breadwinner and mother as angel of the house, but unlike the 1800s there was the added pressure on the father to also be a constant presence in the family unit. This move to the suburbs, with its solidifying of family roles, was accompanied in popular culture with a sense of emasculation. The dual responsibilities of fatherhood and keeping up with the Joneses "clashed with . . . traditional gender models, catching men in a no-win situation."[4]

The crisis of masculinity wasn't the most important crisis at the time, especially in comparison to the travails of African Americans and the general pressures on women to conform to the ideals of femininity. Yet it was predominant enough to become a standard literary theme in the hands of both artists and authors of the day. The pressures felt by the middle-class male suburbanite can be seen in John Cheever's famous short story "The Country Husband" (1958), the hero of which, Francis Weed, embodies this identity crisis. The portrait of his domestic life is one of claustrophobia, a moral emptiness behind a façade of etiquette and dinner parties, where unhappiness is sublimated to manly hobbies like woodworking. His self-defining wartime experience is contrasted to the pettiness of suburbia, where it seems that everyone is "united in their tacit claim that there had been no past, no war."[5] He deals with the emasculation of suburbia, symbolized by his wife, by fantasizing about the new beautiful teen babysitter and a life of travel. As he tries to fight the conformity of the suburban social mores, his life begins to unravel. He finally returns to his family by containing his unhappiness through therapy and retreating to his workshop, losing himself in masculine yet domestic chores.

The opposing worlds of Weed's fantasies of sex and travel and his unsatisfactory role as Mr. Fix-It are both embodied in the different types of men's magazines at this time. The emptiness that Cheever's hero feels, which feeds his fantasies, is exactly what the bachelor magazines pandered to, even hoped to alleviate, by offering, at least vicariously, a means of escape by promoting not the domestic do-it-yourself role but the elevation of the bachelor lifestyle. Outdoorsy adventure magazines like *True* and *Argosy* pandered to the ideals of the suburban male, often featuring how-to articles. Gelber has shown how the do-it-yourself attitude repaired and maintained masculinity because it "permitted the suburban father to stay home without feeling emasculated or being subsumed into an undifferentiated entity with his wife."[6]

The adventure magazines literarily "constructed" the male with advice on bodybuilding. The second issue of *Mr. America,* an adventure magazine

started up and edited by American bodybuilder Joe Weider, is full of such examples. It features articles such as "Elephant Hunting in East Africa" by famous weight lifter, promoter, big-game hunter, and (ironically) raw-foodist Tromp van Diggelen, who contends in the piece that "when I have to decide what sport . . . demands most endurance, determination and physical fitness I unhesitatingly cast my vote for elephant hunting. Here one's very life may depend on the muscular system being tuned so that it will instantaneously respond to every message of the brain." Likewise, the June 1955 *Fury* magazine, another Weider publication, touted as "Exciting True Adventures for Men," featured an exposé on how TV star Dick Strout turned his career around with weight lifting. It is illustrated with Strout explaining numerous posture-improving exercises. This issue is typical in its mélange of male role models, advice, sensationalism, and commercialism.

This emphasis on the image of the suburban adventurer reliant on a leisure-defined masculinity surfaced in rather surreal ways in these magazines, such as in ads for products that flaunted extreme masculinity: underwear, with models holding shotguns; authentic pith helmets (just what every suburbanite needed to mow the lawn); and even a stuffed "'Wild Cat' Big-Game Trophy" replica "for den, club, office, or auto . . . exacting to the last whisker" for only $2.98.[7] These magazines made "masculine" activities vicariously possible: just buying a copy on the newsstand confirmed one's maleness, made the reader an armchair adventurer.

Such DIY adventuring was incidental to the true adventure magazines' specialization in reaffirming accounts of manhood tested. But the bachelor magazines, especially *Playboy,* made the consumption of masculinity their raison d'être by schooling readers on how to look and act like a successful individual. These pinup magazines, like conduct manuals, told men how to dress properly for different occasions, what was new in jazz and the theater, the best and fastest new cars, how to entertain and mix cocktails, and, in hundreds of Kinsey-like articles, how to understand women. Masculinity as outlined in these magazines was defined by play and possessions.

Given the popularity of Hemingway in these magazines, a similar dynamic is at work with his fiction and much-publicized biography. His role in the

Opposite: *Vagabond* captured the bachelor mags' fascination with travel and adventure. This issue featured an article on Hemingway's last bullfight during the dangerous summer of 1960. Another article told the reader how to "get lucky" at the Seville Feria. ©1961 Polo Publishing

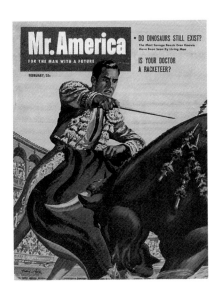

Both *Mr. America* and *Fury* were started by bodybuilder Joe Weider. Both bachelor magazines and adventure magazines such as these "sold" lifestyles of adventure that excluded women, bachelor mags doing so through high style. ©1952 Weider Publications; © 1955 Weider Publications

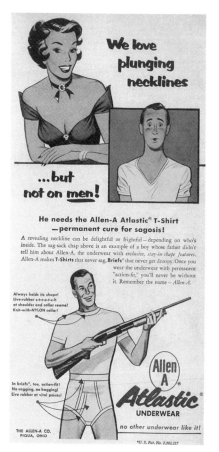

Even the ads, like these from *Adam* (1960) and *True* (May 1952), catered to the armchair adventurer.

bachelor magazines is as the consummate cultured sportsman, the expert and insider who approaches the leisure activities of fishing, hunting, eating, drinking, traveling, and women with the same skill, integrity, respect, and seriousness he approaches a battlefield or a typewriter. His expertise is often flaunted: the cover of the February 1955 *Focus* states, "Hemingway shows how to hunt"; *Sportsman Magazine* (March 1955), "The Magazine of Big Game Adventures," reprints Hemingway's introduction to and an excerpt from François Sommer's *I Hunt Africa,* placing Hemingway's name on the cover rather than Sommer's; the first issue of *GunSport* magazine featured an "Exclusive Interview: Ernest Hemingway Talks About Guns"; in 1956 *Sports Afield* interviewed Hemingway about dove shooting in Cuba; *Tab Magazine* featured an article on "Duck Hunting with Ernest Hemingway"; the issue of *Argosy* that reprints "The Blue River" also reprints Hemingway's specification on tackle. This role of sportsman was an integral part of Hemingway's persona, an image he proudly nurtured and protected, and one that he had established in his fiction and, especially, in his nonfiction written for *Esquire* in the mid-1930s. John Raeburn points out that Hemingway's articles were ultimately practical, they "could teach readers how to catch a marlin, what to look for in a bullfight, how to stalk a lion, where to buy good champagne in Paris, what brand of beer to drink on a fishing cruise."[8]

As *Esquire* correspondent, Hemingway contributed thirty-one "letters," the majority of which offered both personal editorializing and impersonal advice.[9] It is just this play between personal and expert that shaped the persona adopted by and furthered in men's magazines twenty years later. The role *Esquire* played in the construction of Public Hemingway cannot be overstressed, for *Esquire* was the first magazine dedicated to creating a male marketplace and so was the perfect venue for "selling" the Hemingway persona.

ESQUIRE AND MASCULINE MODERNISM

Arnold Gingrich, formerly an editor for men's clothing catalogs and a freelance writer for *Pep, Droll,* and *Breezy Stories* girlie pulps, started *Esquire* in 1933 as a magazine to be sold in men's clothing stores. Its aim was to sell clothes and style to men—a tricky undertaking, because it was generally thought in advertising circles that men only cared about rugged practicality and that any concern with fashion was effeminate. *Esquire* sidestepped this problem by making the magazine overtly masculine in its tone and subject matter. Not surprisingly, the first name listed on the cover of the first issue was Ernest Hemingway. Other articles in the premiere issue were about boxing, bucking broncos, burlesque, and a spy story by the pulpish-sounding "P173 (Captain X)."

Esquire was groundbreaking because it succeeded at creating a commercial venue for male consumption based on travel, fashion, and leisure. For example, advertisements in the February 1936 issue, which published Hemingway's "Tradesman's Return," featured clothing, cars, hotels, nightclubs, liquor, and travel—all ads geared to the man of leisure. Judging by ads and George Petty's pinup cartoons, most of *Esquire*'s readers spent their nights in black tie at the most fashionable clubs.

But judging a magazine's readership solely by ads is misleading, for even though *Esquire* made it "safe" for men to shop, it did so at a time when the majority of American men were not able to: *Esquire* was launched in 1933, at the height of the Great Depression, when between one-third and one-quarter of the American workforce was unemployed.[10] Yet at a time when class- and economic-based male identity was in flux, *Esquire* appealed to a large male audience because, like the pulp magazines of the time, it reaffirmed a life threatened by job losses, home foreclosures, and hungry children. But unlike the pulps, *Esquire* did so by flaunting a conspicuous consumerism. And Gingrich's claim in the inaugural issue, that "Esquire aims to become the common denominator of masculine interests—to be all things to all men,"[11] further explains the magazine's great success: a tone of class elitism, an image of economic security, and a portrait of the successful male.

Hemingway's *Esquire* articles functioned similarly. He wrote and gave advice on African big-game hunting or Cuban fishing when few, if any, of the readers could afford to take that advice. So in a magazine built on masculinity and product consumption, what Hemingway is really selling is his own role as expert on leisure-based masculinity. This posturing—him establishing himself as an expert via "the true gen" or inside track—can be seen as the same effective self-marketing he relied on when establishing his early reputation as a modernist author. It makes perfect sense that Hemingway was integral to *Esquire*'s attempt to construct a male consumer, for it was modernism that blazed the trail of such marketing.

MAKE IT NEW: MODERNISM AND SELF-MARKETING

Modernist literature is marked by revolutionary stylistics and themes consciously pioneered and marketed by small avant-garde groups, such as the Irish Renaissance around Yeats and the Abbey Theatre, the Bloomsbury group around Virginia Woolf, and the diverse Paris salons of Gertrude Stein and Ezra Pound. The publishing venues for these groups have been traditionally seen as little magazines and small press publications unconcerned with large-scale salability. But recent criticism has also pointed to appearances in more popular venues and a more self-conscious pandering to the marketplace.[12] Much of this criticism has focused on the advertising methods used by such modernist movers, shakers, and impresarios as Ezra Pound and Wyndham Lewis—exactly the role models Hemingway took his modernist tutelage from in the early 1920s.

Hemingway's early Paris years were marked (and marketed) by the establishment of his "insider" persona in his dispatches for the *Toronto Star* and his stylistic break with mentors Sherwood Anderson and Gertrude Stein, which resulted in a dynamic of expertise and disavowal, a writerly persona both above and in synch with the literary avant-garde. For example, his 1922 article for the *Toronto Star* "American Bohemians in Paris" reports the inside scoop on the activities of the real poets and painters of Paris, who are not the "strange acting and strange looking breed that crowd the tables of the Cafe Rotonde."[13] In Paris only a few weeks, Hemingway was under the influence of modernist entrepreneurs like Ezra Pound, Ford Madox Ford, and Wyndham Lewis and already establishing his position as one among the avant-garde.

This is also glaringly evident in Hemingway's first novel, the satirical *The Torrents of Spring* (1926), where the author intrudes on the narration to drop names and gossip about prominent modernist authors and little magazines. Though usually considered just a sophomoric satire of Sherwood Anderson and as a means to break his publishing contract with Boni Liveright, *Torrents* can also be seen as another stepping stone in the growing reputation of Hemingway as expert and modernist.

Though the idea of these avant-garde writers, these self-proclaimed literary revoluntionaries, using marketing techniques or being part of the marketplace is traditionally oxymoronic, aspects of the modernist movement were indeed consciously defined by major players like Pound and critics like Malcolm Cowley. Lawrence Rainey, for example, has shown how both Pound and Filipo Marinetti used sensational marketing—bombastic public appearances and extreme printed manifestos—to further their own agendas as well as for monetary support. In this sense, manifestos, reviews, and editorials can be seen as advertisements advocating new trends in art, turning Pound's famous adage "Make It New" to "Make It 'Now, New, and Improved.'"

In teaching their readers to read in a new way, modernists were in fact creating their audience. Hemingway's break with Anderson, which was consciously and publicly manipulated via *Torrents of Spring,* marks a simultaneous disavowal of existing stylistics and a furthering of Hemingway's own reputation.

Years later, Hemingway would utilize a similar technique in *Death in the Afternoon* when he personified the general, unsophisticated reader negatively as an Old Woman. Besides distancing himself from any notion of his pulp beginnings, this characterization contrasted the popular reader with Hemingway's own sophisticated, modern audience, establishing them as privileged, superior.[14] Likewise, modernist little magazines aspired to a tone of intellectual elitism in their marketing, often despite populist leanings. In much the same way, early advertising for the popularly modernist *Vanity Fair* magazine used the term "modernism" to sell subscriptions, telling readers that *Vanity Fair* would make them familiar with the newest trends and authors in the arts, a technique *Esquire*'s Gingrich noticed and took advantage of.

Esquire's tone of modernism was dependent on elite masculinity. Just as Hemingway's Old Woman symbolized popular literature as feminized, so did modernist marketing, especially in little magazines like *The Little Review,* Lewis's *Blast,* and the futurist manifestos. High modernists misogynistically defined themselves against the female reader and consumer. For example, in the March 1913 issue of *Smart Set,* editor Williard Huntington Wright, the modernist predecessor of Mencken and Nathan, wrote, "I believe that this is a day of enlightenment on the part of magazine readers. Men and Women have grown tired of effeminacy and the falsities of current fiction, essays, and poetry." Modernism was strong, masculine, all that which "effeminate" popular fiction was not.[15] This was the strain of modernism that Hemingway subscribed to.[16] More important, in the years between the 1920s and the 1950s, this strain of modernism rose to prominence exactly because of this stance of overt privilege and masculinity. It was not until

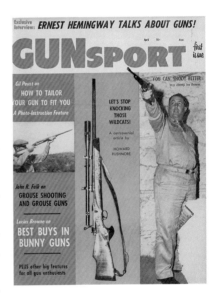

Top: This issue of *Sportsman* excerpted François Sommer's book *Man and Beast in Africa* under the title *I Hunt Africa,* publicizing Hemingway's foreword. ©1955 Male Publishing Co.

Below: In interviews Hemingway set himself up as an expert on almost anything sporting. In the first issue of *GunSport* (1958) it was shotguns. ©1958 Magnum Publications Inc.

the 1970s that the pantheon of modernist authors was opened to women beyond Virginia Woolf and Gertrude Stein.

The efficiency of the marketing techniques of modernism is aptly illustrated (though in a manner perhaps surprising to literary historians) in the pinup variety of 1950s men's magazines, specifically in the presence of modernist fiction and authors within their pages. The publication of modernist writers in these mags was business as usual. *Gent Magazine* published Faulkner, John O'Hara, Joris-Karl Huysman, and even Jean Paul Sartre. *Escapade* featured S. J. Perelman, William Saroyan, Somerset Maugham, and Jack Kerouac. *Dude* offered D. H. Lawrence, James T. Farrell, Faulkner, Budd Schulberg, and Robert Lowry. *High* featured Farrell and Pierre Louys. The list goes on. Many magazines also featured articles *about* famous literary figures, among them Henry Miller, Guy deMaupassant, Lawrence, and Oscar Wilde. Certain authors, like Joyce, Faulkner, and Hemingway, merited both articles about them and fiction by them. Of course, 1950s men's magazines relied on the aura of respectability that republishing modernist authors gave them. But more than this, the fiction of these authors was often concerned with either travel and adventure or sexuality. Such themes are obviously not solely modernist, but when those aspects of 1950s bachelorhood are paired with that stance of self-marketing through expertise as an aspect of modernism, then the 1950s sophisticated men's magazines become intrinsically modernist, a culmination of a certain modernist agenda.

Samuel Roth's pinup digest *Good Times* is an excellent example of the melding of men's magazines and modernism. Roth was a character always on the outskirts of modernism. Though damned by Hemingway and many other modernists in 1927 for pirating *Ulysses* in his *Two Worlds Magazine,* Roth allowed modernist works to reach a larger audience, albeit sometimes under sensational covers. He mixed high brow with erotica, creating the formula that would spell success for Hefner and *Playboy.* Roth's *Good Times,* for example, was a digest magazine started in 1953 that featured nude photography, titillating fiction from around the world, and articles on serious (though mostly nude) art. It was both racy and sophisticated and, again, captured a certain worldly and traveled tone, since each issue was dedicated to a different country, hence its byline "A Revue of the World of Pleasure."

But more than any single magazine can, Hemingway's popularity offers the most successful example of this type of popular modernist marketing. Articles about him in 1950s men's mags feature Hemingway offering his expertise. *Playboy* ran three compendiums of Hemingway advice and mottoes, and *Sir Knight* published "What Life Has Taught Me," another article of quotes lifted from interviews with Hemingway.[17] Stories of his, like his popular interests of fishing, hunting, and war, were marked by their resistance to the feminine or domestic sphere. The conflict of "Hills Like White Elephants," for example, is the American's pressuring of the Girl to get an abortion so that they can continue their life of travel and irresponsible sex, as symbolized by their luggage with "labels on them from all the hotels where they had spent nights."[18] The fantasies of misogyny and travel in "Hills Like White Elephants" are the same that Cheever's Francis Weed falls back on as relief from his suburban life. Such fantasies are, literally, embodied in those nude pictorials of women from around the world in magazines like *Vagabond* and, earlier, in Roth's *Good Times.*

These instances of 1950s modernism are more than a popular form coopting modernism. They point to a genealogy, an evolution of modernism from little magazines through *Esquire* to fifties men's magazines. In this sense, one could even say that the midcentury men's magazines are a culmination of a masculine, misogynistic modernism started in the teens.

The tone of elitism and worldly sophistication that mags like *Playboy* relied on was pioneered by modernism and helps explain the popularity of Hemingway's image at the time. How pervasively this Hemingwayesque modernist attitude spread through consumer-based 1950s hypermasculinity is nowhere better illustrated than in the popularity of the bullfight in the 1950s, especially as tied to the decade's other predominant trope of the Madison Avenue businessman.

HEMINGWAY, MADISON AVENUE, AND SELLING THE ADVENTUROUS LIFE

John Xiros Cooper, in *Modernism and the Culture of Market Society,* contends that early modernists were "revolutionary in the remaking of everyday life" and, however inadvertently, in the making of modern "capitalist society and culture." The end result of this is that the bohemianism of modernism—its symbols, stylistic experimentation, and narrative techniques—became the "preferred cultural style" by the end of the twentieth century.[19] One of the reasons for this is how modernism self-consciously constantly reinvented itself. As Ezra Pound's modernist slogan commands, "Make It New." The midcentury's fascination with modernism is an example of this, as is more pointedly the distinctly modernist marketing stance of privilege.

The trope of travel and expertise, a reoccurring fascination of virile modernism (though often as defined against the female), is nowhere better encapsulated than in Hemingway's use and exploration of the bullfight as a symbol of courage under pressure and artistic expertise. As early as the second paragraph of *Death in the Afternoon,* Hemingway melds his learning about the bullfight with his learning how to write "truly"—both done under the tutelage of Gertrude Stein. And it is in this paragraph, which is perhaps Hemingway's most extended description of his own stylistic goal, that he describes understanding the bullfight as an important step in his learning to describe action "purely enough" to evoke true and lasting emotion.

The bullfight appealed to Hemingway for two reasons: it was an allegory for life and death complete with pomp, tragedy, and dignity; and it was the realm of the aficionado, the knowledgeable and passionate insider, the illuminated audience with privileged knowledge of art and an appreciation for the skillful artist. Hence Hemingway's writing about the bullfight, like his writing about war, established his own expertise and his cultural position as an insider ready and willing to share his knowledge with the audience. Furthermore, it is an extended analogy for the craft of writing, wherein the matador is the artist. It is the author's role to portray life and death gracefully, and it is the privileged artist who understands this battle that makes modernism itself an "aficionado art." This is why modernist artists such as Picasso and Juan Gris used the bullfight as subject matter, as Gris's cubist frontispiece of a matador for *Death in the Afternoon* illustrates.

Whereas his audience was not open to the experience in 1932, as *Death in the Afternoon* was received lukewarmly by readers and critics, bullfighting was such a popular fad by 1959 that *Life* asked Hemingway to write the exposé of the rivalry between two famous bullfighters which eventually became *The Dangerous Summer.* Throughout the decade there was a glut of books dedicated to bullfighting: Barnaby Conrad's *La Fiesta Brava, Gates of Fear, The Death of Manolete,* and translation of *My Life as a Matador;* Sydney Franklin's *Bullfighter from Brooklyn* (in which Hemingway plays a prominent role and which reprints a section of *Death in the Afternoon*); and Vincent Kehoe's *Aficionado!,* Angus MacNab's *Fighting Bulls,* Jack Randolph Conrad's *The Horn and the Sword,* Kenneth Tynan's *Bull Fever,* and Marguerite Steen's novel *Bulls of Parral.*

But the relatively large number of books on the bullfight is nothing in comparison to the number of bullfight-themed articles, fiction, pictorials, and covers in the men's magazines. There were countless articles like *Real Man*'s "Toro, Toreador . . . Terror" or *Men's Pictorial*'s "The Bloody Sands." There were even pictorials featuring pinups in matador outfits, like the one in *Escapade* that flirts, "A Girl Who Makes Passes: Even el toro enjoys a corrida such as this." The predominance of bullfighting articles in men's

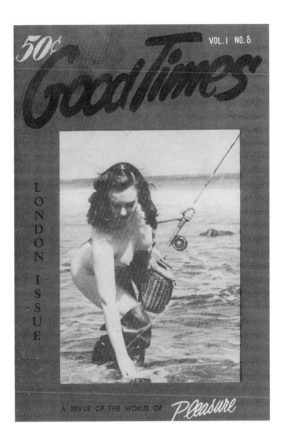

He was a fool to risk his life for a crowd that knew nothing of bullfighting. But he could not resist the challenge of the girl and that magnificent

TORAZO

by Robert L. Trimnell

A cigar brings out the
Matador in you

Cigars have always been a man's smoke. They give you
man-size flavor . . . satisfaction . . . a bold lift of the
spirits that can't be matched. Yet you needn't
inhale to enjoy cigars, and no other pleasure so
great costs so little. Try a few cigars today and . . .

Get that good cigar feeling!

CIGAR INSTITUTE OF AMERICA, INC.

65

Matador in GREY FLANNEL
Fiction By RICK RUBIN

It was to be an inter-office Corrida,

A CLEAN EXECUTIVE-SUITE KILL

FEATURING A GREAT TORRERO, KILLER OF BULLS
ALL THE BLOODY WAY UP FROM THE MAIL ROOM

----- Lawrence TABOR AND Karen OLSEN -----

VS. Mr. Eldon KILLBUCK

magazines indicates how the bullfight was a masculine fascination. The large
number of books on bullfighting illustrates the general cultural fascination
with bullfighting. Taken together, we can see how pervasive the masculine
ideals were in midcentury American culture.

It is interesting to conjecture as to why the bullfight became so popular
in the 1950s. Was it just another aspect of hypermasculinity, an exotic tonic
for the suburban male like the bachelor pad and the sophisticated men's
magazines in general? Since many of the men's magazine bullfight articles
featured Hemingway prominently, what was his role in the spread and popu-
larization of the bullfight? It is perhaps too much to give the credit entirely
to Hemingway, despite quotes in the mags that he "discovered bullfighting"

and "invented bullfighting for the non-Latin world." Unquestionably, both he and the bullfight appealed to a cultural need in the 1950s. The reason that Hemingway initially used the bullfight as a modernist trope was that it appealed to his stance as cultural impresario, as artistic aficionado who dealt in the truth of life and death. This in itself was in keeping with how Pound and Lewis first marketed modernism. If we look closely at how the bullfight was used in men's magazines, it becomes clear that its popularity (along with Hemingway's) was involved with how aspects of modernism, especially its marketing dynamics, infiltrated the general culture of the 1950s.

Whereas the bullfight was popular in men's magazines in general, how it was presented in adventure magazines was different from how it was presented in the sophisticated bachelor magazines. In adventure magazines, the corrida was an extreme test of masculinity, but in the bachelor magazines it was often presented in terms of a travelogue. For example, the 1958 *Hi-Life* ("The Live-It-Up Magazine for Gentlemen") features an article on Venezuelan bullfighting alongside a travel overview on the Caribbean. And in keeping with the conduct manual/cultural guide elements of these magazines, there were also cocktail recipes, car reviews, and a sneak preview of foreign films. It is just this "inside track," inherited from the dynamics of modernist coterie salons, or "focus groups," that was a key dynamic in creating a market in the construction of the male-as-consumer.[20] The pairing of unequivocally masculine themes (bullfight, pinups) with commercialism made it okay for men to define themselves by what they bought, by shopping. This dynamic, initially evident in *Esquire,* came to fruition in the 1950s, a time when men were defined by their possessions and ability to buy, hence the suburban-based ideas of either "keeping up with the Joneses" or differentiating oneself from the Joneses through a lifestyle of travel and cultural fluency. The 1950s were so self-defined by commercialism that the ad salesman, or "man in the gray flannel suit," as he was labeled by novelist Sloane Wilson, became another cultural icon alongside Hemingway and the matador. The 1958 issue of *Hi-Life* also contains "Grey Flannelisms," a list of colloquialisms used by the "advertising and publicity male."

In the 1950s, Madison Avenue's advertising executive became a symbol of modernity, the cultural icon of affluent white-collar middle class. The advertising world became a respectable microculture, one made possible by the subcultural dynamics of avant-garde modernism decades earlier. Ad men played an integral role in constructing wants and representing the culture as a whole. They universalized their own position and dictated social norms.[21] Men's magazines filled their pages with the figure of the ad

Opposite: In the 1950s, the hypermasculine matador became an analogy for the successful male, especially the advertising executive, as seen in this cigar ad in *Argosy* (November 1958) and in Rick Rubin's short story in *Rogue* (July 1961), "Matador in Grey Flannel."

man—in ads, articles, cartoons, and stories. The proliferation of the Madison Avenue executive proves his and advertising's centrality to 1950s culture.

Advertisements such as the 1958 ad for the Cigar Institute of America, which states "A Cigar Brings out the Matador in You" and depicts a gray flannel–suited businessman holding a muletta, illustrate how marketing promoted the idea that it was possible to buy masculinity by simply purchasing a cigar. The ad might as well read, "A Cigar Brings out the Man in You." This is similar to the modernist stance that it was possible to buy cultural expertise by reading modernist authors, by buying little magazines.

This conflation of the ad man and the matador became so institutionalized as to be the running metaphor in the story "Matador in Grey Flannel," by Rick Rubin in the July 1961 *Rogue Magazine*. It concerns a junior ad executive who sees himself as a matador, and his ruthless climb up the corporate ladder as a series of bullfights where he sets up and skewers competitors for their jobs, corner offices, the executive washroom, etc. He is just as ruthless in his pursuit of his secretary, which is eventually his undoing when she reveals his plans to his next victim, his direct superior. As he is fired, the executive thinks, "She unfixed him. . . . That icy Nordic bitch has unfixed him. . . . The goddamned horn is all the way through and now I'm going to have to walk to the infirmary all alone. On the hot sand in the hot sun, with the blood running down my belly, all alone."

The fact that the tone of these magazines depended on the illusion that they were giving the reader inside information helps explain the 1950s adoption of the bullfight both as a metaphor for the advertising executive and as the epitome of masculine performance—with Hemingway as its ambassador, for the position of aficionado was in perfect synch with Hemingway's mantle of expertise. If the bullfight was used to sell products, so was Hemingway. This was the decade of his infamous Ballantine Beer and Pan Am endorsements as well as articles in men's sports magazines on his favorite shotguns and boats.

This merging of the Madison Avenue ad man with the image of the matador is an odd combination unless we contextualize it in terms of marketing, how the bullfight and corporate advertising culture are both "insider sports," how both rely on membership in a men's club of privileged knowledge. It is this dynamic that modernism relied on in its early years to establish itself and that Hemingway adopted and never dropped, as his many examples of advice-giving interviews and journalism illustrate. It is easy to forget that this stance of modernism was initially defined against the feminine sphere of popular magazines, and this is exactly why "bachelor" magazines of the 1950s were so successful and widespread, for they offered the American male escape from what was seen as the feminine sphere of the suburban home and all their domestic responsibilities therein. And within these magazines, Hemingway, with his stories of "Men Without Women," became a symbol for this hypermasculine world.

Vicarious Adventure

Above: Despite the headline for this March 1956 issue of *Uncensored,* the article on "Exposing Safari Sex" had nothing to do with Hemingway. Not only does this demonstrate how synonymous his name was with big-game hunting in the 1950s, but it shows how the safari was a boy's club and he the keeper of insider knowledge. ©1956 Plaza Digest Inc.

Left: The men's magazines of the 1950s offered themselves as a means to alleviate the postwar pressures of suburban conformity and corporate success. The December 1957 issue of *Gent,* which published "The Hemingway I Know," went so far as to call itself "An Approach to Relaxation." ©1957 Excellent Publications

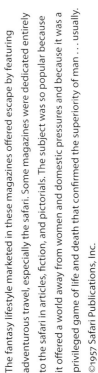

Other magazines were more general but still often pandered to the safari craze. This issue of *Peril* did so sensationally with "Twisted Horns Tore My Guts." ©1958 Jeflin Pub.

The fantasy lifestyle marketed in these magazines offered escape by featuring adventurous travel, especially the safari. Some magazines were dedicated entirely to the safari in articles, fiction, and pictorials. The subject was so popular because it offered a world away from women and domestic pressures and because it was a privileged game of life and death that confirmed the superiority of man . . . usually. ©1957 Safari Publications, Inc.

And of course Hemingway was presented as the expert on
leisure-defined masculinity, the master sportsman. ©1956
Fawcett Publications

CHAPTER FIVE

*Pap*arazzi: Hemingway and the Tabloids

Exposed, Uncensored, Confidential, On the QT, Whisper. The tabloid magazines screamed the dark secrets of the stars: "The Secret Life of Tyrone Power," "Marlon's Marriage Goes Bang," "The Sex Kitten Tells All," "World's Most Amazing Sex Transformation." Lurid, lascivious, and mostly lies, the gossip magazines are the low-watermark of 1950s popular culture. It's hard not to feel sleazy just flipping through their pages, reading accounts of Hollywood pot busts, divorces, drunken orgies, naughty starlets. And Hemingway had as large a presence in the pages of these rags as he did in the adventure and bachelor magazines of the day.

By the 1950s, Hemingway's persona had itself become an icon, a brand name for a certain masculine authorship and lifestyle that had its moorings in intellectual modernism. The evolution of this was spread out over thirty years of publishing, self-invention, and marketing. The articles about him in tabloids of the 1950s are the ramifications of that myth making, the collateral damage of his celebrity status. The extent and fervor of Hemingway gossip during the decade not only stresses exactly how popular he was but also points to the complexity of his celebrity, how it was built on the interplay among the man, his literary reputation, and his public image.

THE RISE OF CELEBRITY CULTURE AND THE BIRTH OF THE TABLOIDS

There have been society gossip rags since the late nineteenth century, but it was the mid-1910s and 1920s that saw the rise of modern celebrity culture with fan magazines like *Picture Play* and *Screenland* that rose to popularity

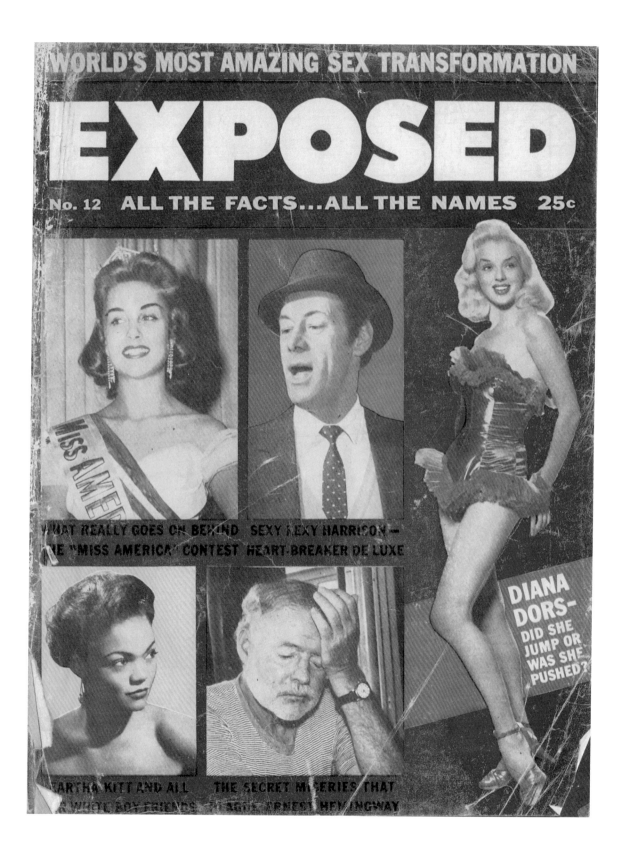

WORLD'S MOST AMAZING SEX TRANSFORMATION

EXPOSED

No. 12   ALL THE FACTS...ALL THE NAMES   25c

WHAT REALLY GOES ON BEHIND
THE "MISS AMERICA" CONTEST

SEXY REXY HARRISON —
HEART-BREAKER DE LUXE

MARTHA KITT AND ALL
A WHOLE BOY FRIENDS

THE SECRET MISERIES THAT
PLAGUE ERNEST HEMINGWAY

DIANA
DORS—
DID SHE
JUMP OR
WAS SHE
PUSHED?

with the proliferation of cinema, the organization of the studio system, and expanded magazine distribution. Such magazines were not limited to film celebrities but also included stage and radio, mirroring the consolidation of the entertainment industry. It is generally taken for granted that celebrity culture—the dynamics of constructing and emulating celebrity—rose exclusively from the movie industry; but what is often overlooked is this consolidation of media, how the popularity and marketing of popular literature, magazines, radio, and film were all interdependent. Novels and magazine short stories were mined for film and radio, the authors themselves writing the scripts. Stars were cross-marketed, acting out adaptations of novels and spotlighted in magazines. Movie stars appeared in radio plays while radio stars jumped to the silver screen. But the most telling marker of the rise of celebrity culture, regardless of media, was the shift of the public's interest from the "role" or work of actors or writers to their personal lives.[1]

The tension between public and private has always been an aspect of celebrity. Press releases and studio-condoned articles in movie magazines pandered to this fascination, featuring voyeuristic glimpses into the home lives of the stars. Even not-condoned, scandalous exposés added to the star's allure. Richard deCordova believes that all "press," whether promotional or scandalous, adds to star status unless it was such that the "discourse" of celebrity culture can't absorb it, as during Roscoe "Fatty" Arbuckle's infamous trial for rape in 1921. The 1930s marked the highpoint of the powerful studio system, where the studios worked hard to create and preserve their properties' images through publicity stunts and other manipulations (such as faux relationships to belie the suspicion of homosexuality). Yet by the 1940s, celebrity culture was such that it could absorb Errol Flynn's 1942 trials for statutory rape—media attention that only added to his image as a dashing scoundrel. This points to a few things. First, celebrity is both subjective and objective, each star's persona is created through the tension between their private and public images. Second, over the first half of the twentieth century, there was a shift in the acceptance and prevalence of scandal and a growing interest in sensationalism and the personal aspects of celebrity.

This trajectory of sensationalism reached its apex in the tabloids of the mid-1950s, which were dedicated almost entirely to scandal. The reciprocal relationship between the traditional fan magazines and the studio system allowed for a certain degree of information (or damage) control. But the tabloids didn't need any studio approval for their stories and, in fact, had not grown out of the fan magazine genre but out of the postwar burlesque

Opposite: "The Secret Miseries That Plague Ernest Hemingway"—no doubt *Exposed* (1957) was one of them. ©1957 Whitestone Publications

Screen magazines were the forerunners of the tabloid and gossip magazines. Hemingway's celebrity had a reciprocal relationship with the studios' publicity system, especially in the 1950s, when numerous films were produced based on his work. ©1934 Tilsam Publishers

magazine. The birth of the tabloid is commonly attributed to Robert Harrison, an editor and publisher who had earlier success with such late-1940s girlie magazines as *Wink, Titter,* and *Eyeful.* His magazine *Whisper* started as a similar burlesque pulp but in the early 1950s became a celebrity scandal rag.

WIDE OPEN VICE in GALVESTON—PHENIX CITY—LOS ANGELES—CHICAGO

EXPOSING AMERICA'S SIN CITIES

No. 1
25¢

MOBSTER RULE

PROSTITUTION

HONKY TONKS

MIAMI—CLEVELAND—NEW ORLEANS—CALUMET CITY—AND OTHERS

The 1950s marked the height (or depth) of tabloid publishing. Exposé magazines like this one from 1955 showed the underside of the popular representation of the decade as golden and worry free. ©1956 Whitestone Publications

It was followed by the hugely successful *Confidential,* which quickly spawned numerous imitators, such as *Top Secret, On the QT, The Lowdown,* and *Hollywood Confidential.*[2] According to a 1955 *Time* magazine article about *Confidential,* "Success in the Sewer," Humphrey Bogart "reports that 'everybody reads it, but they say the cook brought it into the house.'"[3]

Not just confined to Hollywood and celebrity gossip, these magazines also specialized in true crime exposés of gangsters, drugs, and prostitution. Such magazines as *Exposing America's Sin Cities* (1956) delightedly showed the warts on that seemingly placid public face of the 1950s, the cracks in the nostalgic representations of unblemished suburban tranquility. These magazines pandered to the marketplace; they were hypercommercial. This innate sensationalism exposed the extremes of society that were usually ignored by the dominant mass media, which deferred to the accepted mores of the time. And such stories of sleaze were mixed in with the personal foibles of the celebrity.

In addition to pictorials of sexy starlets like Jayne Mansfield and Marilyn Monroe, the stories in these magazines ran a gamut of Hollywood sex orgies, drug busts, celebrity affairs, and unsolved crimes. They were heavy on innuendoes, unanswered questions, and out-of-context photographs. And the "reporters," who could be anyone with the inside scoop, were not above a bit of entrapment—as in the case of Hollywood madam La Quillan, who baited Desi Arnez with two of her call girls in order to get a story.[4]

In 1957, with a circulation of roughly 3.5 million,[5] *Confidential* was indicted by three grand juries on charges of obscenity, and a U.S. Post Office review of the magazine endangered its second-class postage status. Harrison survived most of these charges but was fined multiple times. More troubling for him were the numerous libel suits filed by celebrities such as Robert

Mitchum and Errol Flynn, which eventually forced the publisher to sell his magazines. Little wonder the stars were litigious; the most sensational *National Enquirer* or *Star* of today seems like straightforward ethical journalism compared to any 1950s scandal magazine. Libel was the glue that held them together—that and semi-nude starlets. As Dian Hanson points out in her multivolume *The History of Men's Magazines,* Harrison "soon learned the downside of targeting celebrities: they could afford good lawyers."[6] By the mid-1960s, the Hollywood tabloid died out, giving way to the much less libelous grocery store tabloids aimed at the housewife. But before they died out, they revealed in garish light the downside of celebrity: the drinking, the divorces, the depression, and drugs that too often accompanied the spotlight. And that spotlight shone on Hemingway, like no other author before or since.

HEMINGWAY AND THE CELEBRITY CULTURE OF AUTHORSHIP

"Strictly speaking, modernists like [James] Joyce were not cut from the same celebrity cloth as movie stars like [Marilyn] Monroe," writes Aaron Jaffe.[7] But Hemingway *was* cut from the very same fabric as Monroe and other movie stars of the day. The pattern of his fame, especially in the 1950s, was a patchwork of the rugged canvas of his fictional world cross-stitched with the black satin of his glamorous lifestyle. And it was the interplay between these sides of Hemingway's persona that separated him from the usual writer that allowed him to share magazine space with Monroe as well as with Brigitte Bardot and Diana Dors, Errol Flynn and Marlon Brando.

Hemingway defies the usual dynamics of "literary" celebrity. In the nineteenth century, authorship was a mark of celebrity, thus making writers like Twain and Irving public figures. In the twentieth century, action, acting, image, and lifestyle became signifiers of celebrity.[8] According to Jaffe, modern authors' reputations are not "image-based but predicated instead on a distinctive textual mark of authorship" separate from the marketplace. Yet Hemingway's reputation *was* based on both authorship and image, and this is one of the most fascinating aspects of his reputation, what makes him a celebrity rather than mere public figure. With Hemingway, it seems more appropriate to look at him through the lens of Hollywood stardom, especially in regards to how he was often identified with the characters of his novels. As John Parris Springer puts it, "Any attempt to understand the phenomenon of stardom must begin by recognizing that the identity

This issue of *On the QT* from 1959 ran the article "Hemingway—King of Vulgar Words and Seduction," which states that "'Papa' got the Nobel Prize for 'creating a new style,' but he could have been saluted for his lovemaking scenes alone." ©1959 Barton Magazine Inc.

of the film star is constructed from a variety of texts, most notably their films but also movie posters and promotional material, feature articles and interviews in fan magazines, newspaper stories, publicity photos, and studio press releases."[9] This could just as easily apply to Hemingway.

There is something about Hemingway's fiction that invited comparison, even blurring, between the characters and the author himself. Hemingway's credo was to write what one knows and to make it ring true, hence it was a fashion in 1920s literary salons to guess the real people on whom the characters in *The Sun Also Rises* were based. But any polite backroom conjecture was left behind for the wholesale conflation in the tabloids. "The Twisted World of Ernest Hemingway" from the February 1957 issue of *Exposed* is a perfect example of this. In the article—with the subtitle "Slaughter and Sex Titillate 'Papa's' Pulse!"—Hemingway's writing and person are blurred so that the author of the article claims it is "interesting" to ascribe *The Sun Also Rises*'s Jake Barnes's impotency to Hemingway, that Hemingway shares the same interests of "making love incessantly" and "slaughtering animals" as the protagonist of *Across the River and Into the Trees,* a "self-described 'beat up old bastard' (based on Hemingway?) [who] has been described as an egocentric and narcissistic characterization drawn from adolescent dreams." This portrait epitomizes how in the popular press the characters and situations of Hemingway's fiction are impressed on the real man, much like how an actor and his roles were often conflated in the audience's mind.[10]

It is undeniable that Hemingway in the 1950s was a Hollywood property, as "Hemingway—King of Vulgar Words and Seduction" from *On the QT* makes evident:

HOLLYWOOD movie producers have discovered a golden lode of sexy story material in the red-blooded and full-passioned novels of Nobel Prize winner Ernest Hemingway. The fact that Hollywood has turned to Hemingway for sex source material should come as no surprise to those who have read "Papa's" books. There's plenty of blood and guts in Hemingway's stories of war, insurrection, and big-game hunting— but his leading characters are often hunting another kind of game, the kind that has long, slender legs, voluptuous breasts, beautiful eyes and golden hair that tumbles over a pillow when the hairpins are pulled out.

In 1958, film versions of *The Old Man and the Sea, The Sun Also Rises,* and *A Farewell to Arms* were in production. Leonard Leff contends that the Hemingway legend grew out of both Scribners' marketing and his "adoption" by

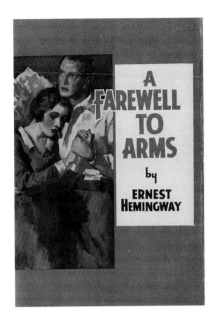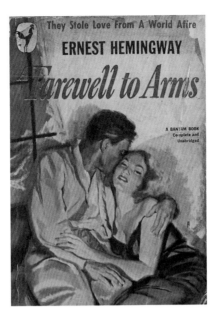

movie companies.[11] Frank Laurence, in *Hemingway and the Movies,* contends that it was Hemingway's films that exposed him to a wide, nonliterary audience, "For many people in among Hemingway's audience at the movies do not read much of anything, certainly not literature as sophisticated as his."[12] Elitist and untrue, this statement ignores both Hemingway's fiction's popular appeal and the numerous popular editions of his work, such as Grosset and Dunlap's numerous reprint editions of *A Farewell to Arms,* the Modern Library editions, the Book-of-the-Month Club edition of *For Whom the Bell Tolls,* and the many paperback editions (not to mention reprints in magazines). Hemingway's readers were exactly the movie-going audience.

The relationship between film and literature was reciprocal: if Hemingway's books were good material for film, Hemingway was good material for film magazines. For example, the story "The Fighter Who Clobbered Ernest Hemingway" appears in the March 1960 *Confidential* alongside an article about Errol Flynn by his last girlfriend, seventeen-year-old Beverly Aadland. A comparison of the lives of Hemingway and Flynn underscores how exceptional Hemingway's celebrity was. There are parallels: both men were symbols of masculinity from the 1930s through the 1950s, both captured a swashbuckling romanticism, both shared a love for Cuba and the sea, and both were excellent at self-invention.[13] But Flynn was an actor, with all the forces of the Hollywood myth machine behind his persona; Hemingway was an author, which is more usually a solitary, insular profession. As Hemingway himself said in his Nobel Prize acceptance speech, "Writing, at its best, is a lonely life."[14] And this difference itself explains part of the

Left: Grosset and Dunlap's photoplay edition of *A Farewell to Arms* went through at least seven printings in 1929. Distributed in drugstores and department stores, this would have outsold Scribners' edition many times over. ©1929 Grosset and Dunlap Publishers

Middle: *A Farewell to Arms* Bantam paperback cover. ©1949 Bantam Books

Right: After WWII, Hemingway was more available to a larger audience than ever before thanks largely to mass paperback editions, like this from Bantam Books. ©1951 Bantam Books

Hemingway allure: unlike acting, the profession of authorship does not lend itself to exoticism and excitement, hence Hemingway's larger-than-life persona was an exception, and so it invited fascination by heightening his individualism. Furthermore, Hemingway's work, both literary and exciting, both commercial and artistic, appealed to all audiences. Such contradictions parallel the contradictory nature of celebrity, which is the state of being both a public and private person. Yet we cannot overlook the part Hemingway played in his own celebrity.

HEMINGWAY PLAYS HEMINGWAY

Hemingway was complicit in his own celebrity making. One of the most tantalizing aspects of Hemingway is exactly that tension between man and celebrity. It is tantalizing because the separation is so often blurred. His writing is personal, full of biographical elements and settings, and his personal life was often fictionalized. But Hemingway's own role in this blurring of man and fiction is most evident in interviews where he seems a caricature of himself. For example, when he tells Jackson Burke in the "Ernest Hemingway—Muy Hombre!" 1953 *Bluebook* interview, "Fact is, I'm still pretty strong. A beat-up old mucker, yes, with my share of scars, but still strong. I drink good liquor, fight big fish, and write hard. That's the way to do it," it is as if he is Hemingway playing the part of "Hemingway."

There is certainly posturing involved even in relatively staid examples of his self-marketing, as evident in a letter he sent to Ray Brock for publication in Brock's profile of Hemingway in *Male Magazine* in 1954:

> Dear Ray:
>
> I don't know what to write to you that would be any good in a piece. But if you use anything from the letter, use it exactly.
>
> Thanks for the gen on the night spots. Here the night places have so many displaced gamblers that you find guys you haven't seen for twenty years, and pretty good gamblers, shilling for the house. There are about four bouncers for every customer. Somehow, I don't think they will be able to handle the nut. Or am I becoming too technical? But when some guy you haven't seen since West Yellowstone comes up and says, "Ernie, what's this they've been giving me that you've gone straight?" I have to reassure him that I have just sort of pulled out of things for awhile and that this writing in stiff covers is just my front.
>
> No, truly, Ray, all I care about is writing as well as I can about

what I know about. It isn't always the same things Henry James knew about. But sometimes it is and there is no harm in writing from the participant's view rather than from the spectator's. I respect Elizabeth Barrett Browning. But it would be rather silly for me to write like her. Besides I do not know Portuguese (and I doubt if she did) and my dogs are hunting dogs or of mixed races. Not one of them has ever been a lap dog.

I respect T. S. Eliot (with reservations) but I respect Ezra Pound more (with more reservations).

All good writers I respect and love, and all good painters. Also the sea (that great whore), mountains, early mornings, nights, days, shooting, fishing, the other sport that starts with F and ends with the big needle, women, men, children with good manners, horses that can jump or pull a load. Also respect and love many of my enemies (although a dead enemy always smells sweet), Venice, Italy, all of the Veneto and much of Frudli, Wyoming, Montana, Idaho, and parts of New Mexico, Arizona (small parts of big states).

I love fighting very much, when it starts, and have avoided, or tried to avoid, the easy and unnecessary ones.

Will not list my contempts. Nor speak about Canasta. Bed seems better.

Also love good airplanes, drinking with good people, record changers that change records, reading, cats, all good music of any epoch or style. Love painting better than music and the same goes—any epoch, any school as long as it is good, and carry with me, always, my built-in s***-detector that tells me if it is good or not.

Of things that are gone I loved the Spanish Republic, the Normandie, Fats Waller, most of my friends, my cat Princessa, a dog named Lugo, and many other animals, peoples and places I would rather not think about this morning.

Think this should hold you. Anyway, I have to get back to work.

Best always,

Ernest Hemingway[15]

Here Hemingway waffles between his writerly persona, mentioning James, Pound, and Eliot, and his persona as a fighter and lover, as in his claim that "a dead enemy always smells sweet" or that he likes "the other sport that starts with F and ends with the big needle." Hemingway feeds into his own celebrity, balancing such grandiose statements with small details

The March 1960 issue of *Confidential* featured the story "The Fighter Who Clobbered Ernest Hemingway," about how "a bully who likes to pick fights when the odds favor him—once got his!" This is representative of the splashy graphics in the tabloids and of their fondness for choosing very unflattering photos of the stars.

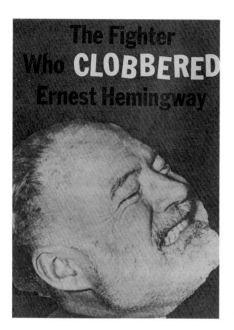

of his personal life. Unlike most of the articles in men's magazines, Brock's actually discusses Hemingway's writing; most of the others expand not the writer persona but the adventurer, womanizer, sportsman, or fighter, all of which Hemingway himself forwarded in interviews, writing, or action. Again, it is the contrast between these two aspects of Hemingway that reaffirms his status as a celebrity.

But another aspect of Hemingway's complicity in his own celebrity, less overt, was his masculine posturing, especially his continued, sometimes literal, sparring with the press. Hemingway's knee-jerk reactions to his critics are infamous—his well-publicized fight with Max Eastman, his numerous beratings of critics in his letters. There is evidence that he took gossip and how it affected his persona with equal seriousness. He complained of how people picked fights with him and how the columnists would make him out to be a loose cannon. He wrote columnist Harvey Breit of one such fight in a Havana barroom, stating that he wasn't like that, that he would be good.[16] It is important to realize that "the star who shuns stardom," according to deCordova, "is as much of a type today as the blond bombshell, and one that meets with much less resistance from the public, since such a star gives the illusion of being a real individual outside of the system."[17] Like when modern stars punch the snooping paparazzi in an effort to preserve some privacy, Hemingway's criticism of the critics had the opposite-than-hoped-for effect by giving the press that much more fodder.

Such anecdotes about Hemingway abound. Howard Rushmore's article from *Whisper,* "When Hemingway Backed Out of a Duel," is a good example and typical of the features on him.[18] It describes the author's fight with journalist Edward Scott and was lifted from the transcripts of Scott's own account on NBC's special radio broadcast "Meet Ernest Hemingway—The Man Who Lived It Up to Write It Down," published in the July 1955 *Picture Week* digest.[19] Scott even read personal letters from Hemingway on the air, confirming Hemingway's accusation of Scott as a publicity seeker.[20] Sensational accounts of Hemingway's fighting, like the more caustic exposés on Hemingway's alcoholism or sexuality, invariably became part of his popular persona. Hemingway's reputation was that of a bully.

The *Confidential* article "The Fighter Who Clobbered Ernest Hemingway" is exactly the type of gossip Hemingway was nominally trying to avoid. After recounting the numerous scuffles Hemingway was involved in, the story describes how he was knocked down while sparring with his friend George Brown.[21] "ERNEST HEMINGWAY is really two people," the article starts out.

THE OLD MAN & THE BOTTLE

A candid analysis of Nobel Prize-winner Ernest Hemingway's heroic exploits

MISTER HEMINGWAY
How come he gets so brave?

THE NOBEL PRIZE for Literature, awarded each year in Stockholm, Sweden, is worth thirty-six thousand bucks plus a flossy diploma. In 1954 it was given to the great author, Mister Ernest Hemingway, for his book called *The Old Man and the Sea.*

Mister Hemingway was unable to journey to Stockholm to pick up the cash and the glory; injuries suffered when his plane cracked up in Africa kept him at home.

These injuries—a ruptured kidney, a cracked skull, three badly damaged vertebrae—would have killed off any average author. But Mister Hemingway is no average author. Mister Hemingway is the bravest, toughest 240 pounds of author that ever lived.

How did he get that way?

By dint of exhaustive research in innumerable smoke-filled rooms,

RAVE is now able to reveal the secret behind Mister Hemingway's fabulous feats of derring-do.

As a beardless but big-chested youth of 18, Mr. Hemingway joined up with the Red Cross ambulance service during World War I and shortly found himself involved in some very sticky doings on the disgraceful Italian front. Here, amidst vast carnage and blood-letting, Mister Hemingway charged around rescuing people until a mortar shell exploded pretty well smack underneath his gallant behind—filling his legs with 237 individual bits of steel.

Following the successful wrapping-up of the Italian front and establishment of permanent Peace and Democracy, Mister Hemingway became interested in bulls, bullfighting, and bullfighters. Bullfighters are noted for their general

guttiness and dame-chasingness. Mister Hemingway demonstrated that in at least a couple of departments, he could do anything any bullfighter could do and do it better.

Mister Hemingway next turned his attention to the so-called sport of killing wild animals and took

the first of his many trips to Africa. Here he slaughtered, the good God knows, how many tons of assorted huge, peevish beasts, standing smack in the path of ferocious, charging lions, rhinos, hippos, etc. and blasting them into bloody smithereens without so much as a quiver of one of the brave Heming-

50

51

[He is] brilliant as a writer and he is a bully as a man. His books, such as *The Sun Also Rises* and *For Whom The Bell Tolls,* are sensitive and compelling masterpieces of American literature. . . . However, as a human being, Hemingway is far from the "ideal" man. Perhaps his worst trait is that of a rough, tough, chip-on-the-shoulder bully. A big man physically, he takes delight in throwing his heavy but well-conditioned body around. His favorite pastime is to goad some unsuspecting patsy into throwing the first punch; then with all the meanness he can muster, Hemingway swings into action—throwing punches.[22]

Though Hemingway claimed that he tried to avoid such publicity, at other times he seemed to seek it. The fact that he wrote Breit, the gossip columnist for the *New York Times,* about a bar fight he was in while claiming

Tabloid articles like this one from *Rave* (May 1955) grew out of Hemingway's own posturing in interviews; they were the collateral damage of his own self-invention.

Milt Machlin's derogatory article in *Argosy* in 1960, "Hemingway and the World's Phoniest Sport," made innuendos about Hemingway's alcoholism, as illustrated by the very unflattering photograph. ©1960 Popular Publications, reprinted by permission of Argosy Communications, Inc.

he really wasn't like that anymore seems somewhat contradictory. Similarly, Hemingway often joked with reporters about his love and capacity for drinking, as when he stated how after one of his plane crashes he emerged from the African jungle with a bunch of bananas and a bottle of gin. It should not be surprising, then, that articles like *Rave*'s 1955 "The Old Man & the Bottle" discuss Hemingway's alcoholism: "Moral of the story: if you just gotta be brave, get cockeyed first. Bring on them goddamn lions."[23] This is the downside of Hemingway's celebrity. As Michael Reynolds says, "His life, no longer his own, had become a public sideshow open to everyone. Always the hunter, he was now the hunted."[24]

THE MYTH AND ANTI-MYTH OF HEMINGWAY'S CELEBRITY

These articles illustrate the high price of fame, what Springer refers to as the "anti-myth" of stardom, the desperate unhappiness underneath and brought on by the condition of celebrity that results in the "inevitable and tragic loss of self" for the star.[25] And despite the fact that Hemingway was complicit in his own image making, there is also plenty of evidence that he revolted under that yoke of his own making. He violently guarded his private life; he generally distrusted journalists and photographers. In 1951 he wrote in a letter about a would-be biographer, "But there has been too damn much written about my personal life and I am sick of it."[26] Citing articles and interviews by Cowley in *Life,* Lillian Ross in *The New Yorker,* and Sam Boal in *Argosy,* Hemingway states he read them with "horror" because they "gave inordinate publicity to my personal life" and affected how people read his stories. At times in the men's magazines interviews, especially those by Milt Machlin in *Argosy* and *Bachelor,* Hemingway either wishes the interview "off the record" or only begrudgingly gives it.

Machlin's case is interesting because he wrote four articles on Hemingway, two of which are interviews, between 1957 and 1960, each one increasingly antagonistic. His attempt at a third interview, for *Argosy,* almost ends in a fist fight, which Machlin quickly describes in his posthumous biography of Hemingway: "There was a scene of violence between us that weekend, outside the Hotel De L'Europe, which is better left unrecorded." Ironically, he had already recorded it in detail in *Argosy*'s February 1960 story "Hemingway and the World's Phoniest Sport," where he describes Hemingway as drunk, cantankerous, moody, and violent. Machlin followed that *Argosy* story a year later with "Dear Beards: An open letter to Hemingway and Castro concerning some very fishy trophies," contending that Castro's winning of the Hemingway Marlin Fishing Prize was rigged and that Hemingway was willing to betray his political and personal ethos for fishing privileges.

In *Remembering Ernest Hemingway,* by James Plath and Frank Simmons, Valerie Hemingway states that

> [Hemingway] was very wary of journalists, except for his personal friends, because he talked of the time a couple of years before, maybe '57, when Milt Machlin had come down, a writer of note at that time for *True,* or one of these popular pulp magazines. And he came down, he met Ernest at the Floridita. Nobody came to the house unless they were formally invited, because unless someone opened the gate they couldn't get in. But they met, and they apparently hit it off, and Machlin was invited to the Finca. He came, must have done an interview, because he had a little notebook, stayed to dinner, and they did have some drinks after dinner. In fact, Machlin was pretty stewed, so they poured him into his car or the chauffeur took him off. But the next day his little notebook was found in the sofa, and in the notebook he had just written these absolutely dreadful things—obviously as part of his article, instead of the answers—and Ernest was absolutely furious. Machlin would have been one of the people where, if he had run into Hemingway again—I think he actually had the effrontery to call the next day and ask, "Have you seen my notebook?"—he would have been a candidate for fisticuffs. That, I know.[27]

And Machlin found that out in Spain in 1959. It is interesting to see how Machlin's articles run the gamut from near-hero worship in the early interviews to deeply negative criticism when Hemingway, the man, didn't live up to what was both Machlin's and the larger public's celebrity image of him.

Obviously, Hemingway's fame was affecting his personal, private life, but it was seemingly more troubling for him that his life had suddenly encroached on his fiction and affected how people read his stories. This could well be a reaction on his part to the largely negative critical reaction to *Across the River and Into the Trees* (1950), which seemed to show how the man was fallible, opening him up for greater criticism throughout the 1950s. The men's magazine *Night and Day,* for example, ran an article, accompanied by an unflattering full-page photo of Hemingway pouring himself a drink, entitled "Is Papa a Flopa?" about the failure of the book with critics.

An open letter to Hemingway and Castro concerning some very fishy trophies
They laughed when Papa hugged Fidel and hooked him the prize

DEAR BEARDS:

"Papa salutes winner Fidel with embrace in fuzz-to-fuzz encounter," reads *Argosy*'s caption to these photographs from a Cuban marlin fishing contest in Hemingway's honor. This "Open Letter" by Milt Machlin contended that Hemingway "sold" the prize for fishing rights. This was the only time Castro and Hemingway met. Photographs by Lillian Tonnaire Taylor, reprinted by permission of Argosy Communications, Inc.

IS PAPA A FLOPA?

HEMINGWAY'S NEW NOVEL— A CRITICAL CATASTROPHE

THE hottest literary war in years has been raging as the result of Ernest Hemingway's new book, "Across the River and Into the Trees." Originator of the tough, hard-biting novel, Hemingway was eagerly imitated by aspiring geniuses who formed a whole new school of writing under the inspiration of their master. Some critics have had a few misgivings all along but never did they all jump to the fore to pounce with lightning swiftness as when the tale of the Colonel and his dreamy Italian countess lady with emeralds in her pocket, first saw light in "Across the River." Immature, undeveloped, shows no mature philosophy, *pulp!*" they screamed. But the fact is, the American public loved it. Book stores were shortly sold out of copies, and it climbed immediately to the top of the best-seller list. The tragic romance of the middle-aged army officer and his young and beauteous love was sopped up by thousands of readers who thought it was all just ducky. But the literary lights were gloomily shaking their heads and mournfully predicting, "That's the end for that bird." Papa, as Hemingway has been better known by each of his four wives, didn't much care. He hunted and fished as usual, gave high-powered interviews to the press with bits of advice such as "keep punching," and "go in fighting" and lounged in the sun in his palatial home in Havana, Cuba. The man who inspired a father complex certainly did well financially. He is now daddy to everything (in latest book, hero is called Father by heroine and in private life everybody but everybody calls him Papa), except a Grade A literary idea. As far as the major critics are concerned, Dear Dad fell on his face with the last epic. Says vitriolic columnist Malcom Bingay in the Detroit Free Press, "He (Hemingway) is still boiling the same piece of cabbage he has been boiling for 30 years, and now, to use his own language, it stinks."

18

With the critically disappointing *Across the River and Into the Trees* came a series of negative features on Hemingway, such as this 1951 article in *Night and Day.* ©1951 Halho Corporation

The many profiles of Hemingway during the 1950s make much of how the book was lambasted but how he came back with *The Old Man and the Sea*—almost always in boxing terminology. In *Rogue's* "Hemingway: A Rogue of Distinction," one piece commented, "Hemingway was accused of 'self-parody' and 'excessive, childish sentimentality' among other charges. The champ was on the mat, but he came back to regain his title in 1952, when he wrote 'The Old Man and the Sea,' winning the Nobel Prize, and the hearts of five million readers."[28] Similarly, Ray Brock wrote in *Male Magazine* in 1954 that "the book was a set-up for [the critics'] bolo punch, and maybe it hurt Hemingway himself, like a sneaky punch by a scientific boxer in a sparring match. Ernie wasn't looking."[29]

It is likely that Hemingway tried, however quixotically, to take control of his out-of-hand persona during the years of 1956 to 1958 by writing *A Moveable Feast,* his memoir about his early Paris years.[30] The writing of this novel can be seen as Hemingway countering the sensationalism of celebrity illustrated in these magazines, this popular public persona in extremis, with a return to his bohemian beginnings. As Rose Marie Burwell points out, Hemingway himself once declared that "it is only when you can no longer believe in your own exploits that you write your memoirs."[31] Hemingway in the 1920s—associate editor of the *Transatlantic Review,* patron of Shakespeare and Company—is continents away from the image of Hemingway forwarded in "The Fighter Who Clobbered Ernest Hemingway" or the Hemingway described as the insecure and egotistical loudmouth in *Uncensored's* "The Secret Life of Ernest Hemingway."[32]

Critics such as John Raeburn, Leonard Leff, and Scott Donaldson have hypothesized that Hemingway's fame and public persona got in the way of his writing, that Hemingway came to believe his own persona. At the very least, as Donaldson has stated, his fame had adverse effects on how his writing was received. It is possible that as Hemingway's fictionalized self became entwined with his fiction, the author "compromised his art." The character of Colonel Cantwell in *Across the River and Into the Trees* equals not Hemingway but "Hemingway's impossible public persona—tough as nails, sensitive as hell, and wise as Jove."[33] After Hemingway's death, many of the eulogies that appeared in the men's magazines ironically make this same point. For example, *Cavalcade*'s 1962 article "Hemingway: A Man called Poppa" starts, "The legend that chose to walk like a man cashed in his blue chips with the sudden flare that had become synonymous with his every single living moment. A gun went off, the lights went out, and the ball game was over. . . . A legend is more a killer than the two torpedoes he sent out in his classic short story, 'The Killers.'"

So just as the gossip magazines confront and counter the nostalgic image of the 1950s as a simple or trouble-free decade, many of their articles on Hemingway hold kernels of truth, even in spite of the purple prose and irony, the unsubstantiated rumors and gossip-mongering. Even in their extremity they capture troubling qualities of the man and legend. Articles like Leonard Bishop's "The Fighter Who Clobbered Ernest Hemingway" and Milt Machlin's "Hemingway and the World's Phoniest Sport" describe the unreasonable, argumentative author late in life, at a time when perhaps the paranoia of his last year was beginning to show itself.[34] Such articles question the line between the Papa the Legend and Hemingway the Man, illustrating the dangers of celebrity and how, in the 1950s, Hemingway's entrepreneurial self-promotion had spiraled away from him.

These derogatory articles capture an innate contradiction in Hemingway's personality, especially pronounced in the last decade of his life. Friends and strangers alike described him as gentle and generous but as having the capacity for bullying and cruelty. His 1959 tour of Spain is an example of such extreme behavior, even according to Mary Hemingway and his good friend George Saviers. Books such as Denis Brian's *The True Gen* spend quite a bit of space trying to account for these extremes in his personality. Explanations range from manic depression to alcoholism. It is ultimately unknowable, perhaps a moot point. But what is interesting is how these personality traits trickle down to or get blown up in the sensational popular press. The 1955 *Time* article describes the tabloids' method: "By sprinkling grains of fact into a cheesecake of innuendo, detraction and plain smut, *Confidential* creates the illusion of reporting the 'lowdown' on celebrities. Its standard method: dig up one sensational fact and embroider it for 1,500 to 2,000 words."[35] Though designed to pander to the sensationalism via stories of the anti-myth of celebrity, and despite their extremities of conjecture, these magazines captured a kernel of truth. They were onto something troubling about Hemingway and the wages of fame.

Early studies of Hemingway were concerned with elevating his reputation, distinguishing the artist from the legend. Consider the titles of two of the earliest extended critical works on Hemingway: *The Writer as Artist* and *The Art of Ernest Hemingway.*[36] In a way, then, much of this popular and sensational material does what the 1950s literary criticism and biography, with its constant affirmation of literary worth, was unwilling to do. And now, with critical hindsight, these articles and magazines offer us, through their very extremity, the opportunity to contextualize a legend and type of literary celebrity so dependent on its time and origin that we shall never see its like again.

"The Twisted World of Ernest Hemingway,"
by Mark Mallory,
Exposed (February 1957)

This particularly malicious tabloid article captures the flavor and tone of this type of journalism. It also epitomizes painfully how in the popular press the characters and situations of Hemingway's fiction are foisted on the real man, attesting to how Hemingway's persona captured the public imagination.

The author Mark Mallory is most likely the pseudonym of Mack Reynolds, who was better known as a mystery and science fiction writer. Reynolds was active during the 1950s and 1960s writing fiction for pulp magazines like *Private Detective* but also such nonfiction articles as "The First Time I Saw Paris," "Europe's Mighty Midgets," and "What Comes After Arthur Miller?" for *Rogue* and *Mr.* He also used the penname Clark Collins for the racier magazines and for porn novels, among them *Counterfeit Cad.*[1]

Slaughter and Sex Titilate "Papa's" Pulse!

The most hotly debated question in literary circles today is "What makes peregrinating, peripatetic Papa run?" In this case it's that whirling dervish of the typewriter, Ernest Hemingway, who would dearly like it believed that he dips his typewriter ribbons into blood before starting a new story.

The Hemingway legend has been lovingly, if inaccurately, built up by a legion of admirers and sycophants—with no little assist from Papa himself. So carefully has it been manufactured, that when you think of Hemingway, a number of images spring to your mind—the devil-may-care Hemingway, with his bare, hairy chest and toothy grin; Hemingway, the killer, standing over a freshly slaughtered beast, a high-powered rifle clenched nonchalantly in his ham-like paw; Hemingway, the intrepid White Hunter, leading his native bearers through an almost impassable jungle, snapping out commands in their native Swahili; Hemingway, the reckless, bravely ignoring almost fatal wounds to pose grinning at his wrecked plane; Hemingway, the war correspondent, calmly knocking out a play in the Hotel Madrid while bombardment is making swiss cheese out of the roof; Hemingway, the one man task force, draped in ammunition belts single-handedly holding an advance post against counter attacks by the "enemy."

These are the carefully fabricated conceptions of Hemingway that have been sold to the public—the great Papa in his many and favorite roles—but how about Hemingway the man? The "Hemingway-Ain't-God" school projects another picture of him—Hemingway, who attacked anyone who'd stand still long enough, to prove to himself he was all man; Hemingway, the failing lover, who told Lillian Ross of the *New Yorker* that he hopes to keep making love until he's eighty, but who, they say, depends on a typewriter to compensate for the damage done by a mortar shell that sent two hundred and thirty seven pieces of shrapnel into his groin and adjoining areas; Hemingway, whose fear of death is lessened by his preoccupation with rendings, gorings and slaughter of animals because he seems to believe that killing is a god-like attribute and makes him triumphant over death; Hemingway, the Peter Pan, who uses action as an opiate and who is addicted to an adolescent overemphasis on violence; Hemingway, who dwells on horror to prove that he can take it and to hide the fact that he is sensitive and hurt.

This latter school, in defiance of the carefully built up legend of Hemingway, insists that it is always Hemingway, talking through his characters—making love incessantly, slaughtering animals and shooting ducks, as in "Over the River and Into the Trees" [*sic*]. The protagonist of this latter book, incidentally, a self-described "beat up old bastard" (based on Hemingway?) has been described as an egocentric and narcissistic characterization drawn from adolescent dreams.[2]

And when Nick Adams in "In Our Time" makes the revealing statement that "everything goes back to childhood" we can see Papa fumbling for some explanation for what has happened to him. It's hard to conceive in the face of the Hemingway legend, but Papa was once a scared and confused kid whose mother was ultra religious and had a fixation for respectability and gentility. His father, whom Hemingway strove to emulate, was a suicide. This latter tragedy, incidentally, made such an impression on him that he based one of the most effective sequences in "For Whom the Bells Toll" [*sic*] on it—the suicide of Robert Jordan's father.

Young Hemingway rebelled against the strictness of his mother's credo and ran away to Chicago. Here, for the first time, he heard the argot of the underworld, the

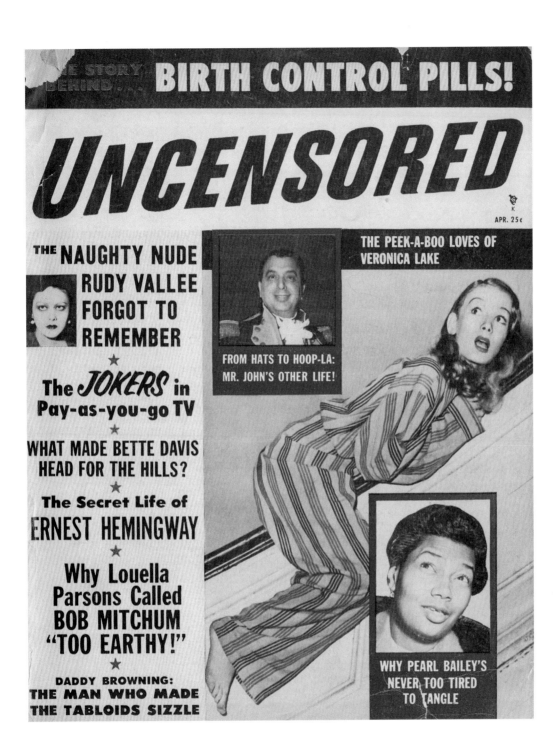

THE STORY BEHIND... **BIRTH CONTROL PILLS!**

UNCENSORED

APR. 25¢

THE **NAUGHTY NUDE** RUDY VALLEE FORGOT TO REMEMBER

★

The JOKERS in Pay-as-you-go TV

★

WHAT MADE BETTE DAVIS HEAD FOR THE HILLS?

★

The Secret Life of ERNEST HEMINGWAY

★

Why Louella Parsons Called BOB MITCHUM "TOO EARTHY!"

★

DADDY BROWNING: THE MAN WHO MADE THE TABLOIDS SIZZLE

FROM HATS TO HOOP-LA: MR. JOHN'S OTHER LIFE!

THE PEEK-A-BOO LOVES OF VERONICA LAKE

WHY PEARL BAILEY'S NEVER TOO TIRED TO TANGLE

This page and overleaf: Another negative article from the gossip tabloids (*Uncensored,* April 1956) contended that Hemingway had become a "slave" to his own legend: "Everybody loves Papa. Momma loves Papa, readers love Papa. But, sshh—Papa loves Papa, too!" ©Plaza-Digest Inc.

THE SECRET LIFE OF
ERNEST HEMINGWAY

Green hills of Africa were far-away hills when he posed for photo with bull taken by Waldo Pierce.

Hemingway and second wife, Pauline Pfeiffer, posed for this in 1934 at start of famous African jaunt.

Third wife was Martha Gellhorn, top. Today, Papa lives in Cuba with fourth, Mary Welsh, nine servants, 16 dogs, 52 cats, cows and a pigeon flock.

Humorist Max Eastman: what Papa did wasn't funny.

Mr. Papa: Though on the ropes many times he's never been counted out—and is confident he never will be!

Everybody loves Papa. Momma loves Papa, readers love Papa. But, sshh — Papa loves Papa, too!

By BEN WEST

"PAPA WOULD be wise to spend more of his time proving to the world that he is a great writer and less of his time in trying to prove that he is the brawling, boozing, battle-scarred monument to masculinity that has become the Ernest Hemingway legend.

This rather caustic criticism of America's greatest living writer and the 1954 Nobel Prize winner for literature came a few weeks ago from one of the author's oldest and closest friends, who recently returned from a visit to Hemingway's Havana hacienda, where he found Papa alternately flexing his biceps and polishing his prose.

"Papa has become so obsessed with the importance of being Ernest—that the Ernest of the amusing anecdotes in Broadway columns—that he is in grave danger of becoming a slave to the legend," the friend said with remarkable candor and an unmistakable affection for his longtime friend. "He shows signs of believing his own publicity. He's too big a boy for that."

Hemingway, now 56, lives at Finca Vigia, a 13-acre estate nine miles from Havana, surrounded by his wife; nine servants; 16 dogs; 52 cats; a flock of pigeons; a parrot; seven cows and whatever house guests might be on hand at the moment.

"I told Papa I can understand a wife, even nine servants, and I can see the value of seven cows and the enjoyment of having house guests. But who the hell needs 52 cats? Why not one cat? Or 16 dogs? And all those pigeons? He just smiled, shrugged and replied that he needs them.'

The bearded novelist, who has always claimed to be the heavyweight drinking champion of the Western Hemisphere, has been obliged to limit his intake of intoxicating beverages since his plane accidents while on safari in Africa two years ago, but he continues to go off on an occasional binge which usually lands him in what he describes as "big trouble."

"When partaking freely of his favorite drink, champagne, or his second or third choices, tequila and bourbon, Papa develops an uncontrollable urge to prove that he is as rough as Rocky Marciano, as loud as Jackie Gleason and as irresistible to the opposite sex as Porfirio Rubirosa. Invariably it turns out he is merely as loud as Gleason," his friend confided.

Hemingway's record as a brawler has been, over the years, unimpressive. Of an estimated two dozen fistic encounters in Havana, New York, Paris, Venice and Africa, there were only two occasions on which he clearly emerged the victor. In one instance he scored a one-punch decision over a drunken broker in the Stork Club's Cub Room (although witnesses reported he had an assist from fellow writer Quentin Reynolds) and a number of years ago he won a hollow victory over a Havana man 10 years his senior and 40 pounds his junior.

Hemingway's most famous fight occurred when he was 38 years of age and had recently completed his novel on bullfighting, Death in the Afternoon.' A critic, Max Eastman, had written a scathing review of the work, in which he said of Hemingway:

". . . some circumstances seem to have laid upon Hemingway a continual sense of the obligation to put forth evidence of red-blooded masculinity . . . a literary style, you might say, of wearing false hair on his chest.'

Chancing upon Eastman in (Continued on page 64)

slang of the pimps and prostitutes, and he learned that "there is honor among pickpockets and honor among whores. It is simply that standards differ."[3]

As a result, Hemingway's world of fiction is peopled with prize fighters, murderers, drunkards, perverts and prostitutes. He has never successfully been able to project an average, normal woman in his works—they have all, like Maria in "For Whom the Bells Toll" [sic] merely served to while away the tedium of their possessors as they go from violence to violence. For all the brutality and recklessness of his heroes during the day and in action, at night they're as wistful and tender with their mistresses as little boys. In fact, the women are so available and so passive that some of his critics accuse him of, infantilism and of indulging "in a boy's erotic fantasies."[4]

In real life, his attitude toward women has shown his confusion. Although he has gone on searching, he has never quite found a flesh and blood woman to be as selfless and as passive as the creatures he manufactures in his mind. When he married his first wife, he sought out a career woman, an accomplished pianist, who retained enough of the gentility and refinement to make her a mother image, a replacement for the mother he had not seen in years. But Hadley Richardson was not a creature of his imagination, but a real woman with a mind of her own. Despite his immature ranting that he could not be tied down by children, she broke the news to him one day that he was soon to become a father. It was the beginning of the end of their marriage, because, as he told her, it was his destiny to live dangerously and to translate that life into fiction. You might just as well be dead, he said, if you could not live dangerously and always on the brink.[5]

His second wife, Pauline Pfeiffer, was a fashion writer on the Paris staff of *Vogue*. In her he thought he saw a woman closer to his ideal—she was modern, emancipated and yet a womanly woman. But she, too, wanted

a home and family and when she bore him two sons, he felt the world closing in again and took flight.

This time his excuse was the outbreak of the Spanish Civil War where he was to lay the foundation for the Hemingway legend. Here, too, he would meet another woman, who was destined to become Mrs. Ernest Hemingway the third. This was Martha Gellhorn, herself a war correspondent who was not afraid of the boom of the big guns, who didn't blanch at the sight of blood and multilation, who could stand the stench of death and still enjoy a drink at a bombed out hotel afterwards. To Hemingway, who associates war with good food, liquor and women, this was more like it—blood, the stench of death, brutality and endless executions, excitement and a woman who shared his love for it all. In 1940, Pauline Pfeiffer Hemingway threw in the sponge, sued for divorce for desertion and a few months later, Papa Hemingway and Martha Gellhorn were married.

But somehow, flesh and blood women were never as acquiescent and as malleable as the lovely creatures that are manufactured on typewriter keys from "boyish erotic fantasies." After a stormy five years of marriage, after the Spanish War was a memory and there was a new war for Papa to cover, Martha Gellhorn reversed the usual procedure and forced Papa to divorce her on grounds of abandonment—a grounds on which he apparently thought he held the patent.

It was during his marriage to Martha Gellhorn that critics started wondering how much was myth and how much was fact about the lustiness and the indestructibility of the peripatetic Papa. It was also during this period that he did some of his greatest work, work in which some critics find more than a little autobiography.

In "Farewell to Arms," we have the situation of two lovers—Frederic Henry and Catherine Barkley.[6] Henry is badly wounded and at the end of the book

Catherine dies. In another book, "The Sun Also Rises," we have a comparable pair of lovers—Jake Barnes and the Lady Brett Ashley. Jake, however, is sexually impotent, whereas Lady Brett is a nympho with probably the roundest pair of heels in the history of literature, and in compensation for Jake's inability to satisfy her, she flounces from one bed to another.

What's the connection?

Some critics seem to think that Papa saw some. They point out that if Frederic Henry's wound had resulted in sexual impotency, he could easily have evolved into the Jake Barnes of the later book. And if Catherine Henry's death had not been a physical death, but spiritual as the result of her lover's incapacity, she could easily have degenerated into Lady Brett of "The Sun Also Rises." Anyway, they point out, in view of Papa's bout with the mortar shell and the resting place of the 237 pieces of shrapnel in his groin and legs, it's interesting to speculate.

Anyway, when Papa shed Mate Number Three, he already had her successor selected. Number Four was to be Mary Welsh, also a war correspondent, whom he had met in London during the Blitz. She is a sweet and smart looking blonde, whom he delights in calling Miss Mary, and who shares his enthusiasm for lusty living. She comes closest to striking the perfect balance between the man's woman and womanly woman he has spent most of his life trying to find. She lived through one of the most violent wars in history, she has walked away from plane wrecks with composure, she has fished with him, drinks with him, lives the kind of life he has selected for himself without complaint.

In 1944, when the Hemingways crashlanded on an elephant track in Africa, he was full of unbounded admiration for her ability to sleep while elephants were less than twelve paces away. The next day they were involved in a plane crash in which the indestructible Papa suffered a fractured skull, a broken back, a smashed kidney and bladder. Miss Mary nursed him through all these, only to have him contract hepatitis shortly afterward, an attack that lasted 40 days. At that time, in 1944, Papa was told by medicos that he could last six months "if he put his mind to it" and a maximum of two years "if he made a career out of it." He laughed at them, refused to turn his back on the bottle from which he has always drawn so much solace, and now—as he recently told columnist Earl Wilson, he's "living on their time."[7]

This past year, Papa has been working on the film script and photography of one of his best efforts, "The Old Man and the Sea." He even interrupted work on his "long book" (already more than 850 manuscript pages) to accompany the shooting crew to Peru for the big fish sequences. Yet, only a few years ago, in answer to a questionnaire sent out by *Time,* Papa lambasted writers who sold out to the movie makers and predicted that he would never be seduced by Hollywood gold.[8]

His contempt for Hollywood writers seems to extend to all denizens of Hollywood with the possible exception of Marlene Dietrich. During World War II, Papa had occasion to meet Marlene while she was entertaining the troops in the Hurtgen Forest, one of the bloodiest battle areas of the war. Here, he marveled at the way she handled herself, at her courage and her determination to bring some joy into the hearts of a bunch of men surrounded on all sides by evidence of war's brutality. With mutilated corpses ringing the area, Marlene sang and joked with the GIs as though she were safely at home on a cabaret stage.

Papa's admiration was boundless. On the spot, he dashed off a poem about war, its horrors and its futility. He sent it up to her and asked her to read it. When she had finished reading it, Marlene broke into tears, demanded to meet the man who had written it.

Here was Hemingway's kind of woman—reacting like a man to the horror of war, overlooking the stench of death to do the job she set out to do—yet woman enough to be moved to tears by a poem. This was Papa's kind of woman.

And the admiration wasn't one sided. Marlene has never made any secret of her devotion to the hairy-chested Papa. When his plane crashed in Africa and his standing obits were being pulled out of the files in every major newspaper in America, Marlene was beside herself with grief. Then, with a dramatic flourish that would have done justice to one of his better characters, Papa beat his way back to civilization, more dead than alive, and proceeded to read his obituaries with delight.

Marlene, almost hysterical with joy, immediately wired to him: "You didn't have to do this to make me realize how much I love you." Needless to say, at this point, Miss Mary did not exactly jump with joy,

although Papa has re-assured her by insisting that he only loves Marlene, the long-stemmed grandma, for her "manly courage under fire" which is a helluva thing to say about any woman.

But then, the comment is typical of the underlying theme of Papa's whole philosophy—a man is judged not by his virtues or his contribution but by how he handles himself in the face of danger and by how well he's able to die. The most important thing in his code is to avoid making a "Bad Show."

Maybe that's the reason why Papa seeks out wars and revolutions, why he is so preoccupied with maiming and slaughter, why he is forever getting himself almost killed—maybe it gives him an opportunity to reassure himself by numerous rehearsals that when he finally does face it, he will give a Good Show.

CHAPTER SIX

Coda—Afterlife

Hemingway's suicide in July of 1961 unleashed the dogs of biography. Memorials, profiles, headlines, and eulogies flooded the world's newspapers and magazines. As James T. Farrell eulogized in *Nugget* magazine (1961), "The death of Ernest Hemingway was blazoned with so much newspaper publicity that it had something of the character of unreality about it." As John Raeburn and other critics state, or as anyone alive in 1961 might recall, the years following Hemingway's death kept him in the spotlight, casting the long shadow of his legend onto the public imagination. By fall, three paperback biographies appeared that, like most of the earlier profiles in popular magazines, were stitched together from articles, hearsay, biographical sketches, and Hemingway's own fiction. These hasty publications relied upon the idea of Hemingway the adventurer, not the writer or the man. As John Raeburn puts it, they were "biographies only in name; they were truly pulp adventure stories, and were published by houses specializing in such literature."[1] With titles like *Hemingway: Life and Death of a Giant, Ernest Hemingway: Life and Death of a Man,* and *The Private Hell of Hemingway,* the type of sensationalism that motivates them is apparent. With cover blurbs like "The incredible story of Hemingway the man, a hard-drinking, thrill-seeking adventurer; bold, virile and violent in life, death, love—a creative genius," these books blended Hemingway's fiction and biography, mythologizing the legend and, in the process, losing the man.

Milt Machlin's biography, *The Private Hell of Ernest Hemingway,* came directly out of the articles he wrote for *Argosy* magazine, and like those earlier stories it advertises Machlin's "inside track" and personal knowledge of the author. It is somehow fitting that a journalist who epitomized everything that Hemingway loathed about his overexposure, who published two scalding exposés of Hemingway, would capture the public emotions after Hemingway's death. Fitting but ironic, since the trajectory of Machlin's four stories, and on which his biography is built, reflects the shifting range of articles in the men's magazines—from the hero worship evident in the early interviews (*Bachelor,* May 1957; *Argosy,* September 1958) to the scalding indictment of Hemingway's behavior and betrayal of his own code of truth (*Argosy,* February 1960, January 1961)—and, finally, his own sensational search for the real man's "secret torment." Furthermore, the shift from idealization to the tone of disillusionment, indignation, and sadness in Machlin's "Phoniest Sport" article evinces the encroaching disillusionment of 1950s hypermasculinity that would mark the mid-1960s reassessment of gender roles, a precursor of how Hemingway's literary reputation would fall into disfavor in conjunction with the feminist movement.

But this is perhaps reading too much into a biography that was obviously written to cash in on Hemingway's death. There are numerous other instances of this "cashing in," the most blatant example of which is a collection of spy stories published in 1961 entitled *The Secret Agent's Badge of*

Within a year of Hemingway's death, three paperback biographies were published—most of them conjecture, all of them sensational. All three covers depict Hemingway similarly, and the two "Life and Death" books taking their inspiration from the same photograph that adorns *The Private Hell of Hemingway*. This was the death mask of Hemingway's masculine persona.

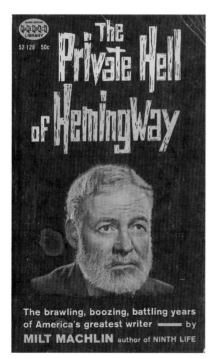

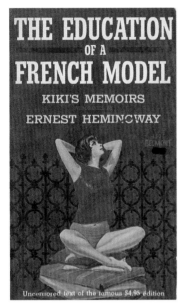

The reprint edition of Kiki's *The Education of a French Model* in 1962 was one of many paperbacks that appeared soon after Hemingway's death, capitalizing on his tragedy. Here, Hemingway receives nearly equal billing as the author.

Courage. Judging by the book's spine and cover, Hemingway is the book's author or editor, or at least integral to the book's composition, rather than just the author of the one-page excerpt (the last page of the book) taken from *Men at War.* Likewise, a paperback edition of *Kiki's Memoirs,* titled *The Education of a French Model,* was published in January 1962 and prominently advertised Hemingway's introduction.

Not surprisingly, after Hemingway's death, there was a flurry of articles in the men's magazines. Some of these, like those paperbacks, were also cashing in on the sensation and resurgence of popularity after his suicide, like *Topper,* which reprinted two "lost" Hemingway stories from the *Toronto Star.* Similarly, many people who had known Hemingway in life, no matter how well—an acquaintance from D day, one of Hemingway's African guides—felt the need to publish reminiscences. Much of this was done under the auspices of "setting the record straight," or finding the "real Hemingway" beneath the legend. *Nugget* ran a eulogy by James T. Farrell; *Climax* interviewed son Patrick Hemingway.

The story "Hemingway's Shillelagh," from *Sir!* magazine, is especially interesting for its defense of the Hemingway persona by proving true an anecdote that A. E. Hotchner's much-maligned 1966 biography, *Papa Hemingway,* denies. The article publishes accounts by both John O'Hara and the bartenders of Costello's bar who witnessed Hemingway break O'Hara's walking stick over his own head. The article even runs a photo of the manager of the bar holding the pieces of the famed shillelagh. *Sir!* in turn takes Hotchner's biography to task, saying that "if the evidence of the blackthorn walking stick Shillelagh is any criterion, then at least some of the material is questionable."[2]

Similarly, many of the articles, such as that in *Sir Knight,* which reprinted quotes by Hemingway on life and death, have an incredulous tone regarding the suicide: "Hemingway had planned to go on a hunting trip on the day of his death. He also had made arrangements to go to his bank vault and take out several unfinished manuscripts and resume work on them. There were rumors of suicide, but would a man with the philosophy of living which we present here—and written shortly before his death—be likely to destroy himself?"[3] Such disbelief is perhaps understandable, since for years men's magazines held Hemingway up as an icon of the kind of masculinity advanced in these magazines, and suicide wasn't part of that mystique. Hemingway's code, according to the February 1957 "Twisted World of Ernest Hemingway" from *Exposed,* was dependent on how well a man is "able to die. The most important thing in his [Hemingway's] code is to avoid making a 'Bad Show.'"

The article even predicted that when Hemingway "finally does face it [death], he will give a Good Show." For a man who sought out dangerous situations for his whole life, suicide was decidedly not a "good show"— at least according to the masculine ethos forwarded by both Hemingway and these magazines.

There is, of course, no definitive answer as to why Hemingway killed himself: his body was failing him and perhaps, unlike with his first taste of mortality in WWI, he didn't see any possibility of bouncing back; he was increasingly paranoid of old friends and the government; it was hereditary, a family trait. But if we can look to the men's magazines that so embodied his persona, that popularized the idea of Hemingway as a male role model and as the public face of the hypermasculine 1950s, then it might be because that larger-than-life persona was unsustainable— impossible for both the man and the genre to keep alive. Indeed, as the 1960s progressed, the market for men's magazines imploded. After devolving into sadistic and hypersensational scare rags, the adventure magazines disappeared. *Bluebook,* one of the last of the holdouts, hung on until the mid-1970s, but by that time it was nothing like the pulp Hemingway submitted stories to in the 1920s. With unavoidable paranoia in stories like "America's Coming Crisis: 20 Million Acid Heads on a One-way Trip," the magazine was a last, pathetic bastion of defense against the cultural revolution of the 1960s and 1970s. The gossip magazines, too, mostly went out of business because of the innumerable lawsuits: reality killed conjecture. And the bachelor magazines like *Gent, Rogue,* and *Dude* devolved into raunchy nudie magazines, keeping their misogyny but losing their pseudo-sophistication and cultural resonance.

Since the 1960s, Hemingway's public persona has been tempered by his academic reputation, one manifested in more sanctioned fictionalizations. Rather than the man being conflated with his writing, Hemingway has become a fiction himself: in novels such as *The Crook Factory, The Hemingway Hoax, I Killed Ernest Hemingway, Papa and Fidel,* and *Toro;* during the carnivalesque Hemingway Days of Key West, Florida, where Hemingway look-alikes become walking characterizations; in the one-man plays so numerous as to be funny, among them "Papa: The One-Man Play," "Just Being

Bluebook was the last surviving, continuously published pulp title, but by 1974 it was only a torrid shade of its former self. ©1974 Q.M.G. Magazine Corp.

Ernest," and "Hemingway: On the Edge."[4] The extreme sensationalism of the 1950s articles on Hemingway is still propagated in print as well. In May of 2008, Hotchner published *The Good Life According to Hemingway,* supposedly a collection of quotes collected by Hotchner during their friendship and recorded on napkins, matchbooks, etc., though some are lifted from published interviews. The quotes are organized by subject headings such as writing, war, sports, hunting, women, life, and death, and they waffle between trite and sensational. The book is in the very same vein as the many such collections and lists published in *Playboy, True,* and other magazines of the 1950s.

Given this continued fascination, it is important to understand the foundations of both his popular and his literary reputations, to examine the cultural machinations that helped in constructing them. "A legend about a writer can kill some or all of his work," writes Farrell in his *Nugget* eulogy about Hemingway, "or it can have the opposite effect. A legend can play a role in the sales rise, and also in the *misreading* of a book." So to understand our own misreading of Hemingway, it is necessary to see the myth and the man in the surroundings of their time, to see the gravitational pull of the legend on the art.

The fictional aspects of Hemingway's persona are nowhere better illustrated than in the many novelizations of the author's exploits, of which *Toro* is the first. The novel, about Hemingway's adventures submarine chasing during WWII, is told in the first person by Morgan, which is obviously a pen name. ©1977 Tower Publications, Inc.

A NOVEL ABOUT
ERNEST HEMINGWAY

BT
51178
CDC
$1.95

TORO

America's most
famous novelist
takes on the Nazis
in Cuba during
World War II.

Henry Morgan

Patrick Hemingway, Ernest's second son, lived as a safari guide in East Africa from roughly 1951 to 1975. Though this article is interesting in its own rights as a story about Patrick, it is fascinating as an example of how, after Hemingway's death, men's magazines such as *Climax* attempted to set "the record straight on Papa." For Patrick to want this is understandable, for he had seen both the real Hemingway beneath the public image and the toll that the pressures of celebrity and success took on his father. Nor was this Patrick's only presence in the men's magazines. Another article on him as a white hunter appeared in *Cavalcade* magazine in 1959, and he wrote an article, "My Papa, Papa," for the December 1968 issue of *Playboy*. Hemingway's brother, Leicester, also serialized his memoirs, *My Brother, Ernest Hemingway,* in *Playboy,* but he already had a long history in the men's magazines, publishing such articles as "How to Make Your Own Wine" in *Man's Illustrated* (December 1958).

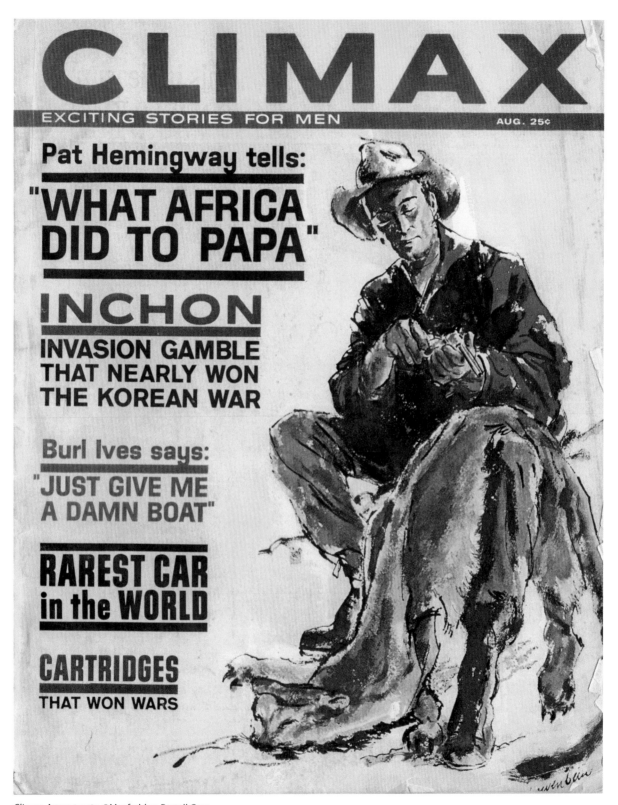

Climax, August 1962. ©Macfadden-Bartell Corp.

The Public has been mislead about his famous writer-father, Pat Hemingway claims—by hoaxsters, moviemakers, mass magazine editors, critics, pals and newsmen, too. In an exclusive interview Pat sets the record straight on Papa

In the pink telephone directory for Tanganyika, East Africa, there is this listing on the top of page 34: "Hemingway, Patrick (Professional Hunter) . . . Arusha 2074." The listing is no gimmick, nor is it for just a *nobody* Hemingway. This Patrick Hemingway is one of the three sons of writer Ernest Hemingway. (Jack is a stockbroker in San Francisco, Gregory is studying medicine at Miami University.) Pat is the only one, so far, who has faced that usually impossible task—following in at least some of a famous father's footsteps. In some ways he has surpassed his old man; in other ways not. At the very least he's at home in Africa and knows it better than Papa ever did—or could.

The 33-year-old Patrick Hemingway lives in a wide-roofed settler's house just off a gravel road in the town of Arusha. The house is right out of Main Street, U.S.A. There are shade trees in front, laundry drying on the line, children playing in the yard and neighbors chatting over the back fence. The house is about 80 miles from the summit of cloud-crowned and snow-swirled Kilimanjaro, the mountain made famous in the Thirties by the already famous "Papa."

Patrick displays paintings by himself on the walls, a lion skin rug in his den, two big maps, one of England the other of Spain, in the living room. But you will find no collection of Hemingway books prominently displayed. Neither does Pat have a trophy room as his father did although he's killed many more wild animals. There are no framed pictures hanging on the walls of him, bare-chested beside a dead elephant.

Though Ernest made Kilimanjaro famous, his youngest son by his second wife, the late Pauline Pfeiffer, has made a living hunting the plains at the foot of the mountain. Pat has also made a go of a profession his father always envied; he's a white hunter, a professional at stalking and killing big game. It was something his father could only play at—and for a price.

The terrain Pat picked as home 12 years ago is rough—the tough green hills of Africa. It teems with wild game, and is studded with the *bomas* (stockades) of tall, majestic Masai warriors. For Pat, there are moments of truth every day on safari. He does not have to go out to seek trophies or buy them or collect them. Hourly they come out of the bushes snorting or out of the grass growling and leaping. Patrick today lives what his father only wrote about two decades ago.

Patrick was born in Kansas City, Missouri, during the noisy Republican National Convention of 1928 which brought forth the winning team of Herbert Hoover and Charles Curtis. His father was covering the convention for a news service. Shortly afterward the Hemingways went to Europe—especially Paris—for three years. When the family returned to the States, they headed for Papa's favorite haunt on the Key West–Cuba run. Pat's earliest memories are of those years with his father, during the Thirties. It was a time of tall tales, fishing and sailing.

"Papa was healthy and always on the hunt for the 'big one' that rarely got away," Pat recalls. "I did not take to the water very well, however. I was always seasick." His father nicknamed him "Mexican Mouse."

Seated in the younger Hemingway's living room, I asked if he had hunted with his father.

"He taught me how to use a shotgun," Pat said.

They hunted mallards. "My brother Jack and I acted as retrievers when we hunted with Papa. What a shot he was! He wanted us to be good shots, too. We even had gun teachers."

It was painful for Pat when his mother, a former Vogue editor, divorced Hemingway in 1934. It meant that he now had to split his time between the two people he loved the most. Always with his father it meant an outdoor life. "We used to fish off the Florida bridges. What times! We had an outboard motor. Then Papa had a sportfishing cruiser built to his specifications." (It was the famed *Pilar,* now without a skipper. It is anchored off the late author's Cuban villa, *Finca Vigia,* and will soon be towed out to sea, and sunk. That was Papa's wish.)

"Papa often didn't have the best of luck fishing," Pat remembers. "He once went one hundred days without a marlin, a run of bad fishing luck that he used in *The Old Man and the Sea.* But once, off Bimini in the Bahamas, I watched him land a tuna without a shark getting it. That took some doing. It was never done before and to the best of my knowledge has not been done since. He holds this record.

"Another time I saw Papa lose seventeen pounds in one day fighting a sailfish. He also holds the record for the largest Atlantic sailfish caught by any means." Chuckling, Pat added, "This one he caught with a Jesuit friend of his."

Recalling his youth, Pat said: "At sports I was never too good in team play, except football. I was a running guard. I would have been a great end but I couldn't catch passes."

Pat insists that Papa never seriously tried to mold him into anything. "Papa wouldn't force anything down our throats. Nothing would have pleased him more than if one of us had been better at athletics. He would have liked one of us to be a good baseball player. He loved that game. In high school I came the closest: I was manager of the baseball team, so I won a baseball letter."

When World War II began Ernest Hemingway approached it in a violent way. In World War I he had been an ambulance driver, in the Spanish Civil War, foreign correspondent. At the beginning of World War II, he decided to seek out submarines in his favorite fishing grounds in the Caribbean and South Atlantic. His *Pilar* was his hunter. For a crew he had a marine wireless operator and two Basque crewmen. For two years Hemingway prowled the waters.

"He never caught one," Pat says with a smile today. "He hunted them with a thirty-caliber machine gun on the foredeck. I was never allowed to go along on these trips. Papa and his crew were a real 'do or die' outfit."

In 1945, shortly after his father (having satisfied his desire to be with U.S. troops in Europe) liberated the Ritz Hotel in Paris, Pat decided to go to Stanford University to take a pre-medical course.

After two years with fair marks, he transferred to Harvard University and a more general program. Pat was never too sure what career to pursue.

"Unlike Papa who knew what he wanted in and out of life, I was unlucky," he says. "I just did not know what I should do with my life. Papa never told me. I had always been an amateur painter so I decided on museum work. Papa liked painting and did a little of it as a kid, but not as a hobby. Mind you, he liked painting, but he figured he would not be successful at it. My grandmother on my mother's side was a painter and our Cuban home always had a lot of paintings around."

Tugging at his drooping knee socks Pat turned to his wife Henny and said: "If anyone ever does a definitive work on my father, it should be called *Man With The Guitar.*

"He had probably one of Juan Gris's best paintings, by that name. Every place Papa moved he took that painting with him. It always hung over his bed. To me it represented Papa perfectly: the artist so careful and conscientious about his craft and thus very much alone, a lone wolf. That was Papa, always lonely."

Graduating from Harvard, Pat went to Spain to see for himself the places he had so often read about in his father's books. He painted in Malaga. He gave

Although Papa was one of world's finest shots and could kill as well as any man, his son Pat claims, "He didn't give two cents for hunting in Africa at the end." Papa got sick at high altitudes.

13

Illustration from the *Climax,* August 1962, interview with Patrick Hemingway. ©Macfadden-Bartell Corp.

bullfighting a try, but it did not take. "I was no *aficionado,* really. If there was nothing to do on Saturdays, we'd go, but I know nothing about them. And I never went out of my way to find out who was who in the bullfight world. I liked the fights—when they were good. I read Papa on bullfighting, but that was about all. I don't know how much Papa really enjoyed the bulls, but I suppose he did."

Pat soon tired of Malaga. His money was running low, so he returned to Cuba to be with his father and think about the future. "Actually we saw little of Papa, then. He was hard at work on *The Old Man and the Sea* and kept pretty much to himself. None of us are in it. He never put his family in his books."

Pat did discuss going to Africa with Papa. "He cautioned me that he did not think Africa was my best business prospect. But in 1952 I came to Kenya on a gentleman's tour with good introductions I had got from Papa. I was pricing farms, but it was sixty thousand for this and a hundred and fifty thousand for that. Henny and I decided to go to Tanganyika and look at the Southern Highlands. I had never planted anything in my life, but we bought some property— eighteen hundred and sixty acres. We still have the land. I was a typical monkey; I had cash to buy and plenty of people were ready to sell."

A burning desire to enter the bush and come face-to-face with big game began to grow in him. "Certainly it's the challenge that excites you," he says. "I liked the way of life in Tanganyika but was too stupid to do anything else but hunt. I also always liked the way of life that Papa described and the life he led."

Pat bought a .375 Winchester and, using an old gun bearer who had once worked for his father, set out daily to stalk big game. He had no fancy equipment or guides; just himself and his Kamba gun bearer.

Pat's first encounter with a wild animal was almost his last. "I had read all the books and listened carefully to Papa. I had taken every precaution. And I got a buffalo on my first hunt—that is, part of a buffalo. But what a time! We came to a dry river bottom. I saw the buff. It was wonderful. I applied the rules I knew: climbed the bank and peeked through the grass. There he was, his nose right in front of me. All I could do was fire. I fired and fell back into the riverbed. The wounded buffalo took off. We tried to find him but couldn't. I went back to my camp and threw up my breakfast. That day I had second thoughts about ever hunting again. 'Now what's wonderful about it,' I asked myself. 'There's a wounded buffalo out there and I can't find it.' (It is the law of the hunter that all means must be exhausted before giving up finding, and finally killing, any wounded animal.) I looked again for five hours. Finally I went to Arusha and reported it. That was like ice skating for the first time. I was awful shaky and had let him get away."

Pat chuckles about this first encounter these days. "You never look back over your shoulder in this game," he says.

About one year after Pat got started in his own safari business, after studying under some of the best Kenya and Tanganyika white hunters, Papa arrived (in 1954) for his ill-fated safari. It was Hemingway's last. During this trip his light plane, flying low to spot game, hit some telephone lines along a stretch of plains in Uganda. In order to get free from the tangled wreck of the cabin Papa had to butt open the door with his head. Later, in the hospital he was delirious for days.

"Papa was hurt a lot worse than anybody knew,"

Illustrated by
Michael Lowenbein

Illustration from the *Climax,* August 1962, interview with Patrick Hemingway. ©Macfadden-Bartell Corp.

says Pat. "He had planned to come back to Africa sometime after that and go on safari with me, but he never did. After that crash he never wanted to fly in a plane again. He planned to come by ship in 1956. But the Suez Canal was closed so that ended that. It depressed him very much."

Many today insist that the crash was the beginning of the end for Ernest Hemingway. He came too close that time to death, which he often described as "my girl, my enemy . . . my brother." Pat puts some of the blame, however, on Hollywood. He thinks that his father's ill-fated depression, which was finally to cause his death, in many ways resulted from the treatment given his stories by the movies. "He had no use for the makers of movies," says Pat, recalling that once a producer sent an urgent cable to Papa saying the book was fine but couldn't he shorten the title of *The Snows of Kilimanjaro*. His father's two-word suggestion was unprintable "even in Hollywood," says Pat.

But while his father was nearing death, Patrick Hemingway prospered as a white hunter. He seemed a natural at it. "I was doing what I wanted to do always. I had a passion for hunting. But I don't kill to inflict pain. It was just one of those things I could work at and succeed," he says. "But I never really have had the feel for it that Papa did."

In his two letters monthly to Pat, Papa gave his son as many hunting tips as possible. "He offered me ideas on hunting and some suggestions. He put me in good with some very famous white hunters. I think the best suggestion he ever gave me, though, was 'Keep good care of your gun.' He told me this over and over again, even as a boy."

"My first customers were Spanish. When a Spaniard is going good he leaves the whole world behind him. But we went for three weeks without a kill. I was depressed and so were they. Then we got two buffalo in three days; then two elephants and a rhino the color of an Andalusian blue fighting cock."

Pat today attributes some of his safari success to the Hemingway name. "Being the son of a famous father is one more added attraction as far as the clients are concerned. But 75 percent of them never talk about Papa to me. Being the son of a famous father is strange. When you are not successful, it's disastrous. When you are, it's a help. That it is a hardship being Papa's son is nonsense."

Pat Hemingway is happiest on safari with honest big-game hunters who don't spend their time drinking too much and talking too much. "I like to go out with somebody who enjoys hunting," he explains. "It's my way of life. I like people who remember the names of animals. I don't like a rum-dumb. Otherwise you're like the headwaiter who serves people who don't appreciate good food."

A safari is not cheap. Take Pat's rates, which are average. For one client with one professional hunter the charge is $3497 for 30 days, $5204 for 45 days, $6911 for 60 days. Booze, tobacco, tips, soft drinks—all are extra along with your hunting licenses (a lion costs $70 and an elephant $280) and the rental of guns.

Pat makes the point, though, that "a safari in Africa is cheaper than a tiger hunt in India or a bear hunt in Alaska. And here you'll always shoot thirty or so animals."

For years now, as a white hunter, Pat has often tried to figure out Papa's hunting ability and his passion for the sport. Though all the pieces have not yet fallen into place—and maybe never will—he does have some penetrating thoughts on it which CLIMAX readers are the first to learn.

"Papa did not just hunt to kill," Pat says. "He was a skillful hunter. An excellent rifle shot and very good with a shotgun. But what so many people forget or don't want to remember is that Papa was, primarily, a fisherman. That was his real love. He spent his whole life at the art of fishing; he spent little time at the art of hunting. He only spent about nine months all told in Africa. During that time he also went fishing, don't forget. Papa was never an expert on Africa. But he had a tremendous capacity to observe. And hunting and fishing, together, never meant to Papa what writing did," Pat observed.

"In hunting I think Papa was sometimes playing up to the image. He did, you know, enjoy being a public figure. Maybe that got out of hand. But he was a lonely man; so he went hunting to relax mainly. Remember this: neither hunting nor fishing were complete poses. Some other things he did in the public eye were."

Many people ask Pat if his father was a better hunter than himself. Pat takes pains to spell out all the qualifications. "Papa was certainly a better shot than me. But he did not have the techniques. One thing he had on me—a basic feeling for it. He did not speak Swahili, however. And to know how to speak to Africans is the important thing while on a safari."

Pat is an honest man—almost too honest. He loved his father dearly and for that reason he wanted to set the record straight for CLIMAX. He detests most of what has been written about Papa. He despises Hollywood for what it has done with his father's stories.

"Papa did not start big-game hunting in Africa. Teddy Roosevelt did; he made big-game hunting in Africa. Maybe Papa did help make people aware of Africa. What Papa did pioneer was big-game fishing. That was his sport, his love. Hunting was not.

"His interests came from the times in which he grew up. It was the age when people were reading about Stanley. He read the books on Africa. He was a romantic. He dreamed. He also read about the Civil War. There was adventure in it all. Africa was simply what would make him happy, Papa thought. It meant freedom. It wasn't civilized. It was a geographical excitement to him: Here you were on the Equator yet there was ice in the wash basin in the morning.

"But when he finally did come to Africa—and some people claim his first safari was paid for, not by himself but by an uncle-in-law—he soon realized a sense of disillusionment. He never did feel the freedom in hunting he did in fishing. On the oceans, he felt, there were no licenses required. He said, 'There are no plains wilder than the ocean. The ocean does not belong to anybody.' That is what he found out in Af-rica. He discovered how much he liked the ocean."

Pat discussed his father's writings to make his point. "Africa to him was an episode. It was one good act and two short stories—out of forty-eight. The public, let's face it, put more emphasis on his Africa than he did. What about his best short story, 'Cat in the Rain'? There were no mountains or big game in it. He did a few short stories for *Esquire* on big-game hunting and that is how all this got started. But I suppose he was responsible, too, in a way, for the myth. Ironically, not one in a hundred stories he wrote dealt with his real love, big-game fishing."

About the mountain his father made famous, Pat seems scornful of it because it has now been discovered by thousands of tourists. "It's a super Fujiyama, that's all. Papa usually despised symbolism. But he used it in *The Snows of Kilimanjaro.* The mountain isn't a symbol now, unless it represents 'The Snows of Zanuck' or something. Papa's story has been worked over by everyone. For me it's in a class with the La Brea tar pits in Los Angeles. Funny, some place Papa read about a *leopard* being in the ice on the mountain. It wasn't. It was a Cerval cat. But then Papa never climbed the mountain to see. He suffered from altitude fever.

I asked Pat whether his father was preoccupied with big-game hunting while in Africa. "For God sakes no!" he retorted. "He was not. And make no bones about it, he didn't give two cents for it at the end.

"How did Papa feel about it?" Pat continued, growing angry. "As a challenge? No. His thought was that big game hunting was not as dangerous as a German division. There was so much pose in the hunting. What Papa really loved, truly, was boxing and military tactics along with the big-game fishing. He was in faultless physical condition which meant a lot to him. Sometimes I think he even hated Africa, because of what the movies did to it."

Right now Patrick Hemingway, professional hunter

and safari outfitter, is sitting pretty. He is working 200 days of the year which is better than average for the professional hunting course. (You must take into account the two rainy seasons totaling usually more than 150 days.) He is grossing about $15,000 per year which is enough to afford him a proper four-bedroom house in Arusha.

Last month he took two professional hunters from Alaska out on their first lion try. They bagged game to their hearts' content. One of them, Dick McIntyre, was so impressed by the game and the white hunter that he wants to come back again next year. That may be tricky as Pat already has his schedule pretty much booked up for next year. He is already booking for 1964.

Often Pat has thought of the famous safari Papa described in *Green Hills of Africa.* He's read the book now several times and agrees with the review of the London *Observer* which appeared in 1936. It said that if Papa were never to write again his name would live as long as the English language for *The Green Hills of Africa.*

Only once did Pat try to actually retrace the steps of that famous safari. He did it with "Karl," the man who actually went with Papa and his wife on the safari that made the book. Pat's safari was a sad experience. For Pat anyway. First of all, many of the areas then lush with game are now barren. Some are in game parks and today unhuntable. Of the places revisited Karl remembered few—if any. Eagerly at first Pat would say "and remember the river where you and Papa shot . . ." Karl could only manage an occasional, "Oh yes, I think so." Nothing more. This pained Pat.

Pat does not admit that his father affected his life in major ways. But it is certainly noticeable. There is a current mystique about his father—very painful for Pat.

"I guess there is no other reason why I am here but because of Father," he says rubbing a brandy glass between his tanned, thin-fingered hands. Thoughtfully, painfully, he gropes for the words. They come in jerks, at first, then in an emotional river. "Being here in Africa has made me free. Now, I can go anywhere. I can go anywhere *I* now want. I am now free of *it.*" You may be sure he means his father's reputation. I asked: "Does this mean, Pat, that you are now going to leave Africa?"

"No, I've grown to love Africa. In fact I've thought about it and have decided I've really had my happiest times *here,*" he said.

I thought for a moment he would add the words "on my own." But he didn't.

THE END

Notes

Introduction

1. Originally published in *The Nation,* July 20, 1957; reprinted in Henry M. Christman, ed., *A View of* The Nation: *An Anthology, 1955–1959* (Freeport, N.Y.: Books for Libraries Press, 1970), 76–79.

2. Ibid.

3. Ibid., 78.

4. Other works on magazines' cultural construction of female roles include Nancy Walker, *Shaping Our Mother's World: American Women's Magazines* (Jackson: Univ. Press of Mississippi, 2000) and *Women's Magazines 1940–1960: Gender Roles in the Popular Press* (Boston: Bedford/St. Martin's, 1998); and Ellen McCracken, *Decoding Women's Magazines* (New York: Palgrave, 1992).

5. See, for example, Elaine Tyler May, *Homeward Bound* (New York: Basic Books, 1988), 58–74; Lynn Peril, *Pink Think: Becoming a Woman in Many Uneasy Lessons* (New York: Norton, 2002), about the women's general socialization in popular culture; Maria Elena Buszek, *Pin-Up Grrrls: Feminism, Sexuality, and Popular Culture* (Durham, N.C.: Duke Univ. Press, 2006), esp. 236–39.

6. Besides Walker's *Shaping Our Mother's World,* others that reenvision the 1950s are Joel Foreman, ed., *The Other Fifties* (Urbana: Univ. of Illinois Press, 1997); Andrew Hoberek, *The Twilight of the Middle Class* (Princeton, N.J.: Princeton Univ. Press, 2005); Stephanie Coontz, *The Way We Never Were: American Families and the Nostalgia Trap* (New York: Basic Books, 1992); Paul Grainge, *Monochrome Memories* (Westport, Conn.: Praeger, 2002); Os Guiness, *The American Hour* (New York: Free Press, 1993), 81–90. See also Barbara Coleman, "Maidenform(ed): Images of the American Woman in the 1950s," in *Forming and Reforming Identity,* ed. Carol Siegal and Ann Kibbey (New York: NYU Press, 1995), 3–29.

7. Richard Simon has even compared *Playboy* to the sixteenth-century *Book of the Courtier.* See his *Trash Culture: Popular Culture and the Great Tradition* (Berkeley: Univ. of California Press, 1999), 101–16. For a cultural reading of the history of *Playboy,* see Bill Osgerby, *Playboys in Paradise: Masculinity, Youth and Leisure Style in America* (Oxford, Eng.: Berg, 2001), one of the few books that examines 1950s men's magazines, even including a few pages on the adventure magazines.

8. The idea of a midcentury trauma affecting masculinity has been a cornerstone of masculinity studies, though a few critics have pointed out inherent dangers in such a reading. Christopher Breu, following in the footsteps of Bruce Traister, warns in *Hard-Boiled Masculinities* (Minneapolis: Univ. of Minnesota Press, 2005) that this obscures the investigation of "the materiality of male power and privilege" (4). Whereas this could very well be true, the goal of *All Man!* is to present and forward an overlooked literary and material signifier of this empowerment: the men's magazine.

9. May, *Homeward Bound,* 28.

10. Peril's *Pink Think* is both entertaining and exhaustive in examining the products of mass culture that constructed the popular ideals of women's roles in the 1950s.

11. The most famous exploration of the voyeuristic male gaze is Laura Mulvey's "Visual Pleasure and Narrative Cinema" (*Screen* 16 [Autumn 1975]: 618), which draws from both Freudian and Lacanian psychoanalysis. A more recent study specific to the pinup is Buszek's *Pin-Up Grrrls.*

12. Coontz, *The Way We Never Were,* 29; see also note 6 above.

13. *The Snows of Kilimanjaro* (Twentieth Century Fox, 1952), *The Sun Also Rises* (Twentieth Century Fox, 1957), *A Farewell to Arms* (Selznick/Twentieth Century Fox, 1958), *The Gun Runners* (United Artists, 1958), and *The Old Man and the Sea* (Warner Brothers, 1958). See Frank M. Laurence, *Hemingway and the Movies* (Jackson: Univ. Press of Mississippi, 1981), 305–10.

14. For example, in the *Sir!* article "Men at War" (June 1952), the author repeatedly refers to Hemingway simply as "Grey Whiskers." An *Argosy* article on Hemingway and Castro is subtitled "Dear Beards" (Jan. 1961).

15. *Man's Illustrated,* Nov. 1960, 34.

16. *The Oxford English Dictionary* (online edition). This latter definition stems from Jungian philosophy.

17. Carl Eby, *Hemingway's Fetishism (*Albany: SUNY Press, 1999); and Robert Scholes and Nancy R. Comley, *Hemingway's Genders: Rereading the Hemingway Text* (New Haven, Conn.: Yale Univ. Press, 1994).

18. See Sandra M. Gilbert and Susan Gubar's reading of "The Short Happy Life of Francis Macomber" in *No Man's Land* (New Haven, Conn.: Yale Univ. Press, 1988), 40–41. Eby's *Fetishism* cites as typical Judith Fetterley's 1978 criticism of Hemingway as a male chauvinist.

1. Hemingway in the Pulp Milieu

1. Robert O. Stephens, *Hemingway's Nonfiction* (Chapel Hill: Univ. of North Carolina Press, 1968), 45–61, is especially good on Hemingway's public mantle of expertise.

2. Michael Kimmel, *Manhood in America: A Cultural History* (New York: Free Press, 1996), 181.

3. Marcelline Hemingway Sanford, *At the Hemingways* (Boston: Little Brown, 1962), 63–64.

4. Suzanne Clark, "Roosevelt and Hemingway: Natural History, Manliness, and the Rhetoric of the Strenuous Life," in *Hemingway and the Natural World,* ed. Robert E. Fleming (Moscow: Univ. of Idaho Press, 1999), 55. Clarke traces the influence of Rooseveltian natural history through Hemingway's fiction. See also Michael Reynolds, *The Young Hemingway* (New York: Norton, 1998), 23–30. Patrick Hemingway implicitly supports this in his interview with *Climax* magazine (August 1962), republished here on pp. 147–55.

5. James Meredith, "Bird Hunting and Male Bonding in Hemingway's Fiction and Family," in Fleming, ed., *Hemingway and the Natural World,* 189–201; Stephens, *Hemingway's Nonfiction;* John Raeburn, *Fame Became of Him* (Bloomington: Indiana Univ. Press, 1986), 80–103.

6. Leicester Hemingway, *My Brother, Ernest Hemingway* (Cleveland, Ohio: World, 1962), 32.

7. Sanford, *At the Hemingways,* 99.

8. Marcelline mentions *St. Nicholas* (ibid., 99), as does Leicester (*My Brother,* 30).

9. Theodore Peterson, *Magazines in the Twentieth Century* (Urbana: Univ. of Illinois Press, 1956), 172–73.

10. Ibid., 255–60. There are also numerous biographies of Macfadden, including Mary Macfadden and Emile Gauvereu, *Dumbbells and Carrot Strips* (New York: Holt, 1953).

11. Peterson, *Magazines in the Twentieth Century,* 300, citing Frederick Lewis Allen.

12. See Reynolds, *The Young Hemingway,* 39.

13. EH letter to William D. Horne, Feb. 3, 1919, box 1, folder 2, The William D. Horne Ernest Hemingway Papers, 1913–1985, Newberry Library, Chicago. I thank Robert Trogdon for bringing this letter to my attention.

14. EH letter to W. Smith, Dec. 4, 1919, box 2, folder 94, item 462, The Charles D. Field Collection of Ernest Hemingway, Stanford Special Collections, Stanford University, Stanford, Calif.

15. For portraits of the life of a pulp writer, see Frank Gruber's *The Pulp Jungle* (Los Angeles: Sherbourne, 1967) and Harold Hersey's *Pulpwood Editor* (Westport, Conn.: Greenwood, 1965), esp. 122–36.

16. In 1915 Hemingway wrote in his high school yearbook

that White was one of his three favorite writers, along with Kipling and O'Henry. For White's influence on Hemingway, see Reynolds, *The Young Hemingway,* 39.

17. Reynolds, *The Young Hemingway,* 179–80. The fact that Hemingway used the theme of disillusionment in his writing long after the war points to two possible writing influences: either he was initially conforming to the pulp formula, which emphasizes the influence of the genre on him; or his later use of disillusionment themes was a conformity to the modernist formula.

18. "The Current" was rejected by *Blue Book* in 1919 (rejection slip, item 352, The Ernest Hemingway Collection, John Fitzgerald Kennedy Library and Museum, Boston, Mass.). "The Current" was finally published in 1985 in Peter Griffin's *Along with Youth* (New York: Oxford Univ. Press, 1985).

19. William Sebelle, "Black Butterfly," *Top-Notch Magazine,* Sept. 1, 1919.

20. For the original opening of "Fifty Grand," see Robert Trogdon, *Ernest Hemingway: A Literary Reference* (New York: Carroll and Graf, 1999), 83; and the typescript in the Hemingway Archive, ms. 388, JFK Library; letter from EH to Edward O'Brien, May 21, 1923, in *Ernest Hemingway: Selected Letters,* ed. Carlos Baker (New York: Scribners, 1981), 82; and Reynolds, *The Young Hemingway,* 89, 179.

21. Charles A. Fenton, "No Money for the Kingbird: Hemingway's Prizefight Stories," *American Quarterly* 4 (Winter 1952): 339–50.

22. Gruber, *Pulp Jungle,* 7–8.

23. In a letter to W. Smith (Dec. 4, 1919, box 2, folder 94, item 462, Field Collection), Hemingway mentions his submissions to numerous pulp editors, including Arthur S. Hoffman, editor of *Adventure* 1912–27. This letter refers to "The Mercenaries" by its first title, "Wolves and Doughnuts"; see Mimi Gladstein's consideration of the name change in "'The Mercenaries': A Harbinger of Vintage Hemingway," in *Hemingway's Neglected Short Fiction,* ed. Susan Beegel (Tuscaloosa: Univ. of Alabama Press, 1989), 29n3.

24. Critics have mined these early stories for hints at the future writer, which ultimately does little to bring a new understanding to the author but just confirms traditional readings. See, for example, Fenton's and Reynolds's descriptions in *The Apprenticeship of Ernest Hemingway* (New York:

Mentor, 1954) and *The Young Hemingway,* respectively. See also Mimi Gladstein, "'The Mercenaries.'"

25. EH letter to Wilson cited in Carlos Baker's *Hemingway and His Critics* (New York: Hill and Wang, 1961), 56. See also Phillip Sipiora's overview of the story in Beegel, ed., *Hemingway's Neglected Short Fiction,* 44–49.

26. Daly started publishing in *Black Mask* in 1922. Many critics cite "The False Burton Combs" (Dec. 1922) and "Knight of the Open Palm" (Sept. 1923) as the first hard-boiled stories, but his earlier story "Dolly" (Sept. 1922) has the cynical, psychological earmarks of a hard-boiled tone. For Hemingway and hard-boiled fiction, see Sheldon Norman Grebstein's "The Tough Hemingway and His Hardboiled Children," in *Tough Guy Writers of the Thirties,* ed. David Madden (Carbondale: Southern Illinois Univ. Press, 1968), 18–41.

27. The best sources for information on *The Smart Set* is Carl Dolmetsch, *The Smart Set* (New York: Dial, 1966), and discussions in H. L. Mencken's autobiography, *My Life as Author and Editor* (New York: Vintage, 1995).

28. See *Ernest Hemingway: Selected Letters,* 154–55.

29. *Chicago Daily Tribune,* Nov. 27, 1926, and *London Observer,* June 12, 1927, both quoted in Audre Hanneman, *Ernest Hemingway: A Comprehensive Bibliography* (Princeton, N.J.: Princeton Univ. Press, 1969), 352 (#57), 354 (#72).

30. See Robert Trogdon's *The Lousy Racket* (Kent, OH: Kent State Univ. Press, 2007) for more on the marketing of TSAR, 44–45.

31. Malcolm Cowley, *The Exile's Return* (New York: Viking, 1964), 225–26.

32. Douglas Ellis, *Uncovered: The Hidden Art of the Girlie Pinup* (Silver Spring, Md.: Adventure House, 2005).

33. For an account of the history of the Mencken pulps, see Mencken, *My Life,* 72–73, as well as Dolmetsch, *The Smart Set,* 47–51. In 1920, Sumner also took the *Little Review* to trial for obscenity for publishing excerpts of James Joyce's *Ulysses.*

34. Ronald Allen Goldberg, *America in the Twenties* (Syracuse, N.Y.: Syracuse Univ. Press, 2003), 94.

35. Liz Conor, *The Spectacular Modern Woman* (Bloomington: Indiana Univ. Press, 2004), 210.

36. Quoted in Trogdon, *Literary Reference,* 69–70.

37. See Sean McCann's excellent *Gumshoe America* (Durham: Duke Univ. Press, 2000) for examples of how Daly, Hammett, and Chandler used their fiction for political commentary.

38. EH, *To Have and Have Not* (New York: Scribners, 1937), 81, 225.

39. EH, *THAHN,* 186.

40. Letters to the Editor, *New York Times,* Mar. 18, 1933, 12.

41. EH, *THAHN,* 262.

"Ernest Hemingway—Muy Hombre!" by Jackson Burke, *Bluebook* (July 1953)

1. First published in *Cosmopolitan,* Sept. 1936; reprinted in *The Fifth Column and the First Forty-Nine Stories* (New York: Scribners, 1938).

2. Hemingway's example of bank clerks and office boys actually has a long-standing history as a marker of middle-class pretension for twentieth-century modernists. Authors such as Aldous Huxley, T. S. Eliot, D. H. Lawrence, and E. M. Forster all rely on the figure of the clerk to symbolize false intellectualism and shallow, fashionable tastes. For more on this, see John Carey, *The Intellectuals and the Masses* (Chicago: Academy, 2002), 46–70.

3. Norbeto Fuentes recounts in *Hemingway in Cuba* (Secaucus, N.J.: Lyle Stewart, 1984) how Hemingway sold Cuban publication rights to "The Old Man and the Sea" to *Bohemia Libre* for "five thousand pesos [to] be invested in the purchase of television sets which he would donate to the patients at El Rincón Sanitarium" (250).

4. Tom Lea, *The Brave Bulls* (Boston: Little, Brown, 1949).

5. "Matadors Die Rich," *Bluebook,* June 1953.

6. Kid Gavilan, the popular name of Gerardo Gonzalez (1926–2003), the world welterweight champion from 1951 to 1954.

2. Pinup Papa: Hemingway and the Rise of Visual Culture

1. Raeburn, *Fame Became of Him,* 54.

2. Amy Henderson, "Media and the Rise of Celebrity Culture," *OAH Magazine of History* 6 (Spring 1992): 49–54.

3. *Ken,* Apr. 21, 1938, 68.

4. "A Way You'll Never Be," in *Byline: Ernest Hemingway,* ed. William White (New York: Scribners, 1967), 219. For the cinematic quality of Hemingway's prose, see Jeffrey Myers, "Conrad's Influence on Modern Writers," *Twentieth Century Literature* 36 (Summer 1990): 186–206; Robert Olen Butler, *From Where You Dream* (New York: Grove, 2005); and Laurence, *Hemingway and the Movies,* 206–22.

5. "Look Ad," *Ken,* Apr. 21, 1938, 96–97.

6. Ibid., 98.

7. See Peterson, *Magazines in the Twentieth Century,* 345.

8. Ibid., 360.

9. See Raeburn, *Fame Became of Him,* 120. Of the few works on Hemingway's public persona, Raeburn's book is the best. Others included Leonard Leff, *Hemingway and His Conspirators* (Lanham, Md.: Rowman and Littlefield, 1999), on the early development of EH's celebrity status via Scribners and Hollywood; and Catherine Turner, *Marketing Modernism* (Boston: Univ. of Massachusetts Press, 2003), who devotes a chapter to Hemingway. Raeburn contends that Hemingway's early machinations for celebrity were a defense against critics.

10. See for examples "The Hemingways in Sun Valley: The Novelist Takes a Wife," *Life,* Jan. 6, 1941, and "Hunting at Sun Valley," *Life,* Nov. 24, 1941. *Town and Country* (Mar. 1941) included photos of the Hemingways en route to the Near East and the drink recipe for "Death in the Gulf Stream" (July 1941), and *Time* ran photos of EH duck hunting (Dec. 16, 1946). For more examples, see Hanneman, *EH Bibliography,* H.

11. *Show,* Feb. 1957, 29, 33.

12. For example, see two different photo profiles of EH in *Pageant Magazine* (Apr. 1953 and Mar. 1955).

13. For the dynamics of role models, see Adeno Addis, "Role Models and the Politics of Recognition," *University of Pennsylvania Law Review* 144 (Apr. 1996): 1377–468.

14. See Leff, *Hemingway and His Conspirators,* 135, 174–75.

15. Matthew Bruccoli, *Conversations with Ernest Hemingway* (Jackson: Univ. Press of Mississippi, 1986), x.

3. Adventure Magazines and the Narrative of Coping

1. *Battle Cry,* Aug. 1956, 16.

2. Christina Jarvis, *The Male Body at War: American Masculinity during World War II* (DeKalb: Northern Illinois Univ. Press, 2004), 169–72.

3. Kaja Silverman, *Male Subjectivity at the Margins* (New York: Routledge, 1992), 54.

4. Quoted in Judith Lewis Herman, *Trauma and Recovery* (New York: HarperCollins, 1992), 25.

5. Ibid., 25. Herman is quoting from the studies of wartime psychiatrists Roy Grinker and John Spiegel and Abram Kardiner and Herbert Spiegel.

6. *Battle Cry,* Aug. 1956, 6.

7. According to Kirby Farrell, *Post-Traumatic Culture* (Baltimore, Md.: Johns Hopkins Univ. Press, 1998), "Most theorists 'speculate that the repetitive reliving of the traumatic experience must represent a spontaneous, unsuccessful attempt at healing'" (6).

8. Robert J. Neborsky "A Clinical Model for the Comprehensive Treatment of Trauma Using an Affect Experience—Attachment Theory Approach," in *Healing Trauma; Attachment, Mind, Body, and Brain,* ed. Daniel J. Siegel and Marion F. Solomon (New York: Norton, 2003), 293.

9. Farrell, *Post-Traumatic Culture,* 12.

10. Robert Finnegan, *The Bandaged Nude* (Middlesex, Eng.: Penguin, 1952), 5.

11. *Man's Daring,* Jan. and Sept. 1962. See Max Allen Collins and George Hageneur, *Men's Adventure Magazines* (New York: Taschen, 2004), 317–18.

12. Buszek, *Pin-Up Grrrls,* 210.

13. Ibid., 236.

14. Farrell, *Post-Traumatic Culture,* 12. The 9/11 terrorist incidents are another such example.

15. *Man's Illustrated,* Nov. 1960, 34.

16. *True,* Feb. 1963; *Man's Illustrated,* Nov. 1960; *Bluebook,* Feb. 1962. *Bluebook* should not be confused with its earlier, more reputable manifestation, *Blue Book.* By 1962 the magazine had devolved into a sensational "sweat," the industry term for a pulpish adventure magazine.

17. John Groth, *Studio: Europe* (New York: Vanguard, 1945); Robert Capa's memoir, *Slightly Out of Focus* (New York: Holt, 1947). "Private War" published in *Man's Magazine* (Sept. 1959), see illustration on p. 97.

18. Hemingway had no official combat role. However, there is some question as to his activities in WWII as an observer accompanying Gen. Buck Lanham both around Paris and in the Hurtgen Forest. Though officially cleared of charges that he broke Geneva Convention rules that a war correspondent cannot carry arms or lead men against the enemy, judging by Hemingway's later accounts, his activities were beyond those of a war correspondent.

19. *Rogue Magazine,* May 1958, 74, 20.

20. *Collier's Weekly,* July 22, 1944, 11.

21. Stephen Ambrose, *Citizen Soldier* (New York: Simon and Schuster, 1997), 340–41.

22. EH, *Byline,* 383.

23. See Hanneman, *EH Bibliography,* A13e, A20. An excellent, short pamphlet on the Armed Service Editions and how they influenced the reading tastes of a generation is John Y. Cole's *Books in Action* (Washington, D.C.: Library of Congress Press, 1984). For a general overview of Hemingway's influence on post-WWII literature, see Morris Dickstein's *Leopards in the Temple* (Cambridge, Mass.: Harvard Univ. Press, 2002), chap. 2.

24. Robert Emmett Ginna, "Life in the Afternoon," in Bruccoli, ed., *Conversations,* 161–62.

25. EH, ed., *Men at War* (New York: Crown, 1942), xi.

26. *Sir! Magazine,* June 1952, 16.

27. Collins and Hageneur, *Men's Adventure Magazines,* 225.

28. EH, *A Farewell to Arms* (New York: Scribners, 1929), 191.

29. Philip Young, *Ernest Hemingway* (New York: Rinehart, 1952).

30. See Joanna Burke, *Dismembering the Male* (Chicago: Univ. of Chicago Press, 1996), as well as the chapter on male neurasthenia in Elaine Showalter, *The Female Malady* (New York: Penguin, 1987).

31. Burke, *Dismembering,* 119.

32. EH, *Complete Short Stories* (New York: Scribners, 1987), 115.

33. John W. Thomason Jr., *Texas Rebel* (New York: Berkley Medallion, 1961); Robert Lowry, *The Last Party* (New York: Popular Library, 1956) and *New York Call Girl* (New York: Popular Library, 1959); Robert Paul Smith, . . . *Plus*

Blood in Their Veins (New York: Avon, 1952); Alan Kapelner, *Lonely Boy Blues* (New York: Lion, 1956); Elio Bartolini, *La Signora* (New York: Lion Books, 1957). The only mention I have found of an "Ernest Hemingway Prize" was awarded in Spain by the *Pueblo* newspaper in 1960 and 1962, which was won by Alfonso Martinez Berganza. EH put up $500 himself for the first year; Antonio Ordóñez put up the money for the second prize, won by Pedro de Lorenzo, but this seems to be the last one given. Also these prizes seem to be Spanish, rather than Italian, and for journalism rather than literature. According to José Luis Castillo-Puche, *Hemingway in Spain* (New York: Garden City, 1974), after Hemingway's death, "The Hemingway Prize was taken over by others and eventually forgotten" (255). Bartolini's win must have come from this later period.

"Hemingway's Longest Day," by William Van Dusen, *True* (February 1963)

1. In civilian life, Van Dusen (1901–1976) was in charge of public relations for Pan American Airlines and, later, Eastern Airlines.

2. Michael Reynolds, *Hemingway: The Final Years* (New York: Norton, 1999), 110–23.

4. Consuming Masculinity in the Bachelor Magazines

1. Quoted in Peterson, *Magazines in the Twentieth Century,* 316.

2. The portrait of Hemingway in these magazines accentuated the general tone of advice and cultural expertise in these magazines. For example, *Playboy* ran three articles of stitched-together Hemingway advice and mottoes (Jan. 1961, Jan. 1963, Jan. 1964). *Sir Knight,* 1961 (vol. 2, no. 10) featured "'What Life Has Taught Me' by Ernest Hemingway," an article of quotes lifted from other magazines' interviews.

3. Warren Susman, "Did Success Spoil the United States?" in *Recasting America: Culture and Politics in the Age of the Cold War,* ed. Larry May (Chicago: Univ. of Chicago Press, 1989), 22.

4. Steven M. Gelber, "Do-It-Yourself: Constructing, Re-

pairing, and Maintaining Masculinity," in *The Gender and Consumer Culture Reader,* ed. Jennifer Scanlon (New York: NYU Press, 2000), 82.

5. *The Stories of John Cheever* (New York: Vintage, 2000), 325–46.

6. Gelber, "Do-It-Yourself," 83.

7. Similarly, Thomas Strychacz, *Hemingway's Theaters of Masculinity* (Baton Rouge: Louisiana State Univ. Press, 2003), writes about how trophy hunting is a "trope of masculinity" in Hemingway's fiction, especially *The Green Hills of Africa,* "The Undefeated," and *The Garden of Eden,* which supports my idea of how Hemingway's themes influenced (if not inundated) the 1950 idea of masculinity.

8. Raeburn, *Fame Became of Him,* 46–47.

9. EH, *Byline,* 202–3.

10. Statistics quoted in Jarvis, *The Male Body at War,* 15.

11. *Esquire,* Autumn 1933, 2.

12. A sampling of this recent criticism includes Lawrence Rainey's *Institutions of Modernism* (New Haven, Conn.: Yale Univ. Press, 1998); Kevin Dettmar and Stephen Watt, *Marketing Modernisms* (Ann Arbor: Univ. of Michigan Press, 1999); Ronald Weber, *Hired Pens* (Athens: Ohio Univ. Press, 1997); Loren Glass, *Authors Inc.* (New York: NYU Press, 2004); Catherine Turner, *Marketing Modernism between the Two World Wars* (Amherst: University of Massachusetts Press, 2003); Jani Scanduri and Michael Thurston, eds., *Modernism Inc.* (New York: NYU Press, 2001); and John Xiros Cooper, *Modernism and the Culture of Market Society* (Cambridge, Eng.: Cambridge Univ. Press, 2004).

13. EH, *Byline,* 23.

14. Innate in this personification is the tension between modernist writing and the marketplace, as explored by Loren Glass (*Authors Inc.,* 143–51), among others. But rather than propagating what I see as an innate class-based prejudice in such arguments, I'm arguing that such tensions were largely posturing or, more applicable to this chapter, marketing as the alternate, popular, and pulpish history of Hemingway's influences and publishing attests.

15. Wright quoted in Dolmetsch, *Smart Set,* 34–35.

16. This is, of course, only one strain of modernism. The concept of a single, male, heterogeneous modernism has been exploded over the past few decades, but what I'm taking to task here is the "idea" or brand name of modernism

as constructed at the hands of the historically largely male academy and major figures of high modernsim. Books such as Bonnie Kime Scott's *Refiguring Modernism,* vols. 1 and 2 (Bloomington: Indiana Univ. Press, 1995) and Shari Benstock's *Women of the Left Bank* (Austin: Univ. of Texas Press, 1986) have illuminated many female key figures of modernism, from editors and writers. This holds true of other liminal types of modernism, from racial and economic. Therefore, modernisms is perhaps more appropriate, as evinced by the title of the journal *Modernisms/Modernity.*

17. *Playboy* articles and *Sir Knight.*

18. EH, *Complete Short Stories,* 214.

19. Cooper, *Modernism and the Culture of Market Society,* 21, 31.

20. Cooper contends that such givens of the corporate system, such as the focus group, stem directly from the dynamics established by successful modernist salons, such as Pound's Imagists or Woolf's Salon.

21. See Andrew Hoberek's reading of the privileging of the middle class by critics such as Richard Ohmann and Jackson Lears in *The Twilight of the Middle Class* (Princeton, N.J.: Princeton Univ. Press, 2005), 4–5.

5. *Paparazzi: Hemingway and the Tabloids*

1. For this shift, see Richard deCordova's *Picture Personalities: The Emergence of the Star System in America* (Urbana: Univ. of Illinois Press, 1990), 98.

2. See Dian Hanson, *The History of Men's Magazines,* vol. 2: *From Post-War to 1959* (Koln, Germany: Taschen, 2004), 43–67.

3. *Time,* July 11, 1955.

4. Ibid., Aug. 26, 1957.

5. Besides Hanson's excellent history, Peterson's *Magazines in the Twentieth Century* (380–82) gives a good account of the history of *Confidential,* including circulation.

6. Hanson, *The History of Men's Magazines,* 47.

7. Aaron Jaffe, *Modernism and the Culture of Celebrity* (London: Cambridge Univ. Press, 2005), 1. Jaffe's comment is on the well-known photo by Eve Arnold of Marilyn Monroe reading *Ulysses.*

8. See Marsha Orgeron, "Making *It* in Hollywood: Clara Bow, Fandom, and Consumer Culture," *Cinema Journal* 42 (Summer 2003): 77–82; Adrienne L. McLean, "'New Films in Story Form': Movie Story Magazines and Spectorship," *Cinema Journal* 42 (Spring 2003): 3–26; and David R. Shumway's "The Star System in Literary Studies," *PMLA* 112 (Jan. 1997): 88.

9. John Parris Springer, *Hollywood Fictions: The Dream Factory in American Popular Literature* (Norman: Univ. of Oklahoma Press, 2000), 95.

10. For more information on Mallory, see the introduction to "The Twisted World of Ernest Hemingway," which is republished after this chapter.

11. See Leff, *Hemingway and His Conspirators,* especially the final chapter, "Winner Take Nothing."

12. Laurence, *Hemingway and the Movies,* 10.

13. Flynn's 1959 autobiography, *My Wicked, Wicked Ways,* published right after his death, attests to his prowess for self-marketing.

14. Trogdon, *Literary Reference,* 297.

15. Ray Brock, "A Letter from Ernest Hemingway," *Male Magazine,* Apr. 1954, 20–21, 80–81.

16. Reynolds, *Final Years,* 292.

17. deCordova, *Picture Personalities,* 10.

18. Author Howard Rushmore was also the editor of *Confidential* in 1955 and was described in a July 11, 1955, *Time* magazine article as a "onetime Communist who was fired as a Hearst reporter . . . partly for contributing in his spare time to *Confidential.*" It is not surprising, in this era of blacklisting, that a "onetime Communist" was fired from the Hearst syndicate and forced into pulp writing, but it is ironic that as editor of such sensational magazines as *Whisper* and *Confidential* Rushmore was not above a little Red-scare journalism himself.

19. The radio program was broadcast in December 1955 as part of "Meet Ernest Hemingway—The Man Who Lived It Up to Write It Down." See Reynolds, *Final Years,* 284; and Hanneman, *EH Bibliography,* H931, 461.

20. The spat was famous enough that Mary Hemingway discussed it, setting the record straight, in her memoir (*How It Was* [New York: Knopf, 1976], 467–69).

21. George Brown owned the New York gym where Hemingway liked to spar and was a good friend, often visiting him in Ketchum. In fact, he ate dinner with Ernest and Mary the night before Hemingway's suicide. The article calls him "Willie" Brown, either out of error or to avoid libel.

22. For more about how such accounts infuriated Hemingway, see Reynolds, *Final Years,* 292.

23. *Rave,* May 1955, 50–54.

24. Reynolds, *Final Years,* 284.

25. Springer, *Hollywood Fictions,* 104.

26. Letter to Thomas Bledsoe about Philip Young, Dec. 9, 1951, in *Ernest Hemingway: Selected Letters,* 744.

27. James Plath and Frank Simmons, *Remembering Ernest Hemingway* (Key West, Fla.: Ketch and Yawl Press, 1999), 84–85.

28. *Rogue Magazine,* May 1958, 80.

29. *Male Magazine,* Apr. 1954, 80.

30. Though recent literary criticism has all but discounted the reason that he started writing his memoirs due to recovered material from the Ritz in Paris and other such nostalgia-evoking events, no one has really offered any satisfactory alternative. Rose Marie Burwell, *Hemingway: The Postwar Years and the Posthumous Novels* (Cambridge, Eng.: Cambridge Univ. Press, 1996), 151.

31. Ibid., 149.

32. While we do not know if Hemingway ever saw any of these articles, we can imagine the effect that such personally violent and discrediting articles would have had on him, given that he was always sensitive and reactionary to criticism of his work. Valerie Hemingway, Ernest's secretary in the late 1950s, and who eventually married Gregory Hemingway, stated in conversation that the author's coterie would have most likely protected him from such sensational articles, but it is undeniable that celebrity did take its toll.

33. Scott Donaldson, *By Force of Will* (New York: Viking Press, 1977), 8.

34. Leonard Bishop was actually an acclaimed hard-boiled author whose first book, *Down All Your Streets* (New York: Dial Press, 1952), became a *New York Times* best-seller in 1952. He attended the New School of Social Research in New York along with Mario Puzo, William Styron, Joseph Heller, Richard Wright, and Harlan Ellison. In 1988 he published *Dare to Be a Great Writer: 329 Keys to Powerful Fiction* (Cincinnati, Ohio: Writers Digest Books, 1988). According to his son, Matthew, Bishop wrote quite a bit for *Confidential* under his own name and also under the pseudonym Louie Bolinger. Bishop passed away in 2002. Matt Bishop, email to the author, July 26, 2005.

35. *Time,* July 11, 1955.

36. Carlos Baker, *The Writer as Artist* (Princeton, N.J.: Princeton Univ. Press, 1952); John Atkins, *The Art of Ernest Hemingway* (London: Spring Books, 1952).

"The Twisted World of Ernest Hemingway," by Mark Mallory, *Exposed* (February 1957)

1. "The First Time I Saw Paris," *Rogue,* Aug. 1957; "Europe's Mighty Midgets," *Rogue,* Nov. 1961; "What Comes After Arthur Miller?" *Mr.,* May 1963; Clark Collins, *Counterfeit Cad* (Los Angeles: Intimate Edition 706, 1962).

2. This is obviously extreme, but it is drawing on the negative reviews of *Across the River and Into the Trees* in 1950. For example, J. Donald Adams's review from the *New York Times Book Review* considered most of Hemingway's heroines "dream-girl type[s]" and "abstraction," and stated that "in this book the narcissism stands fully, and for the reader, painfully revealed." See Robert O. Stephens, *The Critical Reception* (New York: Burr-Franklin, 1977), 311–12.

3. EH, *Death in the Afternoon* (New York: Scribners, 1932), 92. This quote is taken out of context. Hemingway is writing of how honor is "as real as water, wine, or olive oil" to a Spaniard.

4. See Maxwell Geismar's review of *Across the River and Into the Trees* in *Saturday Review of Literature,* Sept. 9, 1950, reprinted in Trogdon, *Literary Reference,* 278–80, 294–95, which cites the novel's "morbid and infantile egotism."

5. This is a classic example of the conflation of Hemingway with his characters. This is notably a theme in "Cross Country Snow" and "Hills Like White Elephants."

6. In the interest of sensationalism, Mallory is combining

the Gellhorn marriage (1940–45) with *AFTA,* published in 1929, and *TSAR,* published in 1926.

7. Earl Wilson was gossip columnist for the *New York Post* and a friend of Hemingway's. See his "A Visit with Papa," *New York Post,* May 26, 1957.

8. *Time,* Aug. 4, 1957, reprinted in Bruccoli, ed., *Conversations,* 50–51.

6. Coda—Afterlife

1. Raeburn, *Fame Became of Him,* 178.

2. *Sir!,* Nov. 1966, 67.

3. *Sir Knight,* 1961 (vol. 2, no. 10): 55.

4. "Ernest: A Salute to Ernest Hemingway," performed at the Manhattan Theatre Club, May 21, 2001; "Papa: The One-Man Play," by John De Groot; "Hemingway on Stage" and "Just Being Ernest," by Brian Gordon Sinclair; "Hemingway Reminisces," by James Mitchell Lear; "Hemingway: On the Edge," by Ed Metzger; Ben Pleasants, *The Hemingway/Dos Passos Wars* (Los Angeles: Engadine Books, 1997).

Bibliography

Archival Sources and Collections

The Charles D. Field Collection of Ernest Hemingway. Stanford Special Collections, Stanford University, Stanford, California.

The Ernest Hemingway Collection. John Fitzgerald Kennedy Library and Museum, Boston, Massachusetts.

The William D. Horne Ernest Hemingway Papers, 1913–1985. Newberry Library, Chicago, Illinois.

Published Sources

Addis, Adeno. "Role Models and the Politics of Recognition." *University of Pennsylvania Law Review* 144 (April 1996): 1377–468.

Ambrose, Stephen. *Citizen Soldier.* New York: Simon and Schuster, 1997.

Atkins, John. *The Art of Ernest Hemingway.* London: Spring Books, 1952.

Baker, Carlos, ed., *Ernest Hemingway: Selected Letters.* New York: Scribners, 1981.

———. *Hemingway and His Critics.* New York: Hill and Wang, 1961.

———. *The Writer as Artist.* Princeton, N.J.: Princeton University Press, 1952.

Beegel, Susan, ed. *Hemingway's Neglected Short Fiction.* Tuscaloosa: University of Alabama Press, 1989.

Benstock, Shari. *Women of the Left Bank.* Austin: University of Texas Press, 1986.

Breu, Christopher. *Hard-Boiled Masculinities.* Minneapolis: University of Minnesota Press, 2005.

Brian, Denis. *The True Gen.* New York: Dell/Delta, 1989.

Bruccoli, Matthew, ed. *Conversations with Ernest Hemingway.* Jackson: University Press of Mississippi, 1986.

———. *Hemingway and the Mechanism of Fame.* Columbia: University of South Carolina Press, 2006.

Burke, Joanna. *Dismembering the Male.* Chicago: University of Chicago Press, 1996.

Burwell, Rose Marie. *Hemingway: The Postwar Years and the Posthumous Novels.* Cambridge, England: Cambridge University Press, 1996.

Buszek, Maria Elena. *Pin-Up Grrrls: Feminism, Sexuality, and Popular Culture.* Durham, N.C.: Duke University Press, 2006.

Butler, Robert Olen. *From Where You Dream.* New York: Grove, 2005.

Capa, Robert. *Slightly Out of Focus.* New York: Holt, 1947.

Carey, John. *The Intellectuals and the Masses.* Chicago: Academy, 2002.

Castillo-Puche, José Luis. *Hemingway in Spain.* New York: Garden City, 1974.

Cheever, John. *The Stories of John Cheever.* New York: Vintage, 2000.

Christman, Henry M., ed. *A View of* The Nation: *An Anthology, 1955–1959.* Freeport, N.Y.: Books for Libraries Press, 1970.

Clark, Suzanne. "Roosevelt and Hemingway: Natural History, Manliness, and the Rhetoric of the Strenuous Life." In Fleming, ed., *Hemingway and the Natural World,* 55–68.

Cole, John Y. *Books in Action.* Washington, D.C.: Library of Congress Press, 1984.

Coleman, Barbara. "Maidenform(ed): Images of the American Woman in the 1950s." *Forming and Reforming Identity.* Ed. Carol Siegal and Ann Kibbey. New York: NYU Press, 1995.

Collins, Max Allen, and George Hageneur. *Men's Adventure Magazines.* New York: Taschen, 2004.

Comley, Nancy R., and Robert Scholes, eds. *Hemingway's Genders.* New Haven, Conn.: Yale University Press, 1994.

Conor, Liz. *The Spectacular Modern Woman.* Bloomington: Indiana University Press, 2004.

Coontz, Stephanie. *The Way We Never Were: American Families and the Nostalgia Trap.* New York: Basic Books, 1992.

Cooper, John Xiros. *Modernism and the Culture of Market Society.* Cambridge, England: Cambridge University Press, 2004.

Cowley, Malcolm. *The Exile's Return.* New York: Viking, 1964.

Davidson, Cathy. *Revolution and the Word.* New York: Oxford University Press, 1986.

deCordova, Richard. *Picture Personalities: The Emergence of the Star System in America.* Urbana: University of Illinois Press, 1990.

Dettmar, Kevin, and Stephen Watt. *Marketing Modernisms.* Ann Arbor: University of Michigan Press, 1999.

Dickstein, Morris. *Leopards in the Temple.* Cambridge, Mass.: Harvard University Press, 2002.

Dolmetsch, Carl. *The Smart Set.* New York: Dial, 1966.

Donaldson, Scott. *By Force of Will.* New York: Viking Press, 1977.

Eby, Carl. *Hemingway's Fetishism.* Albany: SUNY Press, 1999.

Ellis, Douglas. *Uncovered: The Hidden Art of the Girlie Pinup.* Silver Spring, Md.: Adventure House, 2005.

Farrell, Kirby. *Post-Traumatic Culture.* Baltimore, Md.: Johns Hopkins University Press, 1998.

Fenton, Charles A. "No Money for the Kingbird: Hemingway's Prizefight Stories." *American Quarterly* 4 (Winter 1952): 342–47.

Fenton, Charles. *The Apprenticeship of Ernest Hemingway.* New York: Mentor, 1954.

Fetterley, Judith. *The Resisting Reader: A Feminest Approach to American Fiction.* Bloomington: Indiana University Press, 1978.

Finnegan, Robert. *The Bandaged Nude.* Middlesex, England: Penguin, 1952.

Fleming, Robert E., ed. *Hemingway and the Natural World.* Moscow: University of Idaho Press, 1999.

Foreman, Joel, ed. *The Other Fifties.* Urbana: University of Illinois Press, 1997.

Forter, Greg. *Murdering Masculinities.* New York: NYU Press, 2000.

Friedan, Betty. *The Feminine Mystique.* New York: Norton, 1963.

Fuentes, Norbeto. *Hemingway in Cuba.* Secaucus, N.J.: Lyle Stewart, 1984.

Gelber, Steven M. "Do-It Yourself: Constructing, Repairing, and Maintaining Masculinity." *The Gender and Consumer Culture Reader.* Ed. Jennifer Scanlon. New York: NYU Press, 2000.

Gilbert, Sandra M., and Susan Gubar. *No Man's Land.* New Haven, Conn.: Yale University Press, 1988.

Gladstein, Mimi. "'The Mercenaries': A Harbinger of Vintage Hemingway." In Beegel, ed., *Hemingway's Neglected Short Fiction,* 19–30.

Glass, Loren. *Authors Inc.* New York: NYU Press, 2004.

Goldberg, Ronald Allen. *America in the Twenties.* Syracuse, N.Y.: Syracuse University Press, 2003.

Grainge, Paul. *Monochrome Memories.* Westport, Conn.: Praeger, 2002.

Griffin, Peter. *Along with Youth.* New York: Oxford University Press, 1985.

Groth, John. *Studio: Europe.* New York: Vanguard, 1945.

Gruber, Frank. *The Pulp Jungle.* Los Angeles: Sherbourne, 1967.

Guiness, Os. *The American Hour.* New York: Free Press, 1993.

Hanneman, Audre. *Ernest Hemingway: A Comprehensive Bibliography*. Princeton, N.J.: Princeton University Press, 1969.

Hanson, Dian. *The History of Men's Magazines*. Vol. 2: *From Post-War to 1959*. Koln, Germany: Taschen, 2004.

Harry's Bar and American Grill. *The Best of Bad Hemingway*. New York: Harvest, 1989, 1991.

Hemingway, Ernest. *Byline: Ernest Hemingway*. Ed. William White. New York: Scribners, 1967.

———. *Complete Short Stories*. New York: Scribners, 1987.

———. *Death in the Afternoon*. New York: Scribners, 1932.

———. *Farewell to Arms*. New York: Scribners, 1929.

———, ed. *Men at War*. New York: Crown, 1942.

———. *Selected Letters*. Ed. Carlos Baker. New York: Scribners, 1981.

———. *The Fifth Column and the First Forty-Nine Stories*. New York: Scribners, 1938.

———. *The Torrents of Spring*. New York: Scribners, 2004.

———. *To Have and Have Not*. New York: Scribners, 1937.

Hemingway, Leicester. *My Brother, Ernest Hemingway*. Cleveland, Ohio: World, 1962.

Hemingway, Mary. *How It Was*. New York: Knopf, 1976.

Henderson, Amy. "Media and the Rise of Celebrity Culture." *OAH Magazine of History* 6 (Spring 1992): 49–54.

Herman, Judith Lewis. *Trauma and Recovery*. New York: HarperCollins, 1992.

Hoberek, Andrew. *The Twilight of the Middle Class*. Princeton, N.J.: Princeton University Press, 2005.

Hotchner, A. E., ed. *The Good Life According to Hemingway*. New York: Ecco, 2008.

Jaffe, Aaron. *Modernism and the Culture of Celebrity*. London: Cambridge University Press, 2005.

Jarvis, Christina. *The Male Body at War: American Masculinity during World War II*. DeKalb: Northern Illinois University Press, 2004.

Kapelner, Alan. *Lonely Boy Blues*. New York: Lion, 1956.

Kimmel, Michael. *Manhood in America*. New York: Free Press, 1996.

Laurence, Frank M. *Hemingway and the Movies*. Jackson: University Press of Mississippi, 1981.

Lea, Tom. *The Brave Bulls*. Boston: Little, Brown, 1949.

Leff, Leonard. *Hemingway and His Conspirators*. Lanham, Md.: Rowman and Littlefield, 1999.

Loeb, Lori Anne. *Consuming Angels: Advertising and Victorian Women*. New York: Oxford University Press, 1994.

Lowry, Robert. *The Last Party*. New York: Popular Library, 1956.

———. *New York Call Girl*. New York: Popular Library, 1959.

Macfadden, Mary, and Emile Gauvereu. *Dumbbells and Carrot Strips*. New York: Holt, 1953.

Machlin, Milt. *The Private Hell of Ernest Hemingway*. New York: Paperback Library, 1961.

Madden, David. *Tough Guy Writers of the Thirties*. Carbondale: Southern Illinois University Press, 1968.

Marinetti, Fillipo. *Collected Works*. New York: Farrar, Straus and Giroux, 1972.

May, Elaine Tyler. *Homeward Bound*. New York: Basic Books, 1988.

McCann, Sean. *Gumshoe America*. Durham, N.C.: Duke University Press, 2000.

McCracken, Ellen. *Decoding Women's Magazines*. New York: Palgrave, 1992.

McLean, Adrienne L. "'New Films in Story Form': Movie Story Magazines and Spectatorship." *Cinema Journal* 42 (Spring 2003): 3–26.

Mencken, H. L. *My Life as Author and Editor*. New York: Vintage, 1995.

Meredith, James. "Bird Hunting and Male Bonding in Hemingway's Fiction and Family." In Fleming, ed., *Hemingway and the Natural World*, 189–201.

Merrill, Hugh. *Esky: The Early Years at Esquire*. New Brunswick, N.J.: Rutgers University Press, 1995.

Metzger, Edward. *The Hemingway/Dos Passos Wars*. Los Angeles: Engadine Books, 1997.

Morrison, Mark. *The Public Face of Modernism*. Madison: University of Wisconsin Press, 2001.

Moskowitz, Milton. "Newsstand Strip-Tease." In Christman, ed., *A View of* The Nation.

Mulvey, Laura. "Visual Pleasure and Narrative Cinema." *Screen* 16 (Autumn 1975): 6–18.

Myers, Jeffrey. "Conrad's Influence on Modern Writers." *Twentieth Century Literature* 36 (Summer 1990): 186–206.

Neborsky, Robert J. "A Clinical Model for the Comprehensive Treatment of Trauma Using an Affect Experience—Attachment Theory Approach." *Healing Trauma: Attachment, Mind, Body, and Brain.* Ed. Daniel J. Siegel and Marion F. Solomon. New York: Norton, 2003.

Orgeron, Marsha. "Making *It* in Hollywood: Clara Bow, Fandom, and Consumer Culture." *Cinema Journal* 42 (Summer 2003): 76–97.

Osgerby, Bill. *Playboys in Paradise: Masculinity, Youth and Leisure Style in America.* Oxford, England: Berg, 2001.

Parfrey, Adam. *It's a Man's World.* Los Angeles: Feral Press, 2003.

Pendergast, Tom. *Creating the Modern Man: American Magazines and Consumer Culture.* Columbia: University of Missouri Press, 2000.

Peril, Lynn. *Pink Think: Becoming a Woman in Many Uneasy Lessons.* New York: Norton, 2002.

Peterson, Theodore. *Magazines in the Twentieth Century.* Urbana: University of Illinois Press, 1956.

Plath, James, and Frank Simmons, eds. *Remembering Ernest Hemingway.* Key West, Fla.: Ketch and Yawl Press, 1999.

Raeburn, John. *Fame Became of Him.* Bloomington: Indiana University Press, 1986.

Rainey, Lawrence. *Institutions of Modernism.* New Haven, Conn.: Yale University Press, 1998.

Rembar, Charles. *The End of Obscenity.* New York: Random House, 1968.

Reynolds, Michael. *Hemingway: The Final Years.* New York: Norton, 1999.

———. *The Young Hemingway.* New York: Norton, 1998.

Sanford, Marcelline Hemingway. *At the Hemingways.* Boston: Little, Brown, 1962.

Scanduri, Jani, and Michael Thurston, eds. *Modernism Inc.* New York: NYU Press, 2001.

Schneirov, Matthew. *The Dream of a New Social Order.* New York: Columbia University Press, 1994.

Scott, Bonnie Kime. *Refiguring Modernism.* Bloomington: Indiana University Press, 1995.

Scribner, Charles, Jr. *In the Web of Ideas.* New York: Scribner's Sons, 1993.

Showalter, Elaine. *The Female Malady.* New York: Penguin, 1987.

Shumway, David R. "The Star System in Literary Studies." *PMLA* 112 (Jan. 1997): 85–100.

Silverman, Kaja. *Male Subjectivity at the Margins.* New York: Routledge, 1992.

Simon, Richard. *Trash Culture: Popular Culture and the Great Tradition.* Berkeley: University of California Press, 1999.

Smith, Erin. *Hard-Boiled: Working Class Readers and the Pulp Magazines.* Philadelphia, Pa.: Temple University Press, 2000.

Smith, Robert Paul. . . . *Plus Blood in Their Veins.* New York: Avon, 1952.

Springer, John Parris. *Hollywood Fictions: The Dream Factory in American Popular Literature.* Norman: University of Oklahoma Press, 2000.

Stephens, Robert O. *The Critical Reception.* New York: Burr-Franklin, 1977.

———. *Hemingway's Nonfiction.* Chapel Hill: University of North Carolina Press, 1968.

Susman, Warren. "Did Success Spoil the United States?" *Recasting America: Culture and Politics in the Age of the Cold War.* Ed. Larry May. Chicago: University of Chicago Press, 1989.

Strychacz, Thomas. *Hemingway's Theaters of Masculinity.* Baton Rouge: Louisiana State University Press, 2003.

Tal, Kali. *Worlds of Hurt: Reading the Literature of Trauma.* New York: Cambridge University Press, 1996.

Thomason, John W., Jr. *Texas Rebel.* New York: Berkley Medallion, 1961.

Trogdon, Robert, ed. *Ernest Hemingway: A Literary Reference.* New York: Carroll and Graf, 1999.

———. *The Lousy Racket: Hemingway, Scribners, and the Business of Literature.* Kent, Ohio: Kent State University Press, 2007.

Turner, Catherine. *Marketing Modernism.* Boston: University of Massachusetts Press, 2003.

Wagner-Martin, Linda. *A Historical Guide to Ernest Hemingway.* New York: Oxford University Press, 2000.

Walker, Nancy. *Shaping Our Mother's World: American Women's Magazines.* Jackson: University Press of Mississippi, 2000.

———. *Women's Magazines 1940–1960: Gender Roles in the Popular Press.* Boston: Bedford/St. Martin's, 1998.

Weber, Ronald. *Hired Pens.* Athens: Ohio University Press, 1997.

Whiting, Charles. *Hemingway Goes to War.* Stroud, England: Sutton, 1999.

Wicke, Jennifer. *Advertising Fictions.* New York: Columbia University Press, 1988.

Young, Philip. *Ernest Hemingway.* New York: Rinehart, 1952.

Index